Diagnosis in a Multicultural Context

MULTICULTURAL ASPECTS OF COUNSELING SERIES

SERIES EDITOR
Paul Pedersen, Ph.D., *University of Alabama at Birmingham*

EDITORIAL BOARD

VOLUMES IN THIS SERIES

1. **Increasing Multicultural Understanding (2nd edition): A Comprehensive Model** by Don C. Locke
2. **Preventing Prejudice: A Guide for Counselors and Educators** by Joseph G. Ponterotto and Paul B. Pedersen
3. **Improving Intercultural Interactions: Modules for Cross-Cultural Training Programs** edited by Richard W. Brislin and Tomoko Yoshida
4. **Assessing and Treating Culturally Diverse Clients (2nd edition): A Practical Guide** by Freddy A. Paniagua
5. **Overcoming Unintentional Racism in Counseling and Therapy: A Practitioner's Guide to Intentional Intervention** by Charles R. Ridley
6. **Multicultural Counseling With Teenage Fathers: A Practical Guide** by Mark S. Kiselica
7. **Multicultural Counseling Competencies: Assessment, Education and Training, and Supervision** edited by Donald B. Pope-Davis and Hardin L. K. Coleman
8. **Improving Intercultural Interactions: Modules for Cross-Cultural Training Programs, Volume 2** edited by Kenneth Cushner and Richard W. Brislin
9. **Understanding Cultural Identity in Intervention and Assessment** by Richard H. Dana
10. **Psychological Testing of American Minorities (2nd edition)** by Ronald J. Samuda
11. **Multicultural Counseling Competencies: Individual and Organizational Development** by Derald Wing Sue et al.
12. **Counseling Multiracial Families** by Bea Wehrly, Kelley R. Kenney, and Mark E. Kenney
13. **Integrating Spirituality Into Multicultural Counseling** by Mary A. Fukuyama and Todd D. Sevig
14. **Counseling With Native American Indians and Alaska Natives: Strategies for Helping Professionals** by Roger D. Herring
15. **Diagnosis in a Multicultural Context: A Casebook for Mental Health Professionals** by Freddy A. Paniagua

Diagnosis in a Multicultural Context

A Casebook for Mental Health Professionals

Freddy A. Paniagua

Multicultural Aspects of Counseling Series 15

Sage Publications, Inc.
International Educational and Professional Publisher
Thousand Oaks ▪ London ▪ New Delhi

For information:

Sage Publications, Inc.
2455 Teller Road
Thousand Oaks, California 91320
E-mail: order@sagepub.com

Sage Publications Ltd.
6 Bonhill Street
London EC2A 4PU
United Kingdom

Sage Publications India Pvt. Ltd.
M-32 Market
Greater Kailash I
New Delhi 110 048 India

Printed in the United States of America

Library of Congress Cataloging-in-Publication Data

Paniagua, Freddy A.
Diagnosis in a multicultural context: A casebook for mental health professionals / By Freddy A. Paniagua.
p. cm. — (Multicultural aspects of counseling; v. 15)
Includes bibliographical references and index.
ISBN 0-7619-1788-8 (cloth: alk. paper)
ISBN 0-7619-1789-6 (pbk.: alk. paper)
1. Psychiatry, Transcultural. 2. Mental illness—Diagnosis—Cross-cultural studies. I. Title. II. Multicultural aspects of counseling series; v. 15.
RC455.4.E8 P36 2000
616.89'075—dc21

00-009855

01 02 03 04 05 06 10 7 6 5 4 3 2 1

Acquiring Editor: Nancy Hale
Production Editor: Nevair Kabakian
Editorial Assistant: Cindy Bear
Typesetter/Designer: Tina Hill/Barbara Burkholder

Contents

Series Editor's Introduction

Culture is complex and dynamic. Every attempt to capture the cultural dimension or variable in simplistic terms has failed. Because all behaviors are learned in a cultural context and presented in a cultural context, accurate assessment, meaningful understanding, and appropriate intervention must attend to the cultural context. This is a difficult but not impossible task. The application, however, of a "one-size-fits-all" approach to diagnosis, which can be found in far too many clinical textbooks, is an example of a simplistic perspective that degrades the professional image of mental health service providers. The Multicultural Aspects of Counseling series is dedicated to providing resources for counselors and therapists to attend to the complex variables of multiculturalism.

At the same time, a continuing theme of The Multicultural Aspects of Counseling (MAC) series with Sage has been the importance of practical ideas of immediate value to the reader. This is a delicate balance to maintain. Freddy's book on diagnosis is an excellent example of practicality without sacrificing the complexity of cultural constructs. As Freddy puts it at the beginning of Chapter 2, "overdiagnosis, underdiagnosis, or misdiagnosis of psychopathology among clients from the culturally diverse groups" have presented a critical issue in the cross-cultural mental health literature for many years. This book offers a practical utility without oversimplifying the cultural variables by either stereotyping any particular cultural group or minimizing the difficulty of accurate diagnosis.

Freddy takes a uniquely positive perspective on the gradual attention being given to cultural factors in diagnosis generally and in the *Diagnostic and Statistical Manual of Mental Disorders* (4th Edition [*DSM-IV*]; American Psychiatric Association [APA], 1994) in particular. It is easy, of course, to stand by and criticize the diagnostic tools we have as being culturally biased. It is much more difficult to do as Freddy does and come up with positive strategies for making those diagnostic tools work in multicultural populations. Freddy acknowledges the great contribution the *DSM-IV* has made when compared with earlier versions of *DSM*, which gave little or no attention to culture. If progress in culturally relevant diagnostic tools is slow, that indicates the enormous size of the problem. Freddy's book goes a long way toward encouraging those colleagues who, in good faith, are working hard toward developing culturally relevant diagnostic tools.

In reviewing the literature about the *DSM*, Freddy has pulled together many dozens of important published resources and research reports building toward a more culturally relevant perspective of diagnosis. Freddy's book will become a desk reference for any clinician working with multicultural populations. In the broad definition of culture, that includes all therapy providers. He has carefully reviewed the literature for the larger minority groups of African Americans, Hispanic, Asian Americans, and Native American Indians, describing both the similarities across these ethnocultural boundaries and the common ground they all share. Many if not most of these studies have tended to be emic or culture specific in their treatment of diagnostic problems. Freddy does us the service of presenting these data in a larger, more holistic context of modern multicultural society.

In his analysis of the changes in the *DSM* over time, he shows that progress is being made, and he maintains an optimistic viewpoint toward future changes. In looking at alternative futures, he carefully points out the advantages and disadvantages of a so-called cultural axis as an appropriate means of making the *DSM* culturally relevant. He also points out the more promising alternative of a Cultural Formulation, which was included in the Appendix of *DSM-IV*. He also gives credit to the Task Force on Culture and Psychiatry for developing the Cultural Formulation, recommending it for inclusion in the *DSM-IV*, and for continuing to demonstrate the relevance of culture to the diagnostic process. Freddy also gives equal credit to the Task Force on *DSM-IV* for the inclusion of this Formulation in Appendix I of the *DSM-IV*, as well for the inclusion of a significant number of cultural variations across many psychiatric disorders in Axes I and II.

The large number of cases Freddy includes makes his book an excellent text for clinical courses. The discussion of ethnocultural demography and the guidelines for cultural interpretation of *DSM-IV* in the first four chapters give the reader the background necessary to understand the clinical case vignettes in the next four chapters. The wide range of clinical situations and cultural contexts makes this casebook especially valuable.

Of all the books in the MAC series, Freddy's book does the best job of helping the clinician use diagnostic tools in practical and meaningful ways. Freddy's book will do well among the well-intentioned clinicians seeking to be more intentional in providing mental health services to their culturally diverse client populations. It is with great pride that we include Freddy's excellent book among the other books in the MAC series.

Paul Pedersen
University of Alabama at Birmingham

Preface

Prior to 1987, earlier editions of the *Diagnostic and Statistical Manual of Mental Disorders (DSM,* also known as the *Manual)* did not consider the relevance of cultural variables in the assessment and diagnosis of mental disorders (e.g., *DSM-III,* APA, 1980). In 1987, the APA (the institution that owns the *DSM)* included for the first time the term *culture* in the Index (in culture-bound syndromes) and 20 lines, with a discussion of "the use of the *DSM-III-R* in different cultures" (APA, 1987, pp. xxvi-xxvii).

In 1994, the APA made a major decision regarding the recognition of the importance of cultural variations across many mental disorders, in the Multiaxial Classification (APA, 1994). Good (1996) summarized the emphasis on cultural variables across the *DSM-IV* in the following terms:

> Cultural concerns are represented in a *significant manner* [italics added] in the text of *DSM-IV*—in the Introduction, in the introduction to the multi-axial structure, in the test associated with particular categories ("as cultural considerations"), in a glossary of cultural terms ("culture-bound syndromes"), and in an "outline for cultural formulation" appearing in Appendix I. (p. 128)

This significant addition of cultural variables in the *DSM-IV* resulted from recommendations provided by the Task Force on Culture and Psychiatry Diagnosis (also known as the Group on Culture and Diagnosis; Good, 1996; Lewis-Fernandez, 1996) to the Task Force on *DSM-IV,* including specific guidelines to make cultural variations more critical across the entire *DSM-IV.* The Group was composed of "mainly anthropologists and psychiatrists" (Lewis-Fernandez, 1996, p. 133), suggesting minimal representations from other mental health professionals using the *DSM* in clinical and research practices (e.g., psychologists, social workers, marriage and family therapist, Licensing Professional Counselors, etc.). In future revisions of the *DSM,* these other professionals should have a greater representation in the Group (particularly during advisory role of this Group on the expansion of cross-cultural issues in the *DSM-V* or perhaps in the revision of the *DSM-IV* (i.e., *DSM-IV-R*).

Considering the significant amount of cultural materials inserted in the *DSM-IV* relative to prior editions of the *Manual,* it is clear that members of the Task Force on Culture and Psychiatry were extremely successful in their goal to make cultural variables more central in the *DSM-IV.* This Group, however, was not totally pleased with the way its recommendations were used in the *DSM-IV.* For example, the Group recommended that the Cultural Formulation should have "a space of its own" in the *DSM-IV* (Lewis-Fernandez, 1996, p. 138), but the *DSM-IV* Task Force decided to place this formulation in Appendix I (see APA, 1994, pp. 843-844). In addition, this formulation was combined with the Glossary of Culture-Bound Syndromes in Appendix I, which was submitted by the Group to the *DSM-IV* Task Force as a separate section originally titled by the Group the "Glossary of Cultural Syndromes and Idioms of Distress" (Lewis-Fernandez, 1996, p. 138).

That decision from the *DSM-IV* Task Force not only minimized the clinical significance of the Cultural Formulation in the *DSM-IV* (i.e., materials in Appendixes are not required to be used in the diagnosis of mental disorders on pages 37-673 in the *DSM-IV,* APA, 1994), but this formulation "now seems relevant only to 'culture-bound' presentations among non-Western ethnic groups, rather than as an evaluation process applicable to every patient in every cultural setting" (Lewis-Fernandez, 1996, p. 138). Because of that decision from the *DSM-IV* Task Force, Lewis-Fernandez summarized the overall feelings of members of the Group on Culture and Diagnosis advising the *DSM-IV* Task Force in the following terms: "Despite its efforts, therefore, the Group on Culture and Diagnosis was only able to exert *a slight influence* on the *DSM-IV*" (p. 138). The fact of the matter is, however, that this Group actually exerted a *strong* influence on the *DSM-IV,* if one considers the significant amount of cultural issues inserted in the *DSM-IV* relative to nothing on this topic in the *DSM-III* (APA, 1980) and very little consideration of these issues in the revised *DSM-III-R* (APA, 1987).

It should be noted that prior to the publication of the *DSM-III-R* (APA, 1987), in which a brief discussion on cultural variations was included for the first time (see APA, 1987, pp. xxvi-xxvii), several key members of the Task Force on *DSM-IV* were actively involved in the dissemination of information with emphasis on the importance to consider cultural variations in the assessment, diagnosis, and treatment of mental disorders (Holzer, 2000). For example, the book *Critical Issues in Psychiatric Diagnosis* was edited by Robert L. Spitzer and Donald F. Klein (1978) and published 2 years before the publication of the *DSM-III* (APA, 1980). The first paper in this book is titled "The Recognition of

Psychosis in Non-Western Societies" (Murphy, 1978), and it illustrates the role of culture in the diagnosis of psychotic disorders.

Another important text, titled *International Perspectives on DSM-III,* was also edited by Dr. Robert L. Spitzer, with Dr. Janet B. W. Williams and Dr. Andrew E. Skodol as coeditors (1983), and it was published 4 years before the publication of the *DSM-III-R* (APA, 1987). This book provides an excellent example of the applicability of many cultural variables across many countries, including Canada, China, Belgium, France, German-speaking countries, Japan, Latin America, The Netherlands, Spain, and the United States. For example, the paper *DSM-III in Japan* (Honda, 1983) illustrates the culture-bound syndrome *taijin-kyofu,* which includes symptoms resembling Social Phobia in the *DSM-IV* (see APA, 1994, p. 849; the paper "Latin-American perspective on *DSM-III"* [Alarcon, 1983] also deals with cultural factors in mental disorders).

All the editors in the two books just mentioned (Drs. Skodol, Klein, Spitzer, and Williams) were members of different subcommittees that worked on the revision of the *DSM-III* resulting in the *DSM-III-R* (APA, 1987). In addition, Drs. Spitzer and Williams were members of the Work Group to Revise *DSM-III* (chaired by Dr. Spitzer, with Dr. Williams as the text editor), the group responsible for making sure that the revised *DSM* was in accord with the goals of the APA regarding guidelines specifying the overall format of the *DSM-III-R* and its contents. The *DSM-III-R* (APA, 1987), however, did not reflect the outstanding contributions these editors made with the publication of these books.

Drs. Spitzer and Williams also served on the Task Force on *DSM-IV* (again, the committee that decided what exactly to include or exclude and where to place specific materials in the *DSM-IV,* for instance, the placement of the Cultural Formulation in Appendix I instead of placing it at the front of the *Manual* as recommended by the Group). This time, however, this Task Force was more receptive to include a significant amount of cultural considerations across the entire *DSM-IV,* particularly the inclusion of a discussion on "specific culture features" across many disorders (see Paniagua, 1998, pp. 126-143, and Chapter 2 in this text).

The *DSM* is an institution in itself and, like other institutions in this society, it is not an easy task to convince its members (particularly members of the Task Force on *DSM*—see APA, 1994, p. ix) to make drastic changes in the conceptual paradigm (Kuhn, 1962; Paniagua & Baer, 1981) they hold regarding what specific set of criteria is or is not relevant in the diagnosis of people with mental disorders. The smallest variation from this paradigmatic view of categorizing materials across the current (APA, 1994) and future editions of the *Manual* (e.g., *DSM-V*) should be considered *very significant* among clinicians and researchers concerned about the impact of cultural variations as critical or moderator variables in the assessment, diagnosis, and treatment of mental disorders included in the *DSM* (e.g., *DSM-IV,* 1994). In the particular case of clinicians serving culturally diverse clients, the task is to take advantage of this small variation in that paradigmatic view in the *DSM* and use it to enhance their culturally competent skills in the diagnosis of mental disorders. This is, precisely, the overall goal of *Diagnosis in a Multicultural Context: A Casebook for Mental Health Professionals* (henceforth, *Casebook*).

Many excellent texts exist illustrating the applicability of cultural variations to the assessment and treatment of psychiatric disorders. Examples of these texts include *Children of Color: Psychological Interventions With Culturally Diverse Clients* (Gibbs & Huang, 1998), *Clinical Guidelines in Cross-Cultural Mental Health* (Comas-Díaz & Griffith, 1988), *Counseling the Culturally Different: Theory and Practice* (D. W. Sue & D. Sue, 1990, 1999), *Culturally Diverse Children and Adolescents: Assessment, Diagnosis, and Treatment* (Canino & Spurlock, 1994), *Culture and Psychopathology: A Guide to Clinical Assessment* (Tseng & Streltzer, 1997), *Ethnogerocounseling: Counseling Ethnic Elders and Their Families* (Burlingame, 1999), and *Minority Children and Adolescents in Therapy* (Ho, 1992). In addition, the *DSM-IV Casebook* (Spitzer, Gibbon, Skodol, Williams, & First, 1994) includes a chapter dealing with "international cases" (pp. 419-477). (The reference section in this text includes additional examples of excellent books dealing with many cultural issues in mental health practice and research.) These texts provide many clinical cases showing the importance of considering cultural variations in the prevention of bias when diagnosing and treating clients from culturally diverse groups, particularly from the African American, American Indian, Asian, and Hispanic communities.

Casebook contributes with the achievement of a similar goal but with emphasis on the applicability of cultural variations using guidelines provided by the *DSM-IV* (APA, 1994) across most psychiatric disorders in the *Manual,* particularly the applicability of the Cultural Formulation across disorders. Specifically, *Casebook* is designed for clinicians interested in the enhancement of their culturally competent skills during the applications of *DSM-IV* diagnostic criteria, as well as for clinicians who sense in themselves that they are lacking these skills in their clinical practice involving about four culturally diverse groups (Ramirez, Wassef, Paniagua, Linskey, & O'Boyle, 1994).

In addition to *DSM-IV* cultural guidelines, *Casebook* also integrates a significant number of cultural variations not directly covered by the *DSM-IV,* but which are considered of great significance in the assessment, diagnosis, and treatment of clients from these four culturally diverse groups. For example, the *DSM-IV* does not directly deal with the importance of considering *personal prejudice* and *racism* in the assessment and diagnosis of mental disorders as well as the potential impact of these cultural variables in the development of symptoms suggesting a given mental disorder. In Chapter 1, an extensive discussion on these cultural variables is provided (e.g., personal prejudice vs. individual racism). The applicability of these variables is then illustrated across several cases in Chapters 5 through 7. Most of these additional cultural variables across *Casebook* are extensively discussed in *Assessing and Treating Culturally Diverse Clients: A Practical Guide* (Paniagua, 1998).

In several instances, *Casebook* also expands the *DSM-IV* discussions on cultural issues. For example, the impact of acculturation in the assessment and diagnosis of mental disorders is briefly considered in the *DSM-IV* (particularly, the V-Code "Acculturation Problem," APA, 1994, p. 685). Acculturation as an explanatory alternative of symptoms suggesting a mental disorder is extensively discussed across many cases in the *Casebook* (e.g., Chapter 7, "The Case of Susan").

Overview of *Casebook*

Casebook is composed of eight chapters. Chapter 1 provides an overview of demographic variables across the four culturally diverse groups considered throughout the text. This is followed by an overview of cultural variables that are generally reported across all groups (e.g., familism and acculturation) and then by cultural variables specific to each group (e.g., *personalismo* among Hispanics). Chapter 2 summarizes cultural variations in the *DSM-IV*, with emphasis on the Cultural Formulation. Two tables (2.1 and 2.2) in Chapter 2 are designed to assist clinicians with a quick screening of which specific mental disorder received or did not receive a cultural interpretation in the *DSM-IV*, and Table 2.3 provides a summary of culture-bound syndromes discussed in Appendix I of the *DSM-IV* (APA, 1994). Chapter 2 also includes a table (2.4) to help clinicians with a rapid summary of major issues they should consider during the clinical assessment of a case, with emphasis on the Cultural Formulation.

Chapter 3 includes a discussion of culturally competent strategies clinicians should employ when assessing clients from the racial groups considered in *Casebook*. For example, the mental status exam is generally a key element in the assessment and diagnosis process of the case; a detailed discussion is provided regarding culturally sensitive strategies that could enhance the prevention of bias when using this exam with such racial groups. A similar goal is achieved in Chapter 4, with the difference being that culturally sensitive strategies are discussed in terms of the *treatment of the case* (as opposed to its assessment, in Chapter 3). For example, Chapter 4 provides guidelines for the use of individual psychotherapy versus family therapy with these cultural groups, as well as examples of therapies that appear inappropriate (in cultural terms, not in terms of their efficacy) with these cultural groups.

Chapters 5, 6, and 7 include clinical case vignettes with extensive discussions regarding the applicability of many cultural variations in the *DSM-IV*, as well as other cultural variables reported in the literature with African American, American Indian, Asian, and Hispanic clients. Chapter 5 deals with examples of cases involving psychiatric disorders first diagnosed in childhood and adolescence; Chapter 6 includes cases with other disorders across children, adolescents, and adults, and Chapter 7 assists clinicians with the application of a critical guideline in the *DSM-IV:* the application of cultural skills in those cases in which the client does not have a mental disorder but in which "other conditions" associated with specific cultural variables (e.g., acculturation) appear to "be a focus of clinical attention" (APA, 1994, p. 675).

In ethical terms, clinicians are expected to apply that guideline (e.g., cases in Chapter 7); in economic terms, however, it would be very difficult for clinicians to strictly follow this guideline because these so-called other conditions are not reimbursed by most major private insurance companies, Medicaid, or Medicare, which generally cover mental disorders included in the *DSM-IV* on pages 37-673 (APA, 1994). If the client does not receive a diagnostic code in either Axis I (Clinical Disorders) or Axis II (Personality Disorders and Mental Retardation), the diagnostic session (and subsequent treatment sessions) would not be reimbursed by these companies. The same logic applies to the culture-bound syndromes included in Appendix I in the *DSM-IV* (APA, 1994; see Table 2.3 in this text). For example, "koro" (a man's desire to grasp his penis for fear that it might retract into his body, see Cheng, 1996, and Chowdhury, 1996) is not a coded psychiatric disorder in the *DSM-IV* and therefore, would not be covered by most insurance companies.

In the foregoing two circumstances (i.e., cases in Chapter 7 and culture-bound syndromes), reimbursement practices would change in favor of clinicians dealing with such cases (e.g., Chapter 7) and syndromes only when the Task Force on DSM decided that it is time to seriously consider the inclusion of these other conditions and culture-bound syndromes as critical elements in the diagnosis and treatment of clients experiencing such conditions and syndromes. Actually, as noted by Lewis-Fernandez (1996), the Group on Culture and Diagnosis advising the *DSM-IV* Task Force in the present context discussed the possibility of recommending the inclusion of one more axis: Axis VI, initially termed the Cultural Axis (Lewis-Fernandez, 1996, p. 133). Members of the Group, however, did not include this recommendation in its final report because they

> realized . . . that in order to fit the existing multiaxial format, a Cultural Axis would most certainly be reduced to a standardized typology of brief cultural characterizations, a menus of key descriptors listed in the Manual [*DSM-IV*] for use as part of the clinical evaluation. (Lewis-Fernandez, 1996, p. 133)

Another alternative explanation for the exclusion of that recommendation suggested by the Group (Axis VI) could be that the Group also realized that this new Axis would not lead to reimbursement from insurance companies, thus limiting its applicability by most clinicians when making a diagnosis of mental disorder. For example, Lewis-Fernandez (1996) cited the culture-bound syndrome "taijin kyofusho" (see Table 2.3 in this text, and Appendix I in the *DSM-IV*, APA, 1994) as an illustration of "the adequacy of the likely Cultural Axis evaluation of the rich contextual dynamics involved in a presentation of [this syndrome]" (p. 134); the same point could be made in the case of other culture-bound syndromes included by the *DSM-IV* in Appendix I (e.g., *Amok, ataque de nervios, mal de ojo,* and *susto*). Despite the truth value (see Tapscott, 1976, p. 11) of Lewis-Fernandez's argument, at the present moment, it would not be sufficient to convince managed-care companies and federal insurance agencies (e.g., Medicare) about the clinical need to reimburse mental health practitioners for their work involving the assessment of these culture-bound syndromes in their clinical practice.

In the foregoing discussion, the issue is not the importance of considering culture-bound syndromes as critical elements in the diagnosis of a given case but that clinicians do not currently have a mechanism to be reimbursed for citing these syndromes as the main diagnosis in the multiaxial classification of mental disorders in the *DSM-IV*. In general terms, many members of The Task Force on DSM would consider the inclusion of a Cultural Axis a potential battleground with many insurance companies, which are always looking for the best strategy to cut reimbursement costs across all health disciplines (medicine in general, psychiatry, psychology, social work, etc.).

The point is admittedly speculative. But if it is true, it would suggest that the *DSM-IV* Task Force would take many years (and several subsequent editions of the *DSM*) before it has all the ingredients necessary to make a drastic paradigmatic shift (in Kuhn's [1962] usage of the term) leading to the inclusion of a Cultural Axis (Axis VI). For this reason, a better strategy would be to continue shaping the paradigmatic assumptions of the *DSM-IV* toward the acceptance of more cultural materials in the *Manual* in subsequent editions of the *DSM-IV* rather than "threatening" its multiaxial paradigm with the proposal of an additional Axis specifically dealing with diagnosis in cultural terms. In this shaping process, clinicians concerned about cultural issues with their clients could play a major role by publishing cases they sense could assist members of the Group on Culture and Diagnosis in making a more appealing case to the Task Force on DSM regarding the expansion of cultural variations in the *Manual. Casebook* is an example of this strategy.

Chapters 5 through 7 include two discussion sections for each case. (The discussion is provided by the editor, Dr. Freddy A. Paniagua, across cases to ensure commonality in the integration of cultural variables from prior chapters as well as from the current literature cited in the text.) The first section of the discussion is a *general* interpretation of the case in terms of the most likely diagnosis, with emphasis on cultural variations. *Casebook* is not designed to assist clinicians to practice their clinical skills in making a diagnosis; an outstanding text is already available on this topic: *DSM-IV* Casebook by Spitzer et al. (1994). The present *Casebook* places more emphasis either on cultural variables associated with symptoms suggesting a true mental disorder (Chapters 5 and 6) or on cultural variables that could explain such symptoms in those cases when the client does not have a mental disorder (Chapter 7). For example, in Chapter 5, "The Case of Clarence" includes an extensive discussion around the decision to diagnose the client with Posttraumatic Stress Disorder because of specific cultural variations and not only in terms of criteria recommended in the *DSM-IV* in this diagnosis.

The second discussion across cases in Chapters 5 through 7 is a detailed explanation regarding the applicability of specific features of the Cultural Formulation during the design of the treatment plan for the particular case under consideration. For example, in "The Case of Clarence," the V-Code "Identity Problem" (APA, 1994, p. 685) is considered as a potential condition that merits clinical attention; then, during the cultural formulation of this case, the potential impact of personal prejudice and several forms of racism (discussed in Chapter 1) are suggested in the treatment plan. This same approach is used across cases in Chapters 5 through 7, and clinicians (and students of mental health) are expected to apply the same approach when practicing with cases in Chapter 8.

Chapter 8 includes clinical cases that clinicians could use to practice their understanding of cultural variations in the diagnosis of mental disorders. This chapter is also recommended for instructors in undergraduate and graduate programs in the mental health field, as well as in general and child and adolescent psychiatry programs. Chapter 8 is also designed to be used in continuing education programs and in-service education in mental health clinics dealing with cultural issues in the assessment, diagnosis, and treatment of mental disorders.

Last, it is important to point out that *Casebook* is only one step among many current activities in the cross-cultural mental health field, with the goal of shaping a *gradual paradigm shift* in the way the *DSM-IV* is currently using cultural variations in the diagnosis of mental disorders. For example, the journal *Culture, Medicine and Psychiatry* recently initiated a section on Clinical Cases with the explicit purpose to illustrate the feasibility of integrating elements of the Cultural Formulation in given cases (Lewis-Fernandez, 1996). A similar approach is being explored in the journal *Cultural Diversity and Ethnic Minority* (e.g., Takeuchi, 2000). *Casebook* strongly encourages other journals in the mental health field to develop specialty sections dealing with the applicability of cultural variables in the clinical context, particularly with emphasis on the Cultural Formulation (APA, 1994). These efforts could function as exemplary arguments regarding the feasibility of dealing with cultural issues in the clinical context despite social, political, and economical forces preventing clinicians from fulfilling their ethical cultural responsibility toward their clients.

Acknowledgments

I am indebted to all contributors who sent original cases for the *Casebook* as well as those who agreed to have their cases reproduced in this text. The name of all contributors is included so that readers can contact them directly to explore further issues regarding their cases. I want also to thank Sage Publications, Inc., for supporting the publication of *Casebook*. In 1992, Sage took the lead in recognizing the need to organize the cross-cultural literature in *a book series* specifically designed to inform the general public and scholars about *multiculturalism* as a significant variable in understanding differences and similarities across culturally diverse groups, particularly in the field of mental health service and research practice (Pedersen, 1999; D. W. Sue, Bingham, Porche-Burke, & Vasquez, 1999; S. Sue, 1999). This series is termed "Multicultural Aspects of Counseling Series," and it has already made substantial contributions to the field of mental health around many different cultural issues pertinent to the assessment, diagnosis, and treatment of mental disorders experienced by clients from the four cultural groups discussed in *Casebook*.

I thank Dr. Charles E. Holzer, III, for his insightful points regarding many cultural issues we have discussed over the past 15 years, particularly his interpretation of historical events around significant cultural contributions made by several members of the Task Force on DSM, particularly Professors Robert L. Spitzer and his associates (e.g., Drs. Andrew E. Skodol and Janet B. W. Williams).

I thank Paul Pedersen, Series Editor, who was instrumental in the final preparation of this book. I particularly thank Ms. Nancy Hale, Ms. Nevair Kabakian, and Ms. Marilyn Scott for their technical advice.

I especially thank my spouse, Dr. Sandra A. Black, and my son, Robert Alexander Paniagua Black, for their support and patience throughout the duration of this book. *Casebook* is dedicated to them in appreciation of their support.

This book is dedicated to my spouse,
Dr. Sandra A. Black (Sam),
and my son
Robert Alexander Paniagua Black (RAP).

1

Overview of Demographic Findings
and Cultural Variants Across
African Americans, American Indians,
Asians, and Hispanics

The cross-cultural literature includes an extensive description of cultural variables that might directly or indirectly affect the diagnosis of mental disorders
during the assessment of African American, American Indian, Asian, and Hispanic clients seen in mental health services (e.g., Canino & Spurlock, 1994;
Cuéllar & Paniagua, 2000; Dana, 1993b; Friedman, 1997; Gaw, 1993a; Gibbs &
Huang, 1998; Ho, 1987; Ivey, Ivey, & Simek-Morgan, 1996; McAdoo, 1993;
Paniagua, 1998; Pedersen, 1987, 1997; Pedersen, Draguns, Lonner, & Trimble,
1996; Ponterotto, Casas, Suzuki, & Alexander, 1995; Roubideaux, 1999; D. W.
Sue & D. Sue, 1999). This chapter provides an overview of demographic variables across groups, followed by an overview of examples of cultural variants
clinicians should consider across racial groups and within groups to prevent errors when making a diagnosis of psychopathology with clients from these racial
groups. Chapters 5, 6, and 7 include many cases illustrating the applicability of
these variables in clinical practice. Chapter 8 includes cases for self-instruction
activities (e.g., clinicians' self-teaching of cultural variables using this text) and
formal training (e.g., undergraduate, graduate, and continuing education activities with emphasis on cultural issues in mental health).

Demographic Findings

In 1995, the *African American* population was approximately 33.6 million
(U.S. Bureau of the Census, 1996). The majority of African Americans live in

the South, and smaller numbers live in the north central, northeast, and western regions of the United States (U.S. Department of Health & Human Services, 1991). The median income of African American families in 1995 was $24,698, which was below the national U.S. average of $39,276 and below that of white families ($40,884; U.S. Bureau of the Census, 1996). In 1995, 27.3% of African American families and 30.6% of African American persons were below the poverty line (U.S. Bureau of the Census, 1996), in comparison with 9.1% white families and 11.7% white persons below the poverty level.

The *Hispanic* population is the second largest multicultural group receiving mental health services in the United States. In 1995, the total number of Hispanics was approximately 28.3 million (U.S. Bureau of the Census, 1996). In 1995, the majority of Hispanics were Mexican Americans (approximately 18.0 million), Puerto Ricans (2.8 million), and Cubans (1.2 million), and most of them resided in Texas, New York, and Miami, respectively. Other Hispanics with a significant number in the United States include those from the Caribbean island of the Dominican Republic (Cuba and Puerto Rico are the other two Spanish-speaking islands in this region), from Central America (e.g., Nicaragua), and South America (e.g., Colombia), and most live in New York and San Francisco (Marin & Marin, 1991). It is estimated that by the year 2020, approximately between 47 and 54.3 million Hispanics will be residing in the United States (Dana, 1993b; Marin & Marin, 1991). By the year 2050 (Raajpoot, 2000), the Hispanic population in the United States would be 25% of the total population and the largest group among all culturally diverse groups discussed in this text. (In 2050, representation from other cultural groups would be African Americans, 15%; Asians, 9%; American Indians, 1%; and Anglo Americans, 50% [Raajpoot, 2000].) The median income for Hispanic families (including Mexican Americans, Cubans, Puerto Ricans, Central and South American Hispanics, and other Hispanics) was $24,313 in 1995, below the national median of $39,276 and in comparison with $40,884 for white families (U.S. Bureau of the Census, 1996). Among the larger subgroups of Hispanics in the U.S., the Cubans reported the highest median income level in 1995 ($30,584), and the Puerto Ricans reported the lowest level ($20,929). In 1995, approximately 27.8% of Hispanic families and 30.7% of persons were below the poverty level, in comparison with 9.1% of white families and 11.7% of white persons. The Cubans reported the lowest percentage of families below the poverty level in 1995 (13.6%; U.S. Bureau of the Census, 1996).

The *Asian* population is the third largest multicultural group in mental health services in the U.S. In 1995, the Asian population in the United States (all subgroups, e.g., Chinese, Japanese) was 9.6 million (U.S. Bureau of the Census, 1996). Among Asians, the most numerous groups in the 1990 U.S. Census (Kim, McLeod, & Shantzis, 1992) were the Chinese (812,000), Filipinos (782,000), and the Japanese (716,000). The majority of Asians live in California, Texas, and Washington state. In 1995, the median income for Asians was $46,106, which was higher than both the national average ($39,276) and the average income level of whites ($40,884; U.S. Bureau of the Census, 1996). In 1995, 13.1% of Asian families and 14.6% of Asian persons lived below the poverty line (U.S. Bureau of the Census, 1996). Among Asians, the Southeast Asian refugees are the most disadvantaged (Kim et al., 1992).

The *American Indian* population is the fourth major multicultural group in mental health services in the United States (Thompson, Walker, & Silk-Walker, 1993; Walker & LaDue, 1986). In 1995, the American Indian population (all groups) was 2.2 million (U.S. Bureau of the Census, 1996). In 1995, the median income for American Indian families was $21,619 (U.S. Bureau of the Census, 1996). Estimations for Indians living in reservations are much lower (approximately $9,942; Ho, 1992). In 1995, 31.2% of American Indians were living below the poverty level, in comparison with 9.1% white families and 11.7% white persons below the poverty level (U.S. Bureau of the Census, 1996). The majority of American Indians presently live in six states: Alaska, Arizona, California, Oklahoma, New Mexico, and Washington state (U.S. Bureau of the Census, 1996). Among the four groups discussed in this text, the American Indians are presently the most disadvantaged in terms of socioeconomic characteristics, mortality, and life expectancy (Kim et al., 1992; U.S. Department of Health and Human Services, 1991).

Cultural Variables Across Racial Groups

Racial Labels

Racial labels have been a concern to African Americans for many years. Members of this group have been called *colored, Negro, Black,* and *African American* (Smith, 1992). The first three terms emphasize skin color. The last term emphasizes cultural heritage, and it is gaining acceptability in the literature (Dana, 1993b; Griffith & Baker, 1993; Smith, 1992) because it is less stigmatizing (Dana, 1993a), does not emphasize skin color but includes reference to cultural heritage (Griffith & Baker, 1993), and it formalizes the African connection (Fairchild, 1985). Although no empirical findings exist regarding the effect of racial labels on the clinician's effort to obtain a reliable diagnosis of psychopathology among clients from this racial group, a controversy does exist regarding which of the two widely used terms (Black vs. African American) is the most acceptable term (Fairchild, 1985; Smith, 1992). In the assessment and treatment of this culturally diverse group, a clinician should explore which of the two labels the client would prefer to be recorded during the intake session, to minimize the potential negative effect of racial labels during the diagnosis process.

In the case of Hispanics, clinicians serving this group should be aware that the term *Hispanic* has many usages among members of this group. In general, language skill (Spanish speaking), family name (Spanish surname), and ancestry

(Hispanic American) would classify a given client as Hispanic. But some clients within this group would not consider these variants (e.g., language skill) in the inclusion of Hispanics as one of the four major minority groups in the United States. For example, a client from Spain would not be treated as a minority individual by members of the Hispanic community in this country, regardless of the fact that such an individual is Spanish speaking. When the term Hispanic is used by members of this community, it generally refers to individuals from Spanish-speaking Latin American nations, including Central American countries (Mexico, Panama, Costa Rica, etc.), South American countries (Venezuela, Colombia, etc.), and the Caribbean (Puerto Rico, Cuba, Dominican Republic).

Two additional terms commonly used in the present context are *Latino* and *Hispanic American*. The first term implies that a person is from a Latin American country (e.g., from Cuba), and as noted by Dana (1993b), Mexican Americans tend to prefer this term because it "does not signify the conqueror Spain" (p. 66). The second term (Hispanic American) implies that a person is not only of Spanish origin but that he or she was born in the United States (Dana, 1993b; Ho, 1992; Marin & Marin, 1991). It is also important to note that many clients who consider themselves Hispanics and members of a minority group in this country do not speak Spanish. Therefore, it may not be appropriate to label a person Hispanic on the basis of the ability to speak Spanish.

— In the case of Asian clients, racial labels generally include three subgroups (D. W. Sue & D. Sue, 1987, 1990, 1999; Mollica, 1989; Mollica & Lavelle, 1988): Asian Americans (Japanese, Chinese, Filipinos, Asian Indians, and Koreans); Asian Pacific Islanders (Hawaiians, Samoans, and Guamanians), and Southeast Asian refugees (Vietnamese, Cambodians, and Laotians). The generic term, *Asian,* could be used in clinical practice without a concern regarding which specific term should be used when addressing a given client from this racial group.

The American Indian population is also known as *Native Americans,* but this term is not recommended because it does not include other Indian groups in the United States (e.g., Eskimos, Aleuts) and Indians from other countries (e.g., Canadian and Mexican Indians) that have settled in the United States (Fleming, 1992). The preferred terms are *American Indians* and *Alaska Natives* (Fleming, 1992; Thompson et al., 1993). Thompson et al. (1993) suggested that the term *Indian* should be used to "refer to all American Indian, Alaska Natives, and Canadian and Mexican Indian people" (p. 189).

Familism and Role Flexibility

In the diagnosis of African American, American Indian, Asian, and Hispanic clients, *familism* is a critical variable to consider (Boyd-Franklin, 1989; Boyd-Franklin, Aleman, Jean-Gilles, & Lewis, 1995; Canino & Canino, 1993; Ho, 1992; Matheson, 1986; Richardson, 1981; Sandoval & De La Roza, 1986; Smith, 1981; Zapata, 1995).

Many clients from these cultural groups generally turn to family members during times of stress and economic difficulties and often consult with other members in the family before they decide to seek help from a clinician. This consultation sometimes involves members from the *extended family* network who are not related to the family by blood or marriage but tied to the family through special relationships, including, for example, friends, the minister, and church members. For this reason, during the initial evaluation of clients from these culturally diverse groups, the formulation of the *genogram* should emphasize the extended family tree rather than simply the biological family tree (Paniagua, 1996,1998).

In the case of Hispanic clients, the godfather (*padrino*) and godmother (*madrina*) should be included in the genogram. Tribal leaders, the elderly, and the medicine man or woman are important members of the network of extended families among American Indians, and these individuals are often consulted by these families for advice and solutions to family conflicts. This is particularly important in those cases when husband and wife are from two different tribes (e.g., Cherokee and Hopi tribes) and the main conflict involves the discipline of their children (see Chapter 7, "The Case of Ron Tiger"). If the therapist suspects that such conflicts may be the result of different values, norms, or different beliefs between tribes, an elder from either tribe should be consulted to clarify these cultural differences and the contribution of such differences in the manifestation of these conflicts (Ho, 1992). Last, among Southeast Asian refugees, some members of mental health community agencies for Asians (e.g., social workers, case managers) are often perceived as members of the extended family by these clients (Yamamoto, 1986), and these individuals should be listed in the genogram and offered the opportunity to actively participate in the assessment and treatment of the case.

An important issue among many African American families is *role flexibility:* The mother sometimes plays the role of the father and thus functions as the head of the family. In addition, older children sometimes function as parents or caretakers for younger children. In fact, older African American children may drop out from school to work and help younger children to secure a good education (Baker, 1988; Ho, 1992; Smith, 1981). As noted by Boyd-Franklin (1989), the concept of role flexibility among African American families can be extended to include the parental role assumed by grandfather, grandmother, aunts, and cousins. Therefore, the assessment of African American clients should include the identification of the head of the family at the moment of the referral.

In many Hispanic families, the cultural values of machismo and *marianismo* might not permit role flexibility among members of the family. In this cultural group, the father is often perceived as the head of the family, whereas the wife takes care of the children, and it is expected for children to behave according to the father's rules. This cultural value is known as *machismo* (Paniagua, 1998). The phenomenon of *marianismo* is the opposite of machismo (Comas-Díaz, 1988; Comas-Díaz & Duncan, 1985; Martinez, 1988, 1993; Ruiz, 1981):

Women are expected to be submissive, obedient, dependent, timid, docile, senti-mental, gentle, and to remain virgin until marriage. Women are also expected to take care of children at home and to devote their time to cooking, cleaning the house, and doing other activities for the benefit of their children and husband. This *marianismo* is a phenomenon based on the Catholic worship of the Virgin Mary who is considered among Hispanics as both a virgin and a Madonna (Comas-Díaz & Duncan, 1985). The cultural values of machismo and *marianismo* should be considered in the diagnosis of mental disorders among Hispanic women, particularly in the case of Dependent Personality Disorder, in which a female client may have difficulty in making everyday decisions without an excessive amount of advice from her husband or her father (see APA, 1994, p. 668). Partner and parent-child relational problems (two V-Codes in the *DSM-IV*; see APA, 1994, p. 681) could also result from rejection of both machismo and marianismo by some family members versus acceptance of these cultural vari-ables by others in the same family.

Similar to Hispanic families, in many Asian families, the role of the father is to function as the dominant figure in the family and a sense of role flexibility is not generally emphasized among members of the family. Among many Asian families, parents can determine their children's personal desires and ambitions (see Chapter 6, "The Case of Jones"), and any attempt not to comply with par-ents' expectations is seen as a threat toward the parents' authority (Ho, 1992; D. W. Sue & D. Sue, 1990, 1999).

In comparison with Hispanic and Asian families, American Indian families emphasize the *administration* of the family by the father and older relatives rather than the authority (Asians) or machismo (Hispanics) of parents and older relatives. Thus, mutual respect between wife and husband, between parents and children, between family members and relatives, and last, between family mem-bers and the tribe is highly rewarded (Ho, 1992; Matheson, 1986; Richardson, 1981). Strong family relationship is emphasized, but a sense of independence among family members is rewarded, particularly among American Indian chil-dren and adolescents (Ho, 1992). For example, American Indian children are rarely told directly what to do and are often encouraged to make their own deci-sions. Among American Indians, few rules are best, and if they exist, they must be flexible and loosely written (Richardson, 1981). During the assessment and treatment of American Indians, then, it is particularly important to avoid looking for the "head" of the family with the authority to make decisions regarding the entire family. Contrary to the Asian and Hispanic families, in American Indian families, the father (or older adult) only administers the family; he does not control the family in the sense of being authoritarian or macho.

Religious and Folk Beliefs

An assessment of religious and folk beliefs is a critical variable in the process of making a diagnosis of psychopathology and developing treatment modalities with clients from the racial groups discussed in this text (Baker & Lightfoot, 1993; Boyd-Franklin, 1989; Dana, 1993b; Griffith, English, & Mayfield, 1980; Ho, 1992; Koss-Chioino & Vargas, 1999; Levin & Taylor, 1993; Martinez, 1993; Ruiz, 1981; Trimble & Fleming, 1989). The priest (for clients with a Catholic denomination) and the minister (for clients with other church affiliations) are key figures in the assessment and treatment of the case, and they should be consulted, with permission from the client. Many of these clients may believe that mental health problems are caused by evil spirits, supernatural forces, violation of sacred beliefs, or sin (see Chapter 6, "The Case of Felicia Marquez"). Under this circumstance, the church (in the case of sacred beliefs and sins) or folk healers (in the case of evil spirits and supernatural forces) are initially consulted to deal with these problems, not the therapist (Dana, 1993b). Some of these clients may believe that prayers and the use of herbs, teas, and other natural substances will cure a physical or mental health problem, and help from a mental health professional may be sought only after the family has exhausted all religious and folk belief resources to handle the problem.

In addition, some Hispanics believe that certain forms of behavior, such as *envidia* (envy) and *mal de ojo* (evil eye), which is said to result from excessive admiration and attention, might result in physical and mental health problems in themselves and others. These beliefs might be erroneously considered as "delusional" by clinicians that fail to interpret them in cultural terms. Many Hispanic clients may report folk healers, such as *el curandero* (for men) or *la curandera* (for women), and witch doctors, such as *el brujo* (for men) or *la bruja* (for women), as examples of individuals they have consulted in the past to resolve these problems (see Chapter 6, "The Case of the Hex"). Knowledge concerning these beliefs among the Hispanic communities would prevent inaccuracy in diagnosing and unnecessary psychological or psychiatric treatment. (It should be noted that witch doctors [*brujos* or *brujas*] are not used by Hispanics in the same way they use the healers [*curanderos* or *curanderas*]. In general, *brujos* or *brujas* use the power of the devil to resolve problems; *curanderos* or *curanderas* use the power of God, in a spiritual sense [I. Cuéllar, personal communication, January, 1994]. This distinction between the *brujo(a)* and the *curandero(a)* should be kept in mind when communicating with Hispanic clients. It is also important to emphasize that clinicians working with the Hispanic community should not assume that all Hispanic clients share or are familiar with these beliefs. For this reason, the intake interview should include a brief assessment of these beliefs to avoid generalizing them across all Hispanics who come to the clinic seeking professional assistance to deal with their individual or family difficulties.)

In the case of African American clients seeking help for their mental health problems, examples of folk healers include the *old lady* who often deals with common ailments, provides advice, gives medication (e.g., the use of herbs), and is most often consulted by young mothers; the *spiritualist* is the most common folk healer among African Americans seeking help to deal with their problems. The *voodoo priest* or *hougan* who has more formal training in the process of healing, including, for example, selection of plants for healing purposes, may also be consulted and may prescribe the ingestion of organs or parts of certain animals to treat the problem and has skills to deal with individual and family problems (Dana, 1993b).

Acculturation

The term *acculturation* has generally been used to explain changes in behavioral patterns and belief systems resulting from a long-term interaction with the dominant culture (Cuéllar, 2000). In this interaction, immigrants who have lived in the United States for a significant number of years have generally been included in discussions regarding the role of acculturation as a critical cultural variable. Examples of these immigrants include people from the Caribbean (e.g., Dominican Republic), Central (e.g., Panama) and South American (e.g., Venezuela), Asian (e.g., Japan), and Arab (e.g., Egypt) countries (Dana, 1993b; Jackson, 1995; Zapata, 1995).

The possibility of different levels of acculturation among family members seeking mental health services should be assessed during the initial evaluation of the case (Cuéllar, 2000) to rule out the impact of acculturation on symptoms suggesting a given mental disorder (see Chapter 7, "The Case of Susan"). For example, a female Hispanic adolescent might be considered by her parents as "oppositional" because she does not believe in the traditional process of dating held by traditional Hispanic parents, including the participation of parents or relatives in the actual process of dating, for example (see Paniagua, 1998, p. 46). This conflict not only could result in symptoms suggesting Oppositional Defiant Disorder, but it may also lead to the development of mood disorders (e.g., Major Depressive Disorder). In this example, different levels of acculturation could explain parent-child relational problems and symptoms, and these levels should be carefully assessed during the initial evaluation of the case. Many acculturation scales are available to achieve this goal (see Chapter 3, Table 3.1, for examples of these scales). In addition, a quick assessment (less than 5 minutes) of such levels of acculturation during the initial evaluation of the case could be performed with the Brief Acculturation Scale suggested by Paniagua (1998).

In the discussion of acculturation, African Americans are rarely considered (Paniagua, 1998). Some African American clients prefer to identify with the (dominant) Anglo American culture and may display many behavior patterns like those displayed by the Anglo American community, such as styles of dress, music, and language (Dana, 1993b; Ho, 1992). This preference may be acquired through a process of *internal acculturation* (see Paniagua, 1998, p. 9) in which an African American may assimilate behavioral patterns through association with members from a different racial group (e.g., Anglo American).

To determine an African American client's perception of identity with the dominant culture versus the client's perception of racial identity with his or her own culture (Paniagua, 1998), an assessment of the internal process of acculturation is recommended during the initial evaluation of the case. In addition, the same acculturation problem noted earlier in the case of Hispanic families could also be encountered in many African American families seeking mental health services to deal with their children's problem behaviors. For example, Jones (1992) pointed out that some African American adolescents are often referred to therapy because "their parents think that they are mimicking maladaptive white adolescent behaviors such as the wearing of punk-style haircut or interest in heavy metal rock music" (p. 34). In this example, parents would fear that their child may lose his or her racial identity because of the adoption of behaviors of white adolescents and decide to enforce restrictive disciplinary measures resulting in severe parent-child relational problems (e.g., conduct problems, oppositional behaviors). This situation would prompt parents to seek mental health services to deal with these conflicts, and the clinician's task would be to explore the impact of different levels of acculturation as a potential factor in the explanation of such conflicts and, more important, to discuss this explanatory alternative using a culturally sensitive approach.

Racism and Cultural Identity Conflict

In the provision of mental health services to clients from culturally diverse groups, the term *racism* is often interpreted in two different ways. First, this concept is often used to explain why these clients behave the way they do. For example, intelligence test results are generally lower among African Americans, American Indians, Asians, and Hispanics in comparison with scores derived from white subjects (Jenkins & Hunter, 1991). In the case of African American clients, the diagnosis of schizophrenia is frequently used, in comparison to white clients (Kilgus, Pumariega, & Cuffe, 1995; Wilkinson & Spurlock, 1986). The explanation of these results in terms of differences among races is termed racism (De La Cancela, 1993; Paniagua, 1998). The second usage of racism is the reference to "racial prejudice and discrimination used to the advantage of one race and the disadvantage of other races" (Okun, 1996, p. 210). As noted by Miller (1992), prejudice and racial discrimination are in themselves stressful situations that could lead to emotional difficulties among members of the culturally diverse groups discussed in this text. For example, clients from these groups may display low self-esteem and symptoms of depression when they sense that they have been racially discriminated against (see Chapter 7, "The Case of Jones").

During the assessment of culturally diverse clients, it is important to determine whether symptoms reported by the client suggest either personal prejudice or individual racism, cultural racism, or institutional racism (Okun, 1996). *Personal prejudice* deals with beliefs and attitudes "that are not acted out behaviorally" (Okun, 1996, p. 217), including, for example, the sense that one has been excluded from social activities (e.g., parties, conversation, birthday celebrations) and that someone moves away from people who do not share his or her color. In the case of biracial children, they "may experience personal prejudice from the racial group of both parents" (Okun, 1996, p. 217), including the use of racially discriminative labels, such as *oreos* and *zebras* (see Okun, 1996, p. 217).

Individual racism is the opposite of personal prejudice in that the individual would display overt racial discrimination against a given culturally diverse group. Examples of this form of racism include African American children harassed by white children in school and the fact that, regardless of having many white friends in the neighborhood or school, the African American child is never invited into the homes of these white children (see Chapter 5, "The Case of Clarence").

Cultural racism "is based on the assumption that White is the norm, that people of color are inherently inferior, less intelligent . . . [and considered] as uncivilized, emotional labile, and prone to violence" (Okun, 1996, p. 218). When members from the discussed culturally diverse groups "manage to achieve upward mobility [they are considered] as exceptions and are accepted by the dominant white culture as 'You're OK, you're different'" (Okun, 1996, p. 218; see Chapter 5, "The Case of Clarence").

Institutional racism "is represented by the double standards, and differential treatment inherent in our justice, education, medical, government, housing, and other social systems" (Okun, 1996, p. 220). For example, when culturally diverse individuals (e.g., African Americans, Hispanics) are hired to meet affirmative action quotas but are given less significant or powerful responsibilities in the job, this is a case for institutional racism. A similar case of institutional racism is that in which the school system assumes that African American children would perform "less well on academic tasks, tracking them in lower levels and creating a self-fulfilling slow learning prophecy" (Okun, 1996, p. 221). Each of these forms of racism could result in significant emotional difficulties in the individual experiencing them (see "The Case of Clarence" in Chapter 5 and "The Case of Jones" in Chapter 7).

Marsella and Yamada (2000) define *cultural identity* (or ethnocultural identity) as the "extent to which an individual endorses and manifests the cultural traditions and practices of the particular group" (p. 13). A cultural identity conflict would arrive when the individual struggles to identify with his or her own culture but at the same time displays a strong sense of identification with a different cultural group. This conflict is particularly important to assess in the case of biracial children and adolescents (Dana, 1997; Gibbs, 1998b; Koss-Chioino & Vargas, 1999). The importance of considering the cultural identity of the client during the assessment and treatment processes is recognized in the *DSM-IV* in the section dealing with the cultural formulation of the case (APA, 1994, p. 843; see also Chapter 2, Identity Problem, and Table 2.4). Several cases in Chapters 5, 6, and 7 illustrate the need to carefully explore the cultural identity of the client during the diagnosis process (e.g., see Chapter 5, "The Case of Marcia").

Cultural Variables Within Racial Groups

The sharing of cultural variables across the diverse groups discussed in this text is an example of *cultural commonalities* (a term adopted from Chung, 1992). Some cultural variables, however, appear to be more specific within individual racial groups. For example, the "health cultural paranoid" phenomenon (Gregory, 1996; Smith, 1981) is generally associated with the African American community. Many African American clients seen in mental health clinics may appear to the uninformed clinician (culturally speaking) as highly suspicious of others with different colors and values, which may result in the diagnosis of Delusional Disorder, Persecutory Type (APA, 1994, p. 298). This phenomenon, however, has its root in the history of slavery and racism experienced by African Americans in the United States (Gregory, 1996).

In the case of Hispanic clients, their perception of *personalismo* versus the absence of this cultural value could determine the level of trust the clinician wants to develop with the client, particularly during the initial evaluation of the case. Hispanic clients' assessment of *personalismo* (personalism) often includes their attention to both verbal and nonverbal behaviors emitted by the clinician during the evaluation and treatment process, including, for example, the clinician's self-disclosure of "personal" information, such as preferred music, food preference, and hobbies. Lack of *personalismo* could prevent the clinician from gathering the information needed to make a diagnosis of mental disorder (Bernal & Gutierrez, 1988; Canino & Spurlock, 1994; Paniagua, 1998). Hispanics' belief in *fatalismo* (fatalism) is another cultural value to consider in the assessment and treatment of members from this racial group (Neff & Hoppe, 1993). A client would display *fatalismo* when he or she perceives a sense of vulnerability and lack of control in the presence of adverse events, which are associated with a supernatural or divine providence controlling the world. The individual would be involved in religious and folk activities to find ways to handle these fatalistic events but often without success. The individual's interpretation of the origin of these events and his or her ways of dealing with them could lead to "symptoms" that might be perceived by the clinician evaluating the case as examples of a given mental disorder. For example, Hispanic clients who believe in *fatalismo* could show ideas of reference, odd beliefs, and odd thinking and speech suggesting the development of Schizotypal Personality Disorder (APA, 1994, pp. 645). The thought that such events cannot be controlled and that they will negatively affect the life of the individual sensing them could also lead to symptoms resembling mood and anxiety disorders (APA, 1994).

In the case of Asian clients, their efforts to prevent others outside the family from knowing about their emotional problems is one of the most significant variables to consider during assessment and treatment (D. W. Sue & D. Sue, 1990, 1999). Culturally, these problems should be shared only with family members, and the mechanisms of shame and guilt are often used by Asian families to enforce norms preventing members of the family from making these problems public (Dana, 1993b). Violation of these norms may lead to lack of emotional and instrumental support from the extended family; the individual's feeling of shame and guilt resulting from these violations could result in clinical symptoms for anxiety and depression associated with the idea that family support may be withdrawn. Fear that public reports of mental disorder may bring shame and humiliation to the entire family often has a negative impact in the clinician's effort to effectively treat the case: The family would wait for many years before seeking mental health services, which often leads to the presence of a chronic problem at the time the family finally decides to seek help from a mental health professional (Fujii, Fukushima, & Yamamoto, 1993; Gaw, 1993b). Therefore, when an Asian client is brought to the attention of a clinician, it is important to consider the initial evaluation in terms of a crisis the family is experiencing, in which immediate assessment of suicide attempts and thoughts and the development of an emergency treatment plan (e.g., brief hospitalization, contacts with social agencies) should be considered before the client leaves the clinic (Yamamoto, 1986).

Feelings of shame and humiliation and guilt resulting from making mental disorders public may lead to another cultural variable in the assessment and treatment of many Asian clients, namely, their efforts to express symptoms of mental disorder in somatic terms (Gaw, 1993b; Ho, 1992; Hughes, 1993; D. W. Sue & D. Sue, 1990, 1999). Therefore, during the initial evaluation, an Asian client would likely spend a great deal of time talking about physical (medical) complications, such as chest pain, palpitation, nausea, abdominal pain, fatigue, and significant weight loss, but would avoid labeling these symptoms as examples of a given mental disorder (e.g., Panic or Major Depressive Disorder). The reason for refusing to attach these symptoms to a mental disorder is that many Asian clients would consider reports about physical symptoms more acceptable in their community than reports about emotional difficulties (D. W. Sue & D. Sue, 1990, 1999).

Last, in the case of American Indian clients, two important cultural variables to consider are their interpretation of the concepts of *time* and *confidentiality* in clinical practice. Many American Indians treat time as a natural event and do not believe that time should control their natural way of living (Ho, 1992). Among many American Indians, time is not used as a measuring tool (e.g., hours, minutes, seconds) but rather it is related to the holistic task (Arthur L. McDonald, personal communication, August 6, 2000, at the American Psychological Association Presidential Citation awarded to Dr. McDonald, Washington, DC). That is, the event (the task) rather than the clock is what appears critical among members from this racial group. (D. W. Sue and D. Sue, 1990, pp. 127-128, suggested that a similar concept of time may be held by many Hispanics and African Americans.)

In the case of American Indians' interpretation of what is *confidential* in clinical practice, the issue is related with their rejection of pseudosecrecy statements, such as "feel free to tell me . . . " or "You can be assured I will not discuss your problem with . . . ," which resemble promises this cultural group has received in the past but that have been violated in most instances. As noted by Richardson (1981) and Walker and LaDue (1986), American Indians have listened to these statements many times from the Great White Father and federal bureaucrats, and each time, they have been deceived (see Paniagua, 1998, pp. 77-81, for a summary of historical events illustrating this issue). For this reason, clinicians serving American Indian clients should make sure that these clients understand that he or she is aware of historical negative events experienced by American Indians and that such clients' knowledge of these events might negatively affect the client-therapist level of trust in the therapeutic process. Therefore, clinicians serving this cultural group should avoid statements suggesting the applicability of the term *confidentiality* in ways American Indian clients would perceive as suspicious.

2

Cultural Variations in the
Diagnostic and Statistical Manual
of Mental Disorders (DSM-IV)

Overdiagnosis, underdiagnosis, or misdiagnosis of psychopathology among clients from the culturally diverse groups described in the prior chapter have been a critical issue in the cross-cultural literature for many years (Dana, 1993b; Moffic & Kinzie, 1996; Smart & Smart, 1997; Spitzer & Klein, 1978; Spitzer, Williams, & Skodol, 1983). The Task Force on Culture and *DSM-IV* (Lewis-Fernandez & Kleinman, 1995) played a significant role in convincing the APA about the importance of emphasizing the impact of cultural variants across the *DSM-IV* classification of mental disorders (Cervantes & Arroyo, 1995; Lewis-Fernandez & Kleinman, 1995). Clinicians using the *DSM-IV* are now advised that if they are *not familiar* with the impact of cultural variants when diagnosing psychopathology among clients from culturally diverse groups, they "may incorrectly judge as psychopathology those normal variations in behavior, belief, or experience that are particular to the individual's culture" (APA, 1994, p. xxiv). To encourage clinicians' attention to cultural variants in their diagnoses of psychopathology, the *DSM-IV* added four cultural recommendations: (a) emphasis on "Specific Culture Features," (b) a summary of culture-bound syndromes (Appendix I), (c) the Cultural Formulation (Appendix I), and (d) V-Codes dealing with specific cultural variables.

Specific Culture Features

In the *DSM-IV* (APA, 1994), "specific culture features" are either discussed alone or in combination with two additional specific features (also added in the *DSM-IV,* APA, 1994), namely, age and gender features. This combination of culture, age, and gender features is not always discussed across mental disorders, and in the specific case of culture features, not all disorders received a discussion of potential cultural variants associated with symptoms suggesting a given mental disorder. For example, in the case of Attention Deficit/Hyperactivity Disorder and Conduct Disorder, specific culture, age, and gender features are discussed (APA, 1994, pp. 881-82 and p. 88, respectively); but in the case of Oppositional Defiant Disorder, only specific age and gender features were discussed (APA, 1994, p. 92), leaving out the specific culture features. Two additional examples include specific age and gender features in the case of Dysthymic Disorder (APA, 1994, p. 347) and specific gender features in Bipolar II (APA, 1994, p. 360), in which specific culture features were not discussed. The point is this: The *DSM-IV* is not systematic in its discussion of culture, age, and gender features across disorders.

In the particular case of specific culture features, Paniagua, Tan, and Lew (1996) screened the entire *DSM-IV* Classification and found that whereas some disorders included a "discussion . . . of cultural variations in the clinical presentations of those disorders" (APA, 1994, p. xxiv), this was not the case across all disorders. In the next edition of the *DSM* (i.e., *DSM-V* or perhaps a revised *DSM-IV-R*), it would be important to have some commonality with the use of these three features across disorders. The absence of this commonality could be explained in two ways. First, the Task Force on *DSM-IV* was probably already busy with the selection of a significant amount of cultural variables to be considered in the *Manual* and elected to illustrate the applicability of these variables with examples of mental disorders. Second (a more powerful explanation), the Task Force did not find enough materials from the cultural literature to support the inclusion of specific culture features in the case of those disorders that did not receive a discussion regarding such variables. The task of members of the Task Force advisory group on cross-cultural issues (e.g., see Good, 1996; Lewis-Fernandez, 1996) would be to carefully screen the cultural literature to propose the inclusion of cultural variations across those disorders that did not receive a discussion on this topic. For example, in the case of Reactive Attachment Disorder, the *DSM-IV* did not mention potential cultural variations affecting symptoms of this disorder (APA, 1994, pp. 116-118). In Chapter 5, however, the work of Cervantes and Arroyo (1995) is cited to illustrate specific cultural variations clinicians should consider when diagnosing children with this disorder (see "The Case of Clarence," Chapter 5).

Table 2.1 shows mental disorders for which the *DSM-IV* provides a discussion regarding the potential impact of cultural variations in explaining symptoms associated with some disorders. A detailed summary of these variations can be found in Paniagua (1998) and Paniagua et al. (1996). Table 2.2 includes disorders without specific mention of cultural variants in the *DSM-IV*. Both tables are specifically designed for busy clinicians who might not have the time to systematically screen the entire *DSM-IV* to determine the applicability of materials in these tables. Despite this limitation, the inclusion of cultural features across many disorders is a major addition to the *DSM-IV* Multiaxial Classification; the advisory group to the *DSM* on cultural issues would make an even greater contribution by suggesting to the Task Force on *DSM-V* the inclusion of specific culture features (selected from the current cultural literature) across all psychiatric disorders in the *DSM-V.*

Culture-Bound Syndromes

The second cultural recommendation is the inclusion of a glossary of examples of syndromes related to culture, which are generally known as *culture-bound syndromes* (Castillo, 1997; Dana, 1993b; Griffith & Baker, 1993; Guarnaccia, 1997; Ivey et al., 1996; Kirmayer, Dao, & Smith, 1998; Paniagua, 1998; Simons & Hughes, 1993; Smart & Smart, 1997). Table 2.3 shows examples of these syndromes. It is important to note, however, that symptoms suggesting a given psychiatric disorder may be associated with a particular cultural context, but the disorder would not be considered an example of culture-bound syndromes. Under this circumstance, practitioners are encouraged to consider the role of cultural variants in the explanation of such symptoms. This point is not explicitly stated in the *DSM-IV* (APA, 1994; Paniagua, 2000), but a careful analysis of the manner in which the *DSM-IV* integrates cultural variations across most psychiatric disorders suggests a distinction between cultural variables contributing to symptoms in a given *DSM-IV* disorder and culture-bound syndromes. For example, the Task Force on Culture and *DSM-IV* recommended the inclusion of Anorexia Nervosa and Dissociative Identity Disorder as examples of culture-bound syndromes in the Glossary (Lewis-Fernandez & Kleinman, 1995). The Task Force, however, did not include this recommendation in the *DSM-IV,* probably because they were not examples of "locality-specific patterns of aberrant behavior and troubling" (APA, 1994, p. 844) noted in the case of culture-bound syndromes included in the Glossary (Appendix I). In the *DSM-IV,* however, cultural variables were discussed as potential contributors to symptoms suggesting Dissociative Identity Disorder and Anorexia Nervosa. Chapters 5, 6, and 7 include clinical case vignettes with examples of disorders that *were not* specifically included in the *DSM-IV* as examples of culture-bound syndromes but in which culture-specific contexts were considered to assist clinicians with the application of "*DSM-IV* criteria in a multicultural environment" (APA, 1994, p. 843).

It should be noted that in the case of several disorders, the *DSM-IV* suggests that the particular disorder may *resemble* one of the culture-bound syndromes in Appendix I. The term "resemble," however, suggests that in the *DSM-IV,* that disorder is not a culture-bound syndrome per se. For example, *boufee delirante* was included as an example of a culture-bound syndrome in Appendix I and, according to the *DSM-IV,* episodes associated with this culture-bound syndrome "may resemble an episode of Brief Psychotic Disorder" (APA, 1994, p. 845).

Table 2.1 Summary of Psychiatric Disorders With Descriptions of Cultural
Variations in the *DSM-IV* (APA, 1994)

Disorder	Subtype
Adjustment Disorders	All Subtypes
Alcohol-Related Disorders	All Subtypes
Attention Deficit and Disruptive Disorders	Conduct Disorder, ADHD
Amnesic Disorders	All Subtypes
Anxiety Disorders	Social Phobia
	Posttraumatic Stress Disorder
	Panic Disorder (with or without Agoraphobia)
	Obsessive-Compulsive Disorder
	Acute Stress Disorder
	Generalized Anxiety Disorder
Caffeine-Related Disorders	All Subtypes
Cannabis-Related Disorders	All Subtypes
Cocaine-Related Disorders	All Subtypes
Communication Disorders	Expressive Language Disorder
	Mixed Receptive-Expressive Language Disorder
	Phonological Disorder
Delirium and Dementia	All Subtypes
Dissociative Disorders	Dissociative Fugue
	Dissociative Identity Disorder
	Depersonalization Disorder
Eating Disorders	All Subtypes
Feeding and Eating Disorders of Infancy or Early Childhood	Pica
Hallucinogen-Related Disorders	All Subtypes
Impulse Control Disorders	Intermittent Explosive Disorder
	Pathological Gambling
Impulse Control Disorders Not Elsewhere Classified	Trichotillomania
Inhalant-Related Disorders	All Subtypes
Learning Disorders	All Subtypes
Mental Retardation	All Subtypes
Mood Disorders	Major Depressive Disorder
	Bipolar I Disorder
Nicotine-Related Disorders	All Subtypes
Opioid-Related Disorders	All S'ubtypes
Other Disorders of Infancy, Childhood, or Adolescence	Separation Anxiety Disorder
	Selective Mutism
Paraphilias	All subtypes
Parasomnias	Nightmare Disorder
	Sleep Terror Disorder
	Sleepwalking Disorder
Personality Disorders	All Subtypes
Phencyclidine-Related Disorders	All Subtypes
Schizophrenia and Other Psychotic Disorders	All Subtypes

(Continued)

Table 2.1 Continued

Disorder	Subtype
Sedative-Hypnotic or Anxiolytic-Related Disorders	All Subtypes
Sexual Dysfunctions	All Subtypes
Sleep Disorders Related to Another Mental Disorder	All Subtypes
Somatoform Disorders	All Subtypes
Tic Disorders	Tourette's Disorder

SOURCE: From "Culture-Bound Syndromes, Cultural Variations, and Psychopathology" (Table II, pp. 160-161) by Freddy A. Paniagua, in I. Cuéllar and F. A. Paniagua (Eds.), *Handbook of Multicultural Mental Health: Assessment and Treatment of Diverse Populations* (pp. 139-169). Copyright © 2000 by Academic Press, reprinted by permission of the publisher.

The Cultural Formulation

The Outline of Cultural Formulation in Appendix I (APA, 1994) constitutes the third important addition in the *DSM-IV*. Lewis-Fernandez and Kleinman (1995), however, suggested that placing this cultural formulation in Appendix I rather than placing it after the Multiaxial Assessment at the front of the *Manual* would prevent clinicians from seriously considering the relevance of that formulation in their clinical practice. Regardless of this critique, the inclusion of an outline for cultural formulation represents a major step in the *DSM-IV* (Smart & Smart, 1997; Takeuchi, 2000). The *DSM-IV* recommends that clinicians should consider each category in the Cultural Formulation at the moment the particular case is evaluated.

Economic and policy-made reasons, however, might prevent many clinicians from applying that suggestion (Paniagua, 1998). In the first case, an assessment of elements in the Cultural Formulation is not reimbursed by insurance companies, and under this circumstance, clinicians using the *DSM-IV* would not spend time with that formulation during the initial evaluation of the case. In the second case, placing the Cultural Formulation in Appendix I would suggest to many clinicians that they are not required to consider cultural variants during the assessment of the case using the *DSM-IV* (Lewis-Fernandez & Kleinman, 1995). A summary of the elements of the Cultural Formulation follows (*DSM-IV*, 1994, pp. 843-844; see also Takeuchi, 2000, and Tseng & Streltzer, 1997, pp. 248-251).

Cultural Identity of the Individual

This element of the Cultural Formulation generally includes the client's cultural or ethnic preference groups, language use and preference, and in the case of immigrants, the degree of involvement with the culture of origin versus the host

Table 2.2 Summary of Psychiatric Disorders Without Descriptions of Cultural
Variations in the *DSM-IV* (APA, 1994)

Disorder	*Subtype*
Anxiety Disorders	Anxiety Disorder Due to a General Medical Condition
	Substance-Induced Anxiety Disorder
Attention-Deficit & Disruptive Behavior Disorders	Oppositional Defiant Disorder
Communication Disorders	Stuttering
Dissociative Disorders	Dissociative Amnesia
Elimination Disorders	Encopresis
	Enuresis
Factitious Disorders	No subtype listed
Feeding & Eating Disorders of Infant or Early Childhood	Rumination Disorder
	Feeding Disorder of Infant or Early Childhood
Gender Identity Disorder	No Subtype Listed
Impulse Control Disorders Not Elsewhere Classified	Kleptomania
	Pyromania
Mental Disorders Due to a General Medical Condition	Catatonic Disorder Due to a General Medical Condition
	Personality Change Due to a General Medical Condition
Mood Disorders	Dysthymic Disorder
	Bipolar II Disorder
	Cyclothymic Disorder
	Other Mood Disorders
Mood Disorder Due to a General Medical Condition	Substance-Induced Mood Disorder
Motor Skills Disorders	Developmental Coordination Disorder
Other Disorders of Infant, Childhood, or Adolescence	Reactive Attachment Disorder of Infant or Early Childhood
	Stereotypic Movement Disorder
Other (or Unknown) Substance-Related Disorders	All Subtypes
Other Sleep Disorders	Sleep Disorder Due to a General Medical Condition
	Substance-Induced Sleep Disorder
Personality Disorders	Narcissistic Personality Disorder
Pervasive Developmental Disorders	Autistic Disorder
	Rett's Disorder
	Childhood Disintegrative Disorder
	Asperger's Disorder
Polysubstance-Related Disorders	All Subtypes
Psychotic Disorder Due to General Medical Condition	Substance-Induced Psychotic Disorder

(Continued)

Table 2.2 Continued

Disorder	Subtype
Schizophrenia and Other Psychotic Disorders	Shared Psychotic Disorder
Sleep Disorders	Primary Insomnia
	Primary Hypersomnia
	Narcolepsy
	Breathing-Related Sleep Disorder
	Circadian Rhythm Sleep Disorder
Tic Disorders	Chronic Motor or Vocal Tic Disorder
	Transient Tic Disorder

SOURCE: Adapted from Paniagua (1998).

culture. For example, a Latino client might prefer the term *Chicano* rather than *Mexican American* if he or she believes that the first term implies fewer degrees of acculturation to the Anglo American culture (see Skerry, 1993, p. 253). An African American client might report more involvement with the Anglo American culture and display many behavior patterns (e.g., dress, music) *unrelated* to the African American community (Paniagua, 1998). By contrast, another African American client might not only identify himself or herself with the African American community but would also prefer to use Black English in communicating symptoms (Dillard, 1973; Paniagua, 1998; Smitherman, 1995).

Cultural Explanation of the Individual's Illness

This element emphasizes idioms of distress used by the individual to communicate symptoms (e.g., "spirits"), the meaning of the severity of the symptoms as perceived by the client in relation to the cultural reference groups, the client's perception of the cause of the problem, and names applied to symptoms within the client's culture. For example, a Hispanic client would report that he or she feels "depressed" after being exposed to a *susto* (see Table 2.3). Among many Hispanics, a mental disorder (*enfermedad mental*) is less severe than being insane (*estar loco*). In the first case, the client is suffering from a *crisis nerviosa* or *ataque de nervios* (nervous crisis). In the second case, the client shows a complete loss of control or withdrawal or both, requiring hospitalization (Paniagua, 1998).

Cultural Factors Related to Psychosocial Environment and Level of Functioning

Social support and the interpretation of social stressors in cultural terms are two factors clinicians should consider when applying this element of the

TABLE 2.3 Summary of Cultural-Bound Syndromes

Name	*Group*	*Description*
Ataques de Nervios	Hispanics	Out-of-consciousness state resulting from evil spirits. Symptoms include attacks of crying, trembling, uncontrollable shouting, physical or verbal aggression, and intense heat in the chest moving to the head. These ataques are often associated with stressful events (e.g., death of a loved one, divorce or separation, or witnessing an accident including a family member).
Amok, Mal de Pelea	Malaysians, Laotians, Filipinos, Polynesians, Papua New Guineans, Puerto Ricans	A dissociative disorder involving outburst of violence and aggression or homicidal behavior at people and objects. A minor insult would precipitate this condition. Amnesia, exhaustion, and persecutory ideas are often associated with this syndrome.
Brain Fag	African Americans	Problems with concentration and thinking among high school and university students experiencing the challenges of schooling. Symptoms include head and neck pain, blurring of vision, burning, and heat resembling Somatoform, Depressive, and Anxiety Disorder.
Boufee Delirante	Haitians	Sudden outburst of aggression, agitation associated with confusion, psychomotor excitement, and symptoms resembling Brief Psychotic Disorder (including visual and auditory hallucinations, paranoid ideation).
Colera	Hispanics	Anger and rage disturbing body balances leading to headache, screaming, stomach pain, loss of consciousness, and fatigue.
Dhat	East Indians, Chinese, Sri Lankans	Extreme anxiety associated with a sense of weakness, exhaustion, and the discharge of semen.
Falling-out	African Americans	Seizurelike symptoms resulting from traumatic events, such as robberies.
Ghost Sickness	American Indians	Weakness, dizziness, fainting, anxiety, hallucinations, confusion, and loss of appetite resulting from the action of witches and evil forces.
Hwa-byung	Asians	Pain in the upper abdomen, fear of death, tiredness resulting from the imbalance between reality and anger.
Koro	Asians	A man's desire to grasp his penis (in a woman, the vulva and nipples) resulting from the fear that it will retract into his body and cause death.

(Continued)

Table 2.3 Continued

Name	Group	Description
Latah	Asians	A sudden fright resulting in imitative behaviors that appear beyond control, including imitation of movements and speech; the individual often follows commands to do things outside his or her wish (e.g., verbal repetition of obscenities).
Mal de ojo	Hispanics	Medical problems, such as vomiting, fever, diarrhea, and mental problems (e.g., anxiety, depression), could result from the mal de ojo (evil eye) the individual experienced from another person. This condition is common among infants and children; adults might also experience similar symptoms resulting from this mal de ojo.
Mal puesto, hex, root work, voodoo death	African Americans, Hispanics	Unnatural diseases and death resulting from the power of people who use evil spirits.
Ode-ori	Nigerians	Sensations of parasites crawling in the head, feelings of heat in the head, paranoid fears of malevolent attacks by evil spirits.
Pibloktog	Arctic and subarctic Eskimos	Excitement, coma, and convulsive seizures resembling an abrupt dissociative episode, often associated with amnesia, withdrawal, irritability, and irrational behaviors, such as breaking furniture, eating feces, and verbalization of obscenities.
Susto, Miedo, espanto, pasmo	Hispanics	Tiredness and weakness resulting from frightening and startling experiences.
Taijin kyofusho	Asians	Guilt about embarrassing others, timidity resulting from the feeling that the appearance, odor, facial expressions are offensive to other people.
Wacinko	American Indians	Feeling of anger, withdrawal, mutism, suicide from reaction to disappointment and interpersonal problems.
Wind or Cold Illness	Hispanics, Asians	A fear of the cold and the wind; feeling weakness and susceptibility to illness resulting from the belief that natural and supernatural elements are not balanced.

SOURCE: From "Culture-Bound Syndromes, Cultural Variations, and Psychopathology" (Table I, pp. 140-141) by Freddy A. Paniagua, in I. Cuéllar and F. A. Paniagua (Eds.), *Handbook of Multicultural Mental Health: Assessment and Treatment of Diverse Populations* (pp. 139-169). Copyright © 2000 by Academic Press, reprinted by permission of the publisher.

Cultural Formulation. In the specific case of Hispanic clients, the *compadre* (cofather), *comadre* (comother), and the priest are generally consulted by the family experiencing economic and emotional difficulties, and the *compadre* and *comadre* are often responsible for the care of children when their parents are not available (Paniagua, 1998). The minister and church members are important sources of provision of emotional support to African American families (Boyd-Franklin, 1989). In the case of American Indian families, clinicians should always convey to members of the family that he or she is willing to consult with the medicine man or women and tribal leaders regarding emotional difficulties experienced by one or more members of the family and potential treatment alternatives to deal with these difficulties in cultural terms (Trimble & Fleming, 1989). In the mind of many Southeast Asian refugees (Gaw, 1993a), the extended family would include welfare agencies, community support, and individuals providing such services (e.g., social workers, case managers, etc.). In the case of the second factor in this element of the Cultural Formulation, clinicians should carefully screen the client's perception of racial discrimination and the stress resulting from this perception that could lead to symptoms involving a given mental disorder (e.g., Major Depressive Disorder).

Cultural Elements of the Relationship Between the Individual and the Clinician

This element of Cultural Formulation generally includes the assessment of two variables: (a) ethnic and racial differences between the client and the clinician and (b) the negative impact of these differences on the diagnosis and treatment of the client. For example, the fact that the client and the clinician are both African Americans does not necessarily mean that they share the same ethnicity (i.e., values, norms, and lifestyle; Boyd-Franklin, 1989). In this context, an African American client who does not share core values, norms, and styles expected in the African American community would feel uncomfortable with the assignment of the case to an African American clinician with a strong sense of cultural identity with this group. Similarly, culturally identified Hispanic clients would not perceive an appropriate level of care if assessed and treated by Hispanic clinicians who did not believe in the cultural values of machismo and *marianismo* in the regulation of relationships among family members. In the specific case of Hispanic women treated by those clinicians, a failure to appreciate the role of machismo and *marianismo* in this cultural group could result in diagnosing these women with "Dependent Personality Disorder" in those cases when symptoms could be explained in terms of cultural norms these women are expected to accept in the Hispanic community. In this particular context, this diagnosis could result in the programming of "social skills training" (in which Hispanic women would learn self-assertive behaviors and use them in the presence of Hispanic men, particularly husbands). This treatment modality, however, is not culturally appropriate because these women would be asked to perform behaviors (e.g., to openly disagree with their husband's requests to perform a certain behavior, such as staying at home, having sexual relationships when asked to do so, etc.) that compete with the value that Hispanics place on *respeto, machismo,* and *marianismo* (Paniagua, 1998).

Overall Cultural Assessment for Diagnosis and Care

In this category, clinicians are advised to conclude with a formulation that includes a discussion of how cultural variables influence the diagnosis and care of the case. For example, a clinician using this outline for Cultural Formulation would conclude something like the following:

> Cultural variables appear central in the development of the present symptoms. These variables should be considered in the treatment plan. Consultation with clinicians with expertise in the assessment and treatment of clients from the same cultural group should be considered, particularly in the identification of culturally sensitive psychological tests to further explore the role of cultural variations in the development of symptoms. Culturally sensitive treatment should be planned with this case, taking into consideration the client's cultural identity and the culturally normative behaviors this client is expected to display in the referent group.

Culturally Related V-Codes

The fourth cultural recommendation in the *DSM-IV* (APA, 1994) is an emphasis on two culturally sensitive V-codes: Religious or Spiritual Problem (V62.82, p. 685) and Acculturation Problem (V62.4, p. 685). Additional V-codes clinicians should also consider when assessing and treating culturally diverse clients include Partner Relational Problem (V61.1, p. 681), Parent-Child Relational Problem (V61.20, p. 681), and Identity Problem (V313.82, p. 685).

Religious or Spiritual Problem

In general, religious and spiritual beliefs should be considered in those cases when these beliefs lead to "distressing experiences that involve loss or questioning of faith, problems associated with conversion to a new faith, or questioning of spiritual values" (APA, 1994, p. 685). A religious or spiritual problem would also be the focus of clinical attention when this problem interferes with the overall assessment and treatment of the particular disorder (see Chapter 7, "The Case of the Preacher").

Acculturation Problem

An acculturation problem would be the focus of clinical attention when this problem involves "adjustment to a different culture (e.g., following migration)" (APA, 1994, p. 685). Significant difference in the levels of acculturation among family members may be in itself the focus of clinical attention (see Chapter 5, "The Case of Carol," and Cuéllar, 2000). For example, an acculturated Hispanic female residing with less acculturated family members would show symptoms suggesting a given mental disorder (e.g., Major Depressive Disorder) because of a significant difference in acculturation between the client and her parents. This is the problem confronted by many Hispanic adolescent females living with traditional Hispanic parents who do not believe in the American dating process (adolescents are permitted to engage in dating in the absence of parents and with minimal or zero supervision from parents; the opposite is the case among many traditional Hispanic families). In clinical practice, this discrepancy in acculturation levels should be the focus of clinical attention (Paniagua, 1996). Acculturation scales summarized in Chapter 3, Table 3.1 (e.g., Cuéllar, Arnold, & Maldonado, 1995) are recommended to determine whether or not an acculturation problem should be a focus of clinical attention in Axis IV during the management of given disorders in Axis I and Axis II in the *DSM-IV* (APA, 1994).

Partner Relational Problem

This problem could be the result of specific cultural variables, such as marked differences in acculturation levels among family members, rejection of the cultural values of machismo and *marianismo* by some members of the Hispanic community (Paniagua, 1998), and disagreement regarding the discipline of children among parents with two different cultural backgrounds (Ho, 1992). For example, a partner relational problem would result from disagreements between a Hispanic female and her Hispanic husband regarding her rejection of *marianismo* in the marital relationship and her husband's strong belief in these values. These disagreements could be the function of different levels of acculturation between husband and wife, resulting in marital conflicts expressed in terms of negative communication and verbal fights between husband and wife. In this case, the task for the clinician would be to place such disagreements in a cultural context and develop culturally sensitive strategies to assist both partners with an understanding of the impact of cultural variations on their marital conflicts. This point is illustrated in Chapter 6 with "The Case of Bienvenido."

In terms of a partner relational problem around the discipline of their children, a case in point is the assessment of an American Indian family in which husband and wife are from two different tribes. For example, in the Hopi tribe, the wife is primarily responsible for the management of children, whereas in the Cherokee tribe, both husband and wife share the discipline of children. Thus, a Cherokee woman who marries a Hopi man would express marital discord with her husband if he shows no concern regarding the discipline of their children (Ho, 1992; Paniagua, 1998). In Chapter 7, "The Case of Ron Tiger" illustrates this point.

Parent-Child Relational Problem

Parent-child relational problems may include "impaired communication, overprotection, [and] inadequate discipline" (APA, 1994, p. 681). An acculturation problem may lead to parent-child relational problem in the form of impaired communication (see Chapter 5, "The Case of Carol"). For example, later-generation Asian adolescents may disagree with their early-generation parents in certain issues involving customs and lifestyles (e.g., dressing, dating) because parents are less acculturated than their children into the American society (Ho, 1987). The phenomenon of machismo among Hispanic fathers could lead to the overprotection of their children. Inadequate discipline of children and adolescents among American Indian parents may be the result of the parents belonging to different tribes (Ho, 1987).

Identity Problems

Issues related to career choice, long-term goals, moral values, group loyalties, sexual orientation, physical appearance, and child-parent racial differences in adoptions are examples of potential identity problems that clinicians should consider as the focus of clinical attention in the assessment and treatment of mental disorders. This recommendation is particularly important for clients from the four cultural groups discussed in this book (see Chapter 5, "The Case of Marcia"). As noted by Helms (1987),

> in response to discrimination and/or racism in American society, members of minority groups develop strategies for coping with their minority-group status, and the manner in which they come to cope becomes an important part of their personal identity. (p. 339)

It should be noted that the *DSM-IV* (APA, 1994) provides three general guidelines when using these V-Codes. First, the client has a mental disorder, and it is related with a given V-Code. For example, a client meets criteria for Major Depressive Disorder resulting from his difficulty in accepting major behavioral changes displayed by his wife who is acculturated to the American culture. Chapters 5 and 6 include clinical cases illustrating the applicability of this guideline. Second, the client has a mental disorder, but it is unrelated to a particular V-Code. For example, a client meets the criteria for Delusional Disorder, but his or her relational problems with the spouse are not related with the mental disorder (see the Chapter 6, "The Case of Ms. A"). Third, the evaluation clearly shows that the client does not have a mental disorder, but the particular V-Code appears to be the focus of clinical attention. This would be the case of a client who seeks counseling to deal with his or her intention to reduce the level of involvement with church activities (a potential religious or spiritual problem) but does not meet criteria for any of the mental disorders in the *DSM-IV*. All cases in Chapter 7 illustrate the applicability of the third guideline in clinical practice (e.g., see "The Case of the Preacher").

In general, the "cultural formulation is meant to supplement the multiaxial diagnostic assessment and to address difficulties that may be encountered in applying *DSM-IV* criteria in a multicultural environment" (APA, 1994, p. 843). As noted earlier, however, this recommendation is not being followed by most clinicians because managed care insurance companies do not cover description of mental disorders in cultural terms, and the inclusion of the cultural formulation was included in an appendix, suggesting that it is not mandatory to deal with cultural issues when assessing and treating disorders in the *DSM-IV* (Lewis-Fernandez & Kleinman, 1995). The hope is that the current emphasis on multiculturalism as a fourth force in mental health services (the other three are psychodynamic, humanistic, and behavioral theories of behavior; Pedersen, 1999) would provide the theoretical and clinical background needed to move the Outline of Cultural Formulation and the Glossary of Culture-Bound Syndromes from Appendix I (APA, 1994, pp. 843-849) to the multiaxial diagnostic assessment of mental disorders across Axes I and II in the *DSM-IV* (APA, 1994). Table 2.4 shows a general format for a treatment plan combining the traditional clinical assessment of mental disorders with the cultural formulation suggested by the *DSM-IV* (APA, 1994, Appendix I).

A Word of Caution

This chapter and subsequent discussions throughout the text emphasize the importance of considering cultural variations in the assessment and treatment of clients from the four cultural groups described in this *Casebook*. It is also important, however, to remember that placing too much emphasis on such variations may prevent clinicians from diagnosing a true case of psychopathology. Too much attention to cultural variables not only could result in underdiagnosing the case (failure to make the appropriate diagnosis), but it may also result in turning clients over to folk healers for treatment under the assumption that what the client is experiencing is a set of culturally related symptoms resembling a given *DSM-IV* disorder that cannot be treated by mental health professionals. This decision to turn over clients to nonclinicians is considered a major error in clinical practice by experts in the cross-cultural field (e.g., Westermeyer, 1993). One

TABLE 2.4 Clinical Assessment and Cultural Formulation in a Treatment Plan for Culturally Diverse Clients

---

Clinical Assessment
   A. Identifying information (name, age, gender, race)
   B. Summary of present mental disorder
   C. History of present mental disorder
   D. Family history of present mental disorder
   E. Social and developmental issues
   F. *DSM-IV* Multiaxial Classification (Axes I-V)

Cultural Formulation
   1. Cultural Identity of the Client: Client's ethnic-cultural reference groups, immigration status, language preference
   2. Cultural explanation of the individual's illness: *Mal puesto* (hex, root work), *mal de ojo* (evil eye), possessing spirits, fatalism, *susto* (a magical fright), help-seeking experiences (healer = curandero[a], witch doctor = brujo[a])
   3. Cultural factors related to psychosocial environment and level of functioning: Social stressors (recent immigrants, acculturation), available social support (extended family members, the role of the church).
   4. Cultural elements of the relationship between the client and the clinician: Client-therapist ethnic and racial differences, clinician's rejection of cultural values (machismo), failure to distinguish abnormality from normality in the client's culture
   5. Overall cultural assessment for diagnosis and care of the present mental disorder: Symptoms reported by client appear to be culture-related. The following V-Codes should be considered: V62.4: acculturation problem; V62.89: religious and spiritual problems, V61.1: partner relationship problems (machismo versus *marianismo*)

---

way to prevent this error is to emphasize a combination of cross-cultural assessment strategies (e.g., the *DSM-IV* outline for Cultural Formulation) and traditional psychiatric or psychological evaluations to make a differential diagnosis based on the potential impact of cultural variations leading to symptoms suggesting a given mental disorder (Castillo, 1997; Lonner & Ibrahim, 1996; Pope-Davis & Coleman, 1997).

3

Assessment in a Cultural Context

An emphasis on cultural variants suggested in the *DSM-IV* (APA, 1994) could assist clinicians with the prevention of bias during the diagnosis of mental disorders among African American, American Indian, Asian, and Hispanic clients. The *DSM-IV*, however, is only a preliminary step in the application of culturally sensitive strategies to minimize biases when diagnosing psychopathologies in such clients (Arnold & Matus, 2000; Cuéllar, 1998; Geisinger, 1992; López, 1989; Paniagua, 1998; Puente & Perez-Garcia, 2000; Samuda, 1998). Examples of additional strategies include (a) the selection of culturally sensitive instruments to assess acculturation, intellectual functioning, and psychopathology; (b) clinicians' cultural sensitivity in the use of the mental status exam; (c) clinicians' self-assessment of biases and prejudices; (d) the phrasing of culturally appropriate questions during the clinical interview, and (e) clinicians' skills in terms of selecting the least biased assessment strategy among a series of available assessment alternatives.

Assessment of Acculturation, Intellectual Functioning, and Psychopathology

As noted earlier, the *DSM-IV* (APA, 1994, see p. 681) recommends that clinicians should consider the process of acculturation in those cases when a discrepancy in the level of acculturation among family members may be in itself the focus of clinical attention. The next step is to identify acculturation scales, which could assist clinicians with an assessment of acculturation beyond clinical observations. Table 3.1 includes examples of acculturation scales across the culturally diverse groups discussed in this book. The Brief Acculturation Scale suggested by Paniagua (1998) is recommended for clinicians interested in conducting a quick assessment of acculturation with clients before using more elaborate scales in Table 3.1. This brief scale emphasizes three variables: (a) generational status (e.g., first vs. fifth), (b) the language the client prefers to use (e.g., native language vs. English only), and (c) a client's preference of social activities with a particular group (e.g., only within own racial group vs. only with a different racial group). The overall scores range from 1 to 5 points and as the score increases, more acculturation is assumed.

In the case of the assessment of intellectual functioning and psychopathology among culturally diverse groups, *DSM-IV* recommends psychological tests in which the person's relevant characteristics are represented in the standardization sample of the test or by employing an examiner familiar with the aspects of the individual ethnic or cultural background. This recommendation is particularly important during the assessment of Mental Retardation, Learning Disabilities, and Communication Disorders among children and adolescents (APA, 1994; Bernal, 1990; Canino & Spurlock, 1994). Table 3.2 shows examples of tests recommended during the assessment of intellectual functioning and psychopathology among culturally diverse clients. It should be noted that many clinicians are not expert in the use of these tests, particularly psychiatrists who are not generally trained to administer psychological tests. But the issue here is not expertise in cross-cultural testing procedures but knowledge of culturally sensitive psychological tests appropriate for the particular client (see Tables 3.1 and 3.2) and the clinician's efforts to seek appropriate consultation from mental health professionals with expertise in the use and interpretation of such tests. An excellent review of the testing controversy in a cultural context can be found in *Psychological Testing of American Minorities* (Samuda, 1998). In the Appendix (pp. 203-236), Professor Samuda provided a "compendium of tests for minority adolescents and adults" that should assist clinicians with a quick identification of tests "that are designed for, or advertised as being appropriate for, minorities or educationally disadvantaged" (Samuda, 1998, p. 203).

When seeking cultural consultation in the use of tests to assess intellectual functioning and mental disorders, clinicians should be aware of the potential negative impact of the examiner-client racial or ethnic dissimilarity on an accurate assessment of the case. For example, African Americans often obtain lower scores on intelligence tests when such tests are administered by white practitioners rather than by African American clinicians (Jenkins & Hunter, 1991). Other studies have shown that African Americans tend to alter their responses on self-report measures when the race of the examiner changes (Lineberger & Calhound, 1983). In addition, Marcos (1976) suggested that when bilingual Hispanic clients are interviewed in English rather than in Spanish, the probability of errors in assessment and diagnosing of psychiatric disorders may increase (see also Arroyo, 1996). Thus, to minimize biases in the assessment of intellectual functioning and mental disorders among culturally diverse groups, the consultation process should include strategies to minimize the sociocultural gap between the examiner and the client (see Paniagua, 1998, pp. 106-125).

TABLE 3.1 Acculturation Scales

Reference	Name of Scale	Group
Smither & Rodriguez-Giegling (1982)	Acculturation Questionnaire	Vietnamese, Nicaraguan refugees
Cuéllar, Harris, & Jasso (1980) and Cuéllar, Arnold, & Maldonado (1995)	Acculturation Rating Scale for Mexican Americans	Mexican Americans
Pierce, Clark, & Kiefer (1972)	Acculturative Balance Scale	Mexican Americans, Japanese
Szapocznik, Scopeta, Arnalde, & Kurtines (1978)	Behavioral Acculturation Scale	Cubans
Norris, Ford, & Bova (1996)	Brief Acculturation Scale for Hispanics	Mexican Americans, Puerto Ricans
Franco (1983)	Children's Acculturation Scale	Mexican Americans
Garcia & Lega (1979)	Cuban Behavioral Identity Questionnaire	Cubans
Mendoza (1989)	Cultural Life Style Inventory	Mexican Americans
Milliones (1980)	Developmental Inventory of Black Consciousness	African Americans
Masuda, Matsumoto, & Meredith (1970)	Ethnic Identity Questionnaire	Japanese Americans
Ramirez (1984)	Multicultural Experience Inventory	Mexican Americans
Wong-Rieger & Quintana (1987)	Multicultural Acculturation Scale	Southeast Asians, Hispanic Americans, Anglo Americans
Helms (1986)	Racial Identity Attitude Scale	African Americans
Hoffmann, Dana, & Bolton (1985)	Rosebud Personal Opinion Survey	American Indians
Suinn, Rickard-Figueroa, Lew, & Vigil (1987)	Suinn-Lew Asian Self-Identity Acculturation Scale	Chinese, Japanese, Koreans

SOURCE: Adapted from Paniagua (1998)

TABLE 3.2 Tests Recommended for Use With Culturally Diverse Groups

Reference	Name of Test
Tests to Assess Intellectual Functioning	
Anastasi (1988)	Culture-Fair Intelligence Test
Kaufman, Kamphaus, & Kaufman (1985)	Kaufman Assessment Battery for Children (K-ABC)
Anastasi (1988)	Leiter International Performance Scale
Anastasi (1988)	Progressive Matrices
Mercer & Lewis (1978)	System of Multicultural Pluralistic Assessment (SOMPA)
Tests to Assess Psychopathology	
Radloff (1977)	Center for Epidemiologic Depression Studies Depression Scale (CES-D)
French (1993)	Draw-A-Person Test (DAP)
Eysenck & Eysenck (1975)	Eysenck Personality Questionnaire (EPQ)
Holtzman (1988)	Holtzman Inkblot Technique (HIT)
Yamamoto, Lam, Choi, Reece, Lo, Hahn, & Fairbanks (1982)	Psychiatric Status Schedule for Asian-Americans
Spitzer & Endicott (1978)	Schedule for Affective Disorders and Schizophrenia (SADS)
Constantino, Malgady, & Rogler (1988)	Tell-Me-A Story Test (TEMAS)
Kinzie, Manson, Do, Nguyen, Anh, & Than (1982)	Vietnamese Depression Scale

The Mental Status Exam in a Cultural Context

Another important aspect of culturally sensitive assessment of mental disorders is a clinician's effort to minimize biases when using the mental status exam (Rosenthal & Akiskal, 1985) with culturally diverse clients. This exam is extremely important in clinical practice, particularly in those cases when it is critical to carefully assess suicidal ideation or attempts. Cultural variants, however, should be considered when using this exam with culturally diverse clients.[1]

The mental status exam makes the assumption that a series of so-called normal behaviors and cognitive processes are shared by so-called normal people, *regardless of cultural background.* This assumption, however, could lead to misdiagnosis of psychopathology in culturally diverse clients (Hughes, 1993; Mueller, Kiernan, & Langston, 1992; Westermeyer, 1993). For example, clients who fail the serial 7s test (a client is asked to subtract 7 from 100) may be experiencing anxiety, depression, or early symptoms for schizophrenic disorder. If psychological tests used with these clients also show signs for a given mental disorder, the assumption is that this serial 7s test was a good test under this circumstances.

Aside from the fact that the validity of the serial 7s test is questionable by many researchers (see Hughes, 1993, pp. 27-28), many members of multicultural groups would fail this task because they are not versed in the area of counting either forward or backward. In addition, prior studies indicate that normal subjects can make between 3 and 12 errors with this test (Hughes, 1993). Therefore, one should not be surprised if a client fails this test (particularly in a stressful environment, such as a clinic with busy clinicians trying to conduct the entire assessment in less than 1 hour to fulfill managed care requirements). A better (culturally sensitive) strategy would be to instruct the client to select a given number (e.g., 50—it does not need to be 100) and then to subtract whatever individual number the client wants to subtract from that number. In this case, the client is given the opportunity to use his or her level of math skills rather than someone imposing unrealistic expectations on the client's knowledge of the subject.

The assessment of *orientation* allows clinicians to assess negativism, confusion, distraction, hearing impairment, and receptive language disorders. This test emphasizes the assessment of the self (the person), place, and time. For example, a clinician would ask "What is your last name?" "What is the name of this month?" "Where are you right now?" In response to the first question, a Hispanic client, for example, may look confused and distracted because he or she would have to decide which last name to report between the two last names often used by Hispanics, which often includes one last name for the father (e.g., Rodriguez) and another for the mother (e.g., Martinez), as in *Jose Antonio Rodriguez Martinez.* If the client is not familiar with the name of that month in Standard American English, or is not familiar with the name of the building (or cannot remember that name) and he or she appears to provide an incorrect answer in these situations, the client would show negativism, hearing impairment, or receptive language disorder. In this example, a culturally sensitive approach would be to say "You're Hispanic, so you probably have one last name for your father and another for your mother . . . could you tell me these names?" "Do you know the name of this month in English . . . if you don't, you can say it in Spanish." "At this moment, do you know that you are in a hospital and not in your house?"

The assessment of *general knowledge* could be used to assess poor educational background, severe deterioration in intellectual functioning, and the ability to assess remote memory. For example, a clinician would ask "What are the colors of the American Flag?" "What are the names of three countries in Central America?" "Who is the president of the United States?" or "Who was the president before him" "What is the total population of the United States of America," and so on. As noted by Hughes (1993), the answers to such questions imply geographical and public knowledge, and many members of culturally diverse groups do not have this kind of knowledge for two reasons. First, they are too poor to travel (which is one way to answer some of these questions). Second, many members of such groups are illiterate (Westermeyer, 1993). Examples of a culturally sensitive mental status exam in this case would be, "What are the colors of your country's flag?" "Tell me the name of three cities in your country."

"Who is the president in your country?" "Who was the president in your country before him?" "Could you tell me the approximate number of people living in your country today?"

The assessment of *thought process* is a crucial area in that exam. For example, *thought blocking* is a sudden cessation of thought or speech, which suggests schizophrenia, depression, and anxiety (Mueller et al., 1992). Clients who are not fluent in English would show thought blocking. As noted earlier, Hispanic clients with little command of Standard American English would spend a great deal of time looking for the correct word, phrase, or sentence before answering a question from the therapist, and this could lead to anxiety resulting in thought blocking (Martinez, 1986). African American clients who use Black English in most conversational contexts would also spend a great deal of time looking for the construction of phrases or sentences in Standard American English when they feel that Standard American English is expected (Yamamoto, Silva, Justice, Chang, & Leong,1993). In these examples, a culturally sensitive approach would be to interview Hispanic clients using their native language, and African American clients would be told that he or she could use Black English when answering questions during this exam.

Appearance is another important element in the mental status examination that must be carefully screened in cultural terms. For example, lack of eye contact, failure to stare directly into the therapist's eyes, and careless or bizarre dressing and grooming could point to signs of psychiatric disorders (Hughes, 1993). Many Asian clients, however, would avoid eye contact and staring at people's eyes during social interactions (D. W. Sue & D. Sue, 1990, 1999), partially because in such groups it is *impolite* to maintain eye contact or to look directly into the eyes of other persons. Therefore, eye contact as a measure of appearance should be carefully considered during this exam. The definition of what is normal dressing and grooming in the mind of a clinician may not be shared by a client who always comes to the therapist right after finishing a long working day in a grocery store, for example, without enough time to go home to take a shower and change clothes. This client will probably look dirty, with soiled face, hands, and nails, and careless appearance. Lack of self-care skills (e.g., days without taking a shower or changing clothes) is a critical behavior to assess when assessing certain mental disorders (e.g., Major Depression, Alcohol Intoxication, etc.). Under this circumstance, however, the issue is not to assume that the absence of self-care skills is in itself a sign of mental disorder but to assess the absence of such skills in terms of variables preventing a given client from displaying such skills under normal (and expected) conditions. The way a client presents himself or herself in the clinic could be a significant point to consider in the assessment of mental disorders (e.g., a client with symptoms suggesting Major Depressive Disorder might dress carelessly during the first evaluation), but the point here is to also consider environmental variables with the potential of affecting the way that particular client is expected to dress when visiting the clinic (e.g., the earlier hypothetical case with the employee who just finished a long working day at the store).

Self-Assessment of Bias and Prejudice

A self-assessment of bias and prejudice is recommended in those cases when the clinician does not share the racial or ethnic background of the client. This self-assessment could be achieved with the Self-Evaluation of Biases and Prejudice Scale suggested by Paniagua (1998). This scale includes 10 items inquiring about respondents' past and future experiences with specific issues involving African American, American Indian, Asian, Hispanic, and Anglo American communities. Examples of items include "Would you date or marry a member from the following groups?" and "Would you expect a favorable therapy outcome with" (e.g., African American). Each item is scored on a scale ranging from 1 (*very much*) to 3 (*not at all*). The maximum bias-prejudice score is 3.0.

Preliminary results with this scale were reported by Paniagua, O'Boyle, Tan, and Lew (2000) with a sample of 39 professionals, including counselors, teachers, social workers, psychologists, school principals, education diagnostician, and community service administrators. Overall, the alpha coefficient was .87, suggesting acceptable internal consistency for the items. In terms of the mean score of participants' responses to the 10 items, participants reported less bias-prejudice toward clients from their own racial or ethnic background relative to their response in the case of client-professional racial or ethnic differences. For example, Anglo American (mean = 1.6) and Hispanic (mean = 1.6) participants reported more bias-prejudice toward African American clients, in comparison to African American participants' bias-prejudice scores toward these clients (mean = 1.2, p 002, F = 11.32, df = 2). Similar results were found when comparisons were made across participants in relation to clients from their own racial or ethnic background versus participants-clients' racial or ethnic differences: in each case, participants sharing the same race or ethnicity of the client tended to show less bias-prejudice toward these clients relative to their level of bias-prejudice toward clients from different racial or ethnic background. Additional instruments designed to assess multicultural competence among clinicians and with modest reliability and validity results include the Cross-Cultural Counseling Inventory-Revised, Multicultural Counseling Awareness Scale-Form B: Revised Self Assessment, Multicultural Counseling Inventory, and the Multicultural Awareness-Knowledge-and-Skills Survey. A review of each of these instruments can be found in Ponterotto, Rieger, Barrett, and Sparks (1994).

Phrasing Culturally Appropriate Questions

Another important issue in the prevention of cultural bias is the use of culturally appropriate questions during the clinical interview to enhance a culturally sensitive assessment of psychopathology among clients from these culturally diverse groups. For example, Yamamoto (1986) suggests that the following question is not appropriate with Asian clients: "What is your opinion of yourself compared with other people?" The reason to avoid this question is that many

Asians do not like to compare themselves with other people (D. W. Sue & D. Sue, 1999).

Selection of the Least Biased Assessment Strategy

Clinicians working with culturally diverse clients should make an effort to use the least biased assessment strategies first, in a series of available strategies. It should be noted that despite efforts to control bias in the assessment of culturally diverse clients, an assessment strategy that is not biased against specific culturally diverse groups is not yet available (Anastasi, 1988; Rogler, 1999; Zuzuki, Meller, & Ponterotto, 1996). For this reason, Paniagua (1998) recommended that rather than looking for unbiased assessment strategies, a better approach would be to learn how best to select and use these strategies with African American, American Indian, Asian, and Hispanic clients (see Yamamoto, 1986, p. 116).

For example, the question is not whether to avoid the mental status exam but how to use materials that are culturally related to the tasks the client is being asked to solve during this exam. In the assessment of *DSM-IV* criteria for Major Depression, self-report of psychopathology measures, such as the Minnesota Multiphasic Personality Inventory (MMPI) and the Beck Depression Inventory (Dana, 1993b; Zalewski & Green, 1996), are often recommended. The results obtained with these tests could be enhanced with the design of an assessment strategy in which the client could record actual behaviors indicative of "depression" (e.g., did not attend church or any social activities during the past 2 weeks), and this self-monitoring of actual behaviors could be combined with direct observations made by others (e.g., family members, trained observers in clinical settings, etc.) to assess the reliability of the client's self-assessment of symptoms. In this example, self-monitoring is less biased than assessment procedures with the MMPI, for example; direct behavioral observations (e.g., family members recording actual presence vs. absence of the client in social activities) would be the least biased assessment method relative to the MMPI, Beck Depression Inventory, and self-monitoring.

Note

1. In earlier publications (Paniagua, 1994, 1998), the editor of the present text provided an extensive discussion of problems clinicians might encounter when using the mental status exam with clients from the four racial groups discussed in this text. The heading of the pertinent section in those publications, however, was "Avoid the Mental Status," which created an unintended confusion among readers because the author, indeed, did not mean to say that the mental status exam is not a critical approach to use during the overall assessment of clients from these culturally diverse groups. The present text provides the opportunity for the editor to sincerely apologize to readers of his earlier publications for the wrong message he *unintentionally* included in such earlier publications. This section of the present text provides culturally sensitive strategies when using the mental status exam with culturally diverse clients.

4

Treatment in a Cultural Context

In general, clients from the culturally diverse groups discussed in this book prefer treatment modalities that are *directive* (i.e., focusing on what the problem is and what to do to solve it), *active* (what role the client is expected to play in solving that problem), and *structural* (i.e., what exactly is being recommended to the client to solve the problem; Paniagua, 1998; D. W. Sue & D. Sue, 1990). Most treatment modalities have been recommended with clients from such groups (Ho, 1987; Paniagua, 1998, 2000; Tanaka-Matsumi & Higginbotham, 1996). The central point to consider when using these treatment modalities is to ensure that they are used in a cultural context (Canino & Spurlock, 1994). Examples follow of the programming of culturally sensitive therapeutic interventions, which are recommended in the treatment of clinical cases described in Chapters 5 through 8.

Individual Psychotherapy

Individual psychotherapy (i.e., interventions with only the client) is generally recommended with all groups prior to the scheduling of family therapy (a preferred form of intervention across present racial groups, in comparison with individual psychotherapy) in those cases when the phenomenon of acculturation seems to play a major role in the manifestation of the clinical problem. This is particularly important to remember when the clinical problem involves either marital conflict (e.g., discrepancies in values, norms, and worldviews in relationships between less acculturated men and more acculturated women) or family problems involving children and adolescents with high levels of acculturation relative to their less acculturated parents (Jones, 1992).

Family Therapy

Because of the critical role the extended family plays in the lives of many clients from the culturally diverse groups described in this book, several authors suggest that family therapy should be considered among the first treatment approaches with these clients (Berg & Jaya, 1993; Boyd-Franklin, 1989; Ho, 1987). This recommendation should not be generalized across all clients from these groups, however. For example, Boyd-Franklin (1989) pointed out that in the case of marital difficulties, many African American men would not consider family therapy as the first choice of treatment because of fear that their reports about these difficulties may be seen as a sign of weakness in them. Boyd-Franklin (1989) suggests that this observation could be explained in terms of the socialization of African American men, in which the impact of racism, discrimination, and the development of the macho role (Boyd-Franklin, 1989) prevents men from showing weakness during difficult times.

Another point to consider when planning family therapy with these clients is to conduct an assessment of acculturation with each member of the family to be included in this therapy (Paniagua, 1998). At least two reasons exist in the literature to support this point. First, different levels of acculturation among family members may result in different family therapy outcomes (Ho, 1987). For example, communication family therapy would be a treatment choice to manage Hispanic adolescents who reject their parents' rigid discipline resulting in "a recurrent pattern of negative, defiant, disobedient, and hostile behavior" (APA, 1994, p. 91) toward their parents. This modality of family therapy, however, may not achieve its goal without a prior assessment of the level of acculturation in those adolescents versus their parents' level of acculturation (see Chapter 5, "The Case of Janet T."). In this example, acculturated adolescents would display behaviors expected in the dominant culture (e.g., dating without parents present), whereas less-acculturated parents would disagree with such behaviors.

Second, the overall finding in the cross-cultural literature is that many clients from the groups described in this text would prefer to involve the extended family in the treatment of mental disorders (Canino & Spurlock, 1994; Ho, 1987; D. W. Sue & D. Sue, 1990). This point, however, most be carefully evaluated when family therapy modalities are programmed to manage these disorders. Yamamoto (1986) pointed out that acculturated Asian clients may or may not want family members involved in their therapy. In addition to acculturation scales included in Table 3.1, the Brief Acculturation Scale proposed by Paniagua (1998) is recommended in those cases when a quick assessment of acculturation is needed to determine the selection of family therapy as the treatment of choice for the particular family. More extensive acculturation scales (e.g., Cuéllar et al., 1995) could be used during the implementation of family therapy. Additional guidelines involving the use of family therapy modalities with these clients can be found in Paniagua (1996).

Group Therapy

Some modifications in procedures are recommended when group therapy is used to manage mental disorders among African American, American Indian, Asian, and Hispanic clients (Kinzie & Leung, 1993; Martinez, 1993; D. W. Sue & D. Sue, 1990; Thompson et al., 1993). Some African American clients may not agree to participate in group therapy that includes white clients because of the African American history of racism and discrimination by the dominant Anglo American culture. Racial issues between these two groups should be explored during individual psychotherapy sessions before the integration of group therapy in the treatment plan involving African American clients. Another cultural variable to consider in this context is whether the African American client would use Black English versus Standard American English during group therapy sessions (see Smitherman, 1995, for linguistic and grammatical examples between these two language modalities).

In the case of Hispanic clients, acculturated clients should not be mixed with nonacculturated clients in group therapy sessions. More acculturated Hispanics may disagree with traditional cultural values involving *marianismo,* machismo, and dating shared by recent Hispanic immigrants. In addition, if group therapy sessions are conducted in Spanish, it is important to remember that some members of the group may not be able to understand other members because many linguistic and grammatical variants exist in the ways clients from different Spanish-speaking countries use Spanish in daily conversations. In this case, clients should be told that although group therapy will be conducted in Spanish, in some circumstances, it would be necessary for the speaker to explain the meaning of a word, phrase, or sentence that appears difficult for the other members of the group to understand. In addition, Martinez (1993) suggested that group therapy with Hispanics (particularly Mexican Americans) should be (a) flexible in attendance expectations, (b) provide assistance with social problems and medication needs, (c) include a certain degree of therapist's self-disclosure (*personalismo,* discussed in Chapter 1), and (d) scheduled around clients' busy schedules (e.g., biweekly rather than weekly).

Although group therapy has been recommended with Asian clients (e.g., Kinzie & Leung, 1993), the tendency of clients from this racial group to avoid sharing their problems with people outside the immediate family may prevent the integration of this therapy modality in a treatment plan. As noted in Chapter 1, a sense of shame, humiliation, and guilt may be cultural variables preventing Asian clients from reporting emotional problems to people outside the family. These variables should be assessed with these clients prior to their integration in group therapy sessions.

For American Indian clients, group therapy is often recommended in combination with traditional Indian activities (Thompson et al., 1993). With these clients, group therapy should not be scheduled without support or permission or both from tribal leaders. In addition, the medicine man or woman, elders, and other respected tribal members should be invited to participate in some group therapy. Indian mental health professionals (psychologists, psychiatrists, social workers, school counselors) should be involved in group therapy in those cases when the therapist leading the meeting is not an American Indian.

Behavioral Approaches

The overall assumption is that the effectiveness of behavioral interventions (behavior therapy, cognitive-behavioral therapy, applied behavior analysis; Paniagua & Baer, 1981) would be generalized across people, regardless of race or ethnic background (e.g., Paniagua & Black, 1990). These approaches have been recommended with all cultural groups described in this book (Organista & Dwyer, 1996; Paniagua, 1998; Walker & LaDue, 1986). However, clinicians should carefully consider the impact of cultural variables when using behavioral approaches. This point will be illustrated with two cognitive-behavioral therapies often recommended to manage emotional difficulties among African American, American Indian, Asian, and Hispanic clients, namely, problem-solving training and social-skills training.

Problem-Solving Training

This technique teaches clients to identify the critical problem (among a series of problems), to determine alternative responses to deal with that problem, to explore both positive and negative consequences from each alternative response, and to evaluate the results (Kratochwill & Bergan, 1990). During the application of each of these elements, the expected outcome is the achievement of one's goals in the absence of negative consequences. This training is recommended with clients from culturally diverse groups because it emphasizes a directive, active, and structural approach in the management of emotional difficulties (Boyd-Franklin, 1989; Paniagua, 1998). As noted by Schneider, Karcher, and Schlapkohl (1999), however, problem-solving training should be used with caution with culturally diverse clients because this training "emphasizes autonomy and promotion of one's own interests in relationship" (p. 178). For this reason, these authors recommended that this training might not be appropriate in the case of clients who emphasize cooperation in their relationships with other members of the family as well as with clients who are expected to be obedient in the presence of adults.

For example, group consensus in establishing individual goals is a key cultural value among American Indians (Ho, 1987). In this context, problem-solving training would have to be modified to emphasize group consensus in the solution of a client's emotional difficulties. Another example is the case of many Hispanic clients (children and adults) who may not agree with the underlying assumptions of problem-solving training because they believe in the cultural values of machismo and *marianismo* (see Chapter 1). In the case of Asian clients, problem-solving techniques should emphasize a process of negotiation rather than a process of head-on confrontation. In this process of negotiation, the therapist is seen as the mediator who is expected to be an expert in a position of authority (Paniagua, 1998; D. W. Sue & D. Sue, 1999).

Social-Skills Training

The goal of social-skills training (or assertiveness training) is to teach clients to be able to express his or her feelings and legitimate rights in the presence of other members of the community (Lange & Jakubowski, 1976; Schneider et al., 1999), and several authors have pointed out that many members of culturally diverse groups often "cannot speak out or assert themselves" (Yamamoto et al., 1993, p. 116). This being so, many clinicians believe that a solution is the programming of social-skills training in the treatment plan. For example, social-skills training has been recommended with African American and Hispanic clients who are not assertive in their interpersonal relationships with other people (Boyd-Franklin, 1989; Comas-Díaz & Duncan, 1985; Organista & Dwyer, 1996).

Prior to the programming of social-skills training with the discussed racial groups, however, clinicians should consider specific cultural variables that may negatively affect expected clinical outcome. For example, Organista and Dwyer (1996) pointed out that behavior and communication among many Hispanic families are "governed by traditional institutions (e.g., family, community, the church) and values (e.g., deference to authority based on age, gender, social position, etc.)" (p. 135). In this context, Organista and Dwyer (1996) concluded that "assertiveness can run contrary to the culture's emphasis on communication that is polite, personal, nonconfrontational, and deferential" (p. 135). For this reason, assertiveness training would not be recommended for women who have been raised believing that they should be obedient and submissive to men (*marianismo*) or with children and adolescents who are not allowed to argue with their parents, and respect toward the authority of the father is expected (e.g., Asian and Hispanic families).

Pharmacotherapy

Some clinicians do not like to use medication for two reasons. First, they do not believe in the effectiveness of drug therapy in the treatment of mental health problems. Second, if they do believe in the therapeutic effects of medication, clinicians who are not physicians (e.g., psychologists, social workers, etc.) have to depend on the schedule and treatment regimen of a physician (e.g., a psychiatrist). Regardless of any disagreement on the use of medication, three points should be emphasized when considering the use of medication with clients from the four racial groups described in this book (Paniagua, 1998). First, many clients from these groups expect medication for the treatment of their mental disorders. This is particularly true in the case of Mexican American clients (Martinez, 1986). Second, a large set of empirical data exists indicating that certain drugs may be effective in the management of certain mental disorders with all racial groups discussed in this book, such as tricyclic antidepressants in the management of depression (Joyce & Paykel, 1989; Kinzie & Edeki, 1998; Silver, Poland, & Lin, 1993). Third, recommending empirically tested drugs with clients who are *expecting* them during the therapy process may result in a placebo effect (the medication is not actually effective, but the client thinks that it is really effective). If this effect actually works with a client experiencing a severe mental problem (e.g., Major Depressive Disorder), it would be beneficial for the client (e.g., the mental problem is less severe over time), and the clinician may claim that he or she was sensitive to the client's cultural expectation regarding the use of medication as a fundamental approach (in the client's mind) in the treatment of the problem.

Insight-Oriented, Psychodynamic, and Rational-Emotive Therapies

In general, insight-oriented and psychodynamic therapies emphasize internal conflicts and difficulties with the personality of the individual and blame the client for his or her own problems. Many clients from the African American, American Indian, Asian, and Hispanic communities believe that problems in their life emerge because of external conflicts with the environment and that other people should be blamed for their problems. Rational-emotive therapy is an argumentative or logistical talking therapy, which competes with the values and beliefs of clients from these communities (Schneider et al., 1999). For example, Hispanic men who believe in the cultural values of *marianismo* and machismo in their relationships with other people in their community would not agree with the use of therapy procedures aiming to change this belief.

5

Cultural Variables With Childhood and
Adolescent Psychiatric Disorders

Certain mental disorders (e.g., Conduct Disorder) appear to be initially noted in childhood and adolescence. In the *DSM-IV,* however, these disorders are included in a separate section "for convenience only and is not meant to suggest that there is any clear distinction between 'childhood' and 'adult' disorders" (APA, 1994, p. 37). For this reason, the *DSM-IV* points out that "adults may also be diagnosed with disorders included [in the first section of the *Manual*] if their clinical presentation meets relevant diagnostic criteria," (p. 37) such as Adult Attention Deficit-Hyperactivity Disorder (Weiss & Hechtman, 1993).

In addition, when using the *DSM-IV* to diagnose mental disorders in children and adolescents, clinicians are advised (see APA, 1994, p. 37) to consider the entire classification of mental disorders in the *Manual* (Substance-Related Disorders, Mood Disorders, Anxiety Disorders, etc.). This chapter will illustrate the applicability of cultural variables with five examples of mental disorders first diagnosed in children and adolescents, namely ADHD, Conduct Disorder, Oppositional Defiant Disorder, Separation Anxiety Disorder, and Reactive Attachment Disorders. Chapter 6 illustrates the applicability of such variables with other mental disorders in the *DSM-IV* (e.g., Mood Disorders, Anxiety Disorders) across children, adolescents, and adults.

Psychiatric Disorders, Clinical Cases, and Discussion

Attention Deficit-Hyperactivity Disorder

Attention Deficit-Hyperactivity Disorder (ADHD) is known to occur in various cultures (APA, 1994, p. 81). Variations in the prevalence of the disorder have been reported, however. Two hypotheses have been proposed to explain these variations (Barkley, 1990). According to the first hypothesis, a high rate of ADHD in developing countries (e.g., United States) relative to underdeveloping countries (e.g., Caribbean, Central American, and South American countries) is a result of an increase in the cultural tempo in developing countries, which leads to increases in environmental stimulation and significant increases in impulsivity, inattention, and overactivity among individuals exposed to that cultural tempo. In the second hypothesis, ADHD is a function of consistent versus inconsistent expectations in the "demands made and standards set for child behavior and development" (Barkley, 1990, p. 16). Cultures that are consistent not only provide clear and reliable expectations and consequences for behaviors that follow expected societal norms, but they also minimize individual differences among children. These two elements of consistent culture are said to result in fewer children with a diagnosis of ADHD. By contrast, inconsistent cultures would result in more children with diagnosis of ADHD because they emphasize individual differences and provide unclear expectations and consequences to children regarding which behaviors conform to expected norms.

Conduct Disorder

A diagnosis of Conduct Disorder might be erroneously applied to individuals residing in settings where undesirable behaviors could be considered protective (e.g., threatening, high-crime, impoverished areas). In addition, immigrant youth from countries with a long history of wars, resulting in aggressive behaviors necessary for survival in such countries, would not warrant the diagnosis of Conduct Disorder. Behaviors that are the result of a reaction to the immediate social context would not be considered as examples of Conduct Disorder (APA, 1994, p. 88).

Oppositional Defiant, Reactive Attachment, and
Separation Anxiety Disorders

The *DSM-IV* (APA, 1994) did not mention cultural variables in the cases of Oppositional Defiant Disorder and Reactive Attachment Disorder. As noted in Chapter 1, symptoms of Oppositional Defiant Disorder could result from a child-parent difference in levels of acculturation. Regarding Reactive Attachment Disorder, Cervantes and Arroyo (1995) pointed out symptoms suggesting that this disorder

> may be common among children in some inner city neighborhoods and rural areas where the child experiences severe isolation, lack of stimulation, and deprivation. Immigrants children are often prohibited by their parents from socializing beyond the household out of fear for child's safety. These may be children from neighborhoods where community violence occurs. (p. 145)

Last, the *DSM-IV* suggests that in the diagnosis of Separation Anxiety Disorder, clinicians should assess the extent to which anxiety resulting from separation from home or parents is tolerated in a given culture. Thus, the *DSM-IV* specifically recommends that "it is important to differentiate Separation Anxiety Disorder from the high value some cultures place on strong interdependence among family members" (APA, 1994, p. 111).

The following case vignettes illustrate the application of cultural variants across the aforementioned examples of disorders first noted in childhood and adolescence. As noted in the Preface, the two-part discussion of each vignette (general and cultural formulation) is provided by the editor, Dr. Freddy A. Paniagua, to ensure the commonality of the discussion across cases around specific cultural issues.

The Case of Clarence
Andrés J. Pumariega, MD

Clarence was a 5-year-old biracial male presented to a child and adolescent psychiatry clinic for the evaluation of hyperactivity, impulsivity, and mood disturbance. He was brought by his foster mother, who reported that he had difficulty in paying attention in his kindergarten class and in Sunday school, was fidgety and restless in classroom situations, and required multiple reminders and prompts to follow directions or commands. His behavior had become increasingly difficult to manage: He demonstrated aggressive behaviors towards peers, and at times even towards his foster mother, without clear provocation.

The foster mother described Clarence's mood as mostly being "irritable," though at times, he cried for no reason and looked quite sad. He isolated himself from most of his peers and complained that they did not like him because he was "different" from them. His sleep was disrupted by nightmares from which he awoke frequently, but his appetite was normal and his energy level was normal to elevated. However, he did not demonstrate any periods of elation or grandiosity. He often referred to himself as a "bad kid" and had made suicidal statements on two occasions in the prior 4 weeks, though he had not made any attempt to hurt himself. He also demonstrated startle responses when exposed to loud noises or voices.

Clarence was the product of a relationship between a white woman and an African American man with whom she shared a substance abuse habit, reportedly to alcohol and cocaine. Little was known about the natural father's background except that he was not in the child's life for very long, having left the natural mother shortly after his birth. The natural mother was well known to the local community as a troubled youth, being in frequent trouble with the law with juvenile court appearances and having substance abuse problems from her early teens. It was suspected but not confirmed that she was using cocaine and alcohol during the pregnancy. The natural mother had kept Clarence until he was 3 years of age, when protective services stepped in and removed him, due to the poor living conditions he lived in as a result of mother's substance abuse as well as suspicions of physical abuse by the mother's boyfriend at the time. The natural mother had not had any physical contact with Clarence since the removal and reportedly had moved to the Southwest. She managed to track Clarence to the home of his foster parents, however, and called him about twice a year, sounding intoxicated and promising to come back for him. After these phone calls, Clarence's mood was even more labile, ranging from anger to despair and becoming more aggressive and impulsive.

When he was first placed with the foster parents, Clarence was malnourished, had limited language skills, avoided eye contact and much human contact, was not yet toilet trained, and often foraged for food and hoarded food in the home. He had made much progress since then, with language skills being at age level, interacting with the foster parents, eating normally and having normal weight for height, and having been toilet trained. Little was known about his earlier development. Psychological testing at a developmental clinic in which he was evaluated prior to referral showed him to be of normal intelligence and without any significant learning disabilities but showing much anxiety, depression, and inattention.

The foster parents were a well-educated African American couple, the father a college educator and community organizer and the mother an elementary school teacher. They had three older children, all of whom had - already completed college and were successful on their own rights. The foster parents lived in a small university town in the Southeast United States with a predominantly white population and few minority families. The foster mother felt that Clarence was definitely seen as different by his mostly white schoolmates and did experience much harassment about his biracial background. She expressed much sensitivity to the plight of African American males, feeling that she needed to instill within Clarence a strong African American identity, and she expressed her fear that her foster child would be additionally "labeled" with a psychiatric diagnosis. She was quite intense in her devotion to Clarence and believed that strict discipline (and at times, corporal punishment, though nonabusive) and religious teaching were necessary to help him to overcome the impact of his past trauma and abandonment. She often considered adopting Clarence, feeling that he deserved a "second chance," but feared the stress on her marriage during a time in their lives in which they hoped to "slow down." She also had multiple physical problems that at times left her unable to keep up with Clarence. The father was similarly attached to Clarence but was also concerned about his failure to respond to their guidance and structure.

On mental status examination, Clarence appeared as a well-groomed and initially well-mannered child who was cooperative in interviews. During this exam, Clarence was extremely hyperactive, including fidgeting in his chair and, after a few minutes, moving about the room. His speech was coherent, with no pressure or looseness, with normal content and no delusions, and with good articulation. His mood was calm and even at first, but he became more agitated as interviews progressed, with his affect ranging from sad to anxious to angry at turns, with little provocation. He had poor eye contact with the interviewer and anyone else except his foster parents, and he limited affectionate physical contact with them even when they hugged him. He demonstrated above-average intellectual abilities, being able to read some phrases and add simple numbers. His attention span was quite short, shifting play activities after a couple of minutes. Clarence was well oriented to person, day, month, and year. He demonstrated much impulsivity and aggression in his play, having family doll figures fighting each other and experiencing accidents (crashing cars and falling off roofs). When asked about friends, he expressed feeling "bad" about being different and how both black and white kids made fun of him, having few friends. He avoided questions about his natural mother and stated that his foster parents were "nice" to him. He did acknowledge that he had frequent nightmares and fears of people hurting him, with his feeling nervous at times.

Clarence was diagnosed with ADHD, Mixed-sub-type, and Post-Traumatic Stress Disorder (PTSD). Depressive Disorder Not Otherwise Specified (NOS) and Reactive Attachment Disorder were also considered in the differential diagnosis. The diagnostic team recommended that Clarence receive individual play therapy with a focus on trauma resolution, from a white female therapist, and family psychoeducational therapy with a focus on behavioral skills training, from a Latino child psychiatrist. Pharmacotherapy was also recommended, including Ritalin, 5 milligrams twice a day, for his ADHD symptoms and Prozac, 10 milligrams daily, for his mood and anxiety symptoms. The latter recommendations were quite upsetting to the foster mother, who felt that Clarence should be helped without the use of medications. We worked with the foster parents on the decision about the use of medications, including her concerns about excessive use of medications with children of color, fears of addiction, and their being stigmatizing. The parents were empowered to make the decisions and actively question the recommendations, with the Latino child psychiatrist empathizing with their fear of loss of control. After much consideration and discussion about risks versus benefits (including side effects and fears and myths about medications), they agreed to a medication trial, with a clear delineation that the decision to proceed or cease medications was totally up to them.

Clarence demonstrated improvement in his inattention and hyperactivity, with his foster parents being able to take him to services at the African American church they attended, for the first time. His mood was less labile, and he began to experience less frequent nightmares and less anxiety. However, his aggressiveness continued unabated, with continued oppositionalism on his part towards his foster parents. In individual therapy, he continued to focus on play that reenacted family conflicts and trauma, with white parent dolls giving their children to black parent dolls but also, both parent dolls hitting and leaving their babies. Clarence's adoptive parents were counseled on the frequent testing that adoptive children demonstrate towards surrogate parents as part of their fear of attachment after prior abuse and abandonment. They in turn were able to explore their own ambivalence as to whether they would be able to adopt Clarence, given his problems and their limitations. The parent counseling also focused on the parents' rather strict and rigid approach to childrearing. They were supported on their culturally traditional beliefs about child obedience to parental authority and structure, which particularly fit Clarence's needs. Clarence's adoptive parents, however, learned about more effective techniques of limit setting (such as response cost and time-out removal from environmental reinforcers), careful selection of target behaviors to avoid unnecessary control struggles, and the use of contingent positive reinforcers as a foundation for shaping positive behaviors. The foster mother's urgency to deal with his behavior was addressed, pointing out the many liabilities that Clarence started out with, his progress under their care, and the need for a longitudinal approach.

Further improvements were noted over a period of a year, during the continued programming of individual and family therapy in combination with pharmacotherapy. Visits began to be tapered down to once monthly. Clarence, however, experienced a sudden relapse of his problems with aggression and oppositionalism, as well as a return of his anxiety and mood symptoms (though his attentional problems did not relapse). He also began to refuse to participate in individual psychotherapy, becoming aggressive in each visit to the clinic. Because of these sudden changes in Clarence's behaviors, a decision was made to reevaluate him, with emphasis on the potential sources for these changes. Three significant contributing factors were identified. First, the natural mother had suddenly appeared at Clarence's school, asking to see him and going up to him unannounced in the school playground to talk with him, then disappearing just as suddenly. Second, the foster mother had a relapse of health problems, which limited her time and availability to Clarence. Third, the foster parents revealed that they had been overcoming their reservations about adopting Clarence as he showed more open affection towards them, but with his renewed problems and foster mother's health problems, they were again reconsidering. His behavior worsened to the point that the parents had to obtain home-based behavioral technician services for 2 months, from a case management agency for children in state custody, to help them manage Clarence in their home and school.

Therapy sessions were increased in frequency again, and the doses of Ritalin and Prozac were adjusted upward to 10 milligrams twice daily and 20 milligrams daily, respectively. In addition, the issues of Clarence's biracial heritage now were more clearly focused in both individual and eventually in joint family sessions. The foster parents recognized that they needed to encourage Clarence to socialize with white as well as African American children, and they needed to expose him to a more mixed racial environment socially. When he began to express his bewilderment about his natural mother's visit, Clarence's adoptive parents also were able to express their understanding that she loved him and wanted to care for him but was unable to do so. Under this circumstance, the adoptive parents made sure that Clarence understood that they would continue providing emotional and instrumental support to him. The parents were also supported in maintaining their behavioral skills and maximizing their flexibility with him. The foster father also began to take a more active parenting role with Clarence, both in terms of recreational activities as well as behavior management. A turning point was a trip to the West Coast for a professional meeting that they all took together, which facilitated their bonding and interaction. The foster mother expressed feeling less pressured about her parenting, and Clarence began to demonstrate much less mood lability, anxiety, and aggression. The foster parents finally decided to legally adopt Clarence, and shortly thereafter, he began to express less aggression in his individual sessions, and his play was much more relaxed and cooperative. Both the individual sessions and the Prozac were terminated before the second year of treatment.

Clarence is now 9 years of age. He continues on Ritalin, 10 milligrams twice a day and 5 milligrams in the afternoon as needed for homework completion. He is seen every 3 months for medication management and family behavioral support. He has excellent academic performance and no behavioral problems and shows much maturity for his age, able to sit and converse with the child psychiatrist and his parents. He is engaged in sports and church activities with peers and helps his father with home chores. He shows open affection towards his adoptive parents, with both of them expressing much pride in his accomplishments. He identifies himself as African American but can talk about his white natural mother comfortably, at times wondering where she is but expressing hope that she will "get better" and some day visit him.

Discussion of the Case of Clarence
Freddy A. Paniagua

General Discussion

The diagnostic team concluded that Clarence met the criteria for ADHD (APA, 1994, pp. 83-84) and PTSD (APA, 1994, pp. 427-428). In the differential diagnosis, Depressive Disorder NOS (APA, 1994, 350) and a Reactive Attachment Disorder (APA, 1994, p. 116-118) were also considered. Some clinicians may argue that criteria for PTSD were not as evident as those of ADHD. In addition, for these clinicians, it would appear that this case does not provide a clear-cut example of the applications of cultural variants the *DSM-IV* recommends in the case of PTSD. According to the *DSM-IV,* the main feature of PTSD is the development of symptoms (e.g., distressing recollection of the event, recurrent distressing dreams of the event, persistent avoidance of stimuli associated with the traumatic event)

> following exposure to an extreme traumatic stressor involving direct personal experience of an event that involves actual or threatened death or serious injury, or other threat to one's physical integrity, or witnessing an event involves death, injury, or a threat to the physical integrity of another person. (p. 424)

Symptoms pointing to a PTSD could also develop when an individual learns about an extreme trauma (e.g., violent death) experienced by a friend or family member (see APA, 1994, p. 424). Consideration of cultural variables when diagnosing PTSD, the *DSM-IV* emphasizes the impact of "social unrest and civil conflicts" on immigrants with prior traumatic experiences associated with wars in other countries.

In terms of the aforementioned stipulations, Clarence did not experience those extreme traumatic stressors, and he did not emigrate from a country in social unrest or civil conflict. The diagnostic team did identify several critical social stressors affecting Clarence's overall symptoms, namely, his poor living conditions and suspected physical abuse by his mother, who probably was emotionally disturbed, his biracial status, and his foster parents' decision to continue living in an environment with a predominantly white population after taking Clarence into their home. Clarence's symptoms of nightmares, startle response, and some elements of reliving the trauma are clinical manifestation for the diagnosis of PTSD. In addition, aggression and rage are frequent symptoms seen in PTSD (and Reactive Attachment Disorder [RAD]), and these are indicative of the intensive anxiety and mood disturbance associated with PTSD (and RAD). Furthermore, anxiety symptoms are not only difficult to differentiate from those of ADHD, but such symptoms are often comorbid with PTSD (Cuffe, McCullough, & Pumariega, 1994).

In general, children often show disruptive behavioral symptoms in conjunction with internalizing disturbances. The comorbid internalizing disorder is often missed in children of color, however, due to the clinician's bias and lack of understanding of cultural context, which could lead to misdiagnosis and ineffective or incomplete treatment (Kilgus et al., 1995). Therefore, in this case, the diagnostic team appropriately included in the differential diagnosis the possibility of a Depressive Disorder NOS (APA, 1994, p. 350).

The *DSM-IV* did not discuss potential cultural variants that clinicians should consider when diagnosing children with RAD (another possible diagnosis considered in this case). As noted earlier, Cervantes and Arroyo (1995) pointed out that symptoms suggesting this disorder may be experienced by children with a history of "severe isolation, lack of stimulation, and deprivation" (p. 145). Clarence definitively experienced severe isolation, lack of stimulation, and deprivation throughout the first 3 years of his life, which resulted in the action taken by Child Protective Services because of Clarence's poor living conditions, exposure to mother's substance abuse, and suspicions of physical abuse. Clarence's adoptive parents provided a more rewarding environment that enabled Clarence to engage in developmentally appropriate social relatedness in most contexts (sports and church activities with peers), suggesting substantial reduction in symptoms for RAD (see APA, 1994, p. 118, Criteria 1 and 2 for RAD).

It should be noted that another alternative diagnosis is Adjustment Disorder with Mixed Disturbance of Emotion and Conduct (APA, 1994, p. 624). This diagnosis, however, requires that "symptoms must be developed within 3 months after the onset of the stressor(s)" (APA, 1994, p. 623), whereas with Clarence, symptoms were developed over a period of 5 years. The diagnostic team felt that PTSD was probably the best alternative diagnosis, given the impact of those traumatic events over a long period (birth to 5 years of age, the age at which Clarence was first evaluated by Dr. Pumariega). Last, in the overall diagnosis of this case, two V-Codes to consider in Axis V are Neglect of Child (APA, 1994, p. 682) and Identity Problem (APA, 1994, p. 685).

Cultural Formulation

An important issue addressed in the treatment plan, from the perspective of the cultural formulation, was Clarence's cultural reference involving two racial groups (a white mother and an African American father). Psychologically, Clarence struggled with two intertwined conflicts: his conflict over his abandonment by his white mother and efforts to integrate his biracial identity into his self-concept. The fact that Clarence's adopted parents were both African Americans constituted a major factor in helping Clarence to adjust both to his biracial status and the development of a strong African American identity over time. For example, after 4 years of intensive treatment with emphasis on cultural issues, Clarence (then 9 years old) was able to identify his main cultural reference group as African American and at the same time was able to talk about his white natural mother with the absence of emotional difficulties.

His adoptive parents were clearly culturally sensitive to Clarence's identification with the African American community. In addition, the adoptive parents' decision to continue living in a predominantly white community with few minority families may be interpreted as their efforts to ensure that Clarence would develop over time an appreciation for the other side of his biracial background (i.e., the integration of his white identity). Placing Clarence in that community, however, probably constituted a social stressor leading to his early maladaptive behaviors at the age of 5 in response to harassment about his biracial background, according to the adoptive parents' reports. The treatment team, however, elected to avoid an emphasis on the adoptive parents' choice to live in that predominantly white community, and it appears that those efforts were culturally adaptive for Clarence; this decision from the treatment team was culturally sensitive in this particular case. Another culturally sensitive treatment strategy leading to Clarence's adjustment to his biracial status was to encourage the adoptive parents to engage Clarence in social activities involving white and African American children as well as to explore a more mixed racial environment for the family.

It should be noted that Clarence was treated by a Latino child psychiatrist and a white female therapist and that this client-psychiatrist-therapist racial difference did not affect the selection of the most culturally sensitive treatment to manage Clarence's emotional difficulties. For example, the alliance with the adoptive parents and their sense of empowerment and participation in all aspects of treatment was crucial. This was true both in terms of addressing their mistrust of mainstream culture institutions and interventions (such as pharmacotherapy) and also in terms of supporting their parenting roles in terms of recognizing the need to provide opportunities for Clarence's involvement with both the white and African American cultures. The approach to pharmacotherapy was not only introduced as an alternative treatment modality, but it also addressed the power differential that parents of color feel in dealing with physicians and psychiatrists from different racial or ethnic backgrounds. In addition, the dose of serotonin reuptake inhibitor was titrated carefully to prevent potential difficulties with the slow metabolism of these agents among some African American clients (Smith & Mendoza, 1996).

During individual psychotherapy with the white therapist, sessions centered around Clarence's feelings of abandonment and anger toward the biological mother who was not accessible physically and psychologically to Clarence's needs, as well as with Clarence's difficulty in dealing with his biological mother's sudden presence and absence from school, his struggle to be loyal to his adoptive parents, and his difficulty in determining his cultural identity. It should be noted that regardless of racial or ethnic considerations, few biological mothers actually forget or put in the past their abandoned children, and most of them make an effort to contact their children after coming "to terms with this loss and progressing through a mourning and grieving process" (Okun, 1996, p. 25). Therefore, the reevaluation of Clarence's sudden relapse of his problems was an important decision taken by the treatment team to explore the reasons for these sudden changes in Clarence's progress.

Another culturally sensitive approach in the treatment of Clarence was the selection of a behavioral approach during counseling of the parents, which was practical and problem oriented (Paniagua, 1998; Pumariega & Cross, 1997). Within this context, Clarence's adoptive parents were introduced to more effective (and less punitive) behavioral interventions, which they eventually incorporated into their repertoire. It was also important to address Clarence's need for empathy with the white aspect of his identity, which the parents were able to accomplish through their expressed empathy for his white biological mother.

Last, in this case and other cases where racism appears to play a significant role in the explanation of emotional difficulties, it is important to discuss with the client or the family (e.g., Clarence's adoptive parents) issues regarding personal prejudice, individual racism, and cultural racism (see Chapter 1), as well as the role of one or more of these in the present case (Okun, 1996). As noted earlier (Chapter 1), one form of personal prejudice is abandonment of a child by the biological mother because the child is biracial. As noted by Okun (1996), "children of interracial couples may experience personal prejudice from the racial groups of both parents" (p. 217). In the case of Clarence, this was a possibility in explaining why his biological father was not in Clarence's life for very long.

Harassment by white children directed against African American children in school is one example of individual racism, and Clarence's adoptive parents reported this situation in this case. Another example is when an African American child (or a child from another culturally diverse group) has many white friends at school, but he or she never receives an invitation to visit the homes of these friends. The fact that Clarence lived in a predominantly white community suggests that he went to a school with a large percentage of white children. The question, "How many of his white friends invited him to their house to spend the night?" suggested in Chapter 1 to assess this type of racism, would assist the treatment team to further explore the negative impact of this form of racism on Clarence's emotional difficulties.

Last, as noted in Chapter 1 in the discussion of cultural racism, people of color who manage to be successful and move up in their academic and social lives might be seen as different from other individuals of color who do not achieve in similar contexts and are thus accepted by the predominant culture (Okun, 1996). Clarence's adoptive parents may be an example of this type of achievement perceived by the dominant culture, and further exploration of this point would help to understand the parents' decision to raise Clarence in a predominantly white community.

The Case of Lisa
Angela S. Lew, PhD

Lisa is a 14-year-old female from the Dominican Republic, referred by the school for allegedly drinking beer in the bathroom, poor grades, physical aggression toward other students, skipping classes, and oppositional behaviors directed toward male teachers. These problems started at the beginning of her school year and worsened approximately a month before she was referred for evaluation.

Lisa comes from a single-parent household consisting of her mother and 5 siblings. Her parents were born in the Dominican Republic, grew up in the United States during their childhood, but later returned to the Dominican Republic. When Lisa was 10 years old, her mother took her children and left the father by leaving the Dominican Republic and returning to the states. The father maintained sporadic contact with the children. The separation affected Lisa the most because she was "daddy's girl." Mother reported a long history of conflictual marital relationship, including father's alcohol abuse, verbal abuse toward her when intoxicated, and suspected infidelity. Family-related stressors include recent deaths of extended family members due to illness and the father undergoing extensive medical diagnostic tests. Lisa was close to her extended family. She had a difficult time mourning the losses of family members. Lisa had a difficult time coping with her fears related to her father's illness and a recent revelation involving an intimate relationship between her father and another woman resulting in children from this relationship, unknown to Lisa.

The mother appeared very tearful, depressed, and overly emotional and dramatic. She reported feeling overwhelmed in her care-giving role, particularly in managing her children's varied reactions to the stressors. Her oldest son at home took on the parental role, and this caused friction between Lisa and him. Lisa defied his requests at home, resulting in verbal and physical fights at home between Lisa and her oldest brother. The mother seemed to conform to her culturally based female role to be passive and deferent to males, and she was relinquishing her authority to her oldest son against Lisa's defiant behavior.

Given the family dynamics and the importance of the family in the Dominican culture, Lisa, her mother, and siblings were invited for a preliminary session to perform an extended assessment, with the goals of exploring the need for family therapy to address unresolved mourning; to restructure roles within the family (i.e., empower and restore mother's parenting role); and to enhance communication, coping, and problem-solving skills. The mother, however, reported that she could not get all her children to attend this preliminary session. Therefore, the therapist decided to conduct weekly individual psychotherapy with Lisa, with emphasis on short-term goals due to the short-term nature of the treatment.

During the individual psychotherapy process, Lisa reported additional emotional difficulties, including feelings of worthlessness, depression, irritable mood, social withdrawal, and impaired concentration. She also reported overeating, leading to significant weight gain, and sleep disturbance. Lisa kept the therapist at a distance during early individual psychotherapy sessions by carefully selecting what she was going to reveal, at times telling lies but most of the time venting incessantly about her anger related to her perceptions of unfair treatment by school staff and of other girls initiating fights with her. She also reported being angry at her mother because of the parental role the mother gave to the brother. In school, Lisa was invested in portraying herself in a bravado or macho manner. She would provoke others so that she could fight with them, or she would gravitate toward other students' fights, claiming that she was loyal and would defend her friends.

Therapeutic interventions involved the exploration of her feelings and the connection between her anger and other unexpressed feelings and her acting out. She was also confronted with her self-destructive and provocative behaviors and how she was putting herself in danger. The meaning of her macho or bravado ways of expressing her verbal and physical aggression toward others were also explored. Lisa admitted that these ways of expressing her aggression were sources of tremendous self-esteem for her, given the attention she was getting for her "bad" reputation in school. She did, however, acknowledge that peers' perception of her bravado or macho personality isolated her further from her peers in school and other settings. In addition, Lisa reported that she was interested in boys but that her macho or bravado image accompanied with her tendency to fight with other students (regardless of their gender) probably scared these boys away.

During the course of individual psychotherapy, Lisa was confronted with the idea that her anger and bravado or macho manner in dealing with her peers were probably the mechanisms that allowed her to keep a distance from others for fear of being hurt, disappointed, or being rejected by other students. Lisa was also encouraged to talk about the possibility that this feeling of rejection could have led to her feeling of worthlessness, irritability, and social withdrawal. Over the course of treatment, she was able to talk about her depression and disappointments as well as her anger related to her interactions with family members, peers, and school staff. The number of fights decreased, though her grades were still poor, and some defiant behaviors toward male teachers persisted, though less frequently. She also displayed a more appropriate insight into the negative impact of her macho or bravado ways of dealing with others, which were not culturally expected by her peers, particularly non-Hispanic boys who were afraid to socially interact with Lisa because of their fear of being hurt by her. Lisa continued to deny the seriousness of her father's medical condition and could not talk about the intensely ambivalent feelings she harbored toward him.

Discussion of the Case of Lisa
Freddy A. Paniagua

General Discussion

Lisa's problem behaviors in school and at home suggest either Conduct Disorder, Adolescent-Onset Type (APA, 1994, pp. 85-91) or Oppositional Defiant Disorder (APA, 1994, pp. 91-94). In its present format, however, this vignette does not appear to include sufficient symptoms for Lisa to meet required criteria for such disorders. For this reason, the most likely diagnosis would be Disruptive Behavior Disorder NOS (APA, 1994, p. 94). Two alternative diagnoses that should be ruled out include Major Depressive Disorder (APA, 1994, pp. 339-345) and Adjustment Disorder with Mixed Disturbance of Emotions and Conduct (APA, 1994, p. 624). In Axis IV, psychosocial and environmental problems to consider include "problems with primary group support" (APA, 1994, p. 29), such as illnesses among family members, discord with siblings (particularly Lisa's oldest brother), and father's involvement with another woman, resulting in another extended family Lisa did not know; "problems related to the social environment" (APA, 1994, p. 29), such as Lisa's difficulty in accepting the parental role mother gave to her oldest son, students' rejection of Lisa because of her bravado or macho approach in school; and "educational problems" (APA, 1994, p. 29), such as discord with classmates and teachers and poor academic performance. Specific V-Codes to consider across these broader psychosocial and environmental problems include V61.20: Parent-Child Relational Problem, V61.8: Sibling Relational Problem (APA, 1994, p. 681), and V62.81: Relational Problem NOS, for instance, difficulties with peers (APA, 1994, p. 681).

Cultural Formulation

In terms of the cultural identity of this client (see APA, 1994, p. 843), Lisa is Hispanic, but she elected to play a macho role in her relationship with her oldest brother and classmates, which is not culturally accepted among many members of the Hispanic community. As noted in Chapter 1 (see also Paniagua, 1998, pp. 40-41), men are expected to be the dominant authority in a Hispanic family (the cultural role of machismo); women are expected to be submissive, obedient, dependent, and gentle (the cultural role of *marianismo*) toward the machismo role expected among Hispanic men. Lisa's mother applied these cultural variables in her designation of her oldest son as the individual to play a parental role in the family; Lisa inversed these roles, which led to significant discord with her brother. In school, Lisa also threatened her classmates by playing a *machista* role unexpected among both Hispanic and non-Hispanic students. This *machista* role not only led to social rejection directed at Lisa, but it also forced Lisa to display maladaptive behaviors for her to self-validate that culturally rejected role among Hispanic women. Therefore, in terms of the cultural explanation of the present symptoms (see APA, 1994, pp. 843-844), Lisa's difficulty in accepting the *marianismo* role and her defiant behaviors in support of a *machista* role probably led to her malapdative behaviors in school and at home.

In terms of cultural elements in the relationship between the clinician and Lisa, it should be noted that the clinician was Asian and that racial or ethnic differences between Lisa and her therapist did not significantly affect the diagnosis of the case and selection of culturally sensitive treatment strategies in the management of Lisa's emotional difficulties. For example, mother's sense of *marianismo* (her recognition of her oldest son as someone with the authority to provide a parental role in the family) was not questioned but supported throughout the treatment. Similarly, Lisa was not directly confronted with her *machista* role but encouraged to understand the negative consequences of this role among Hispanic women. These examples (and others across this text) illustrate the applicability of the universalistic argument in the assessment and treatment of culturally diverse clients (Paniagua, 1998; Paniagua, Wassef, O'Boyle, Linares, & Cuéllar, 1993; S. Sue, Fujino, Hu, Takeuchi, & Zane, 1991; Tharp, 1991). This argument states that "effective assessment and treatment will be *the same across all multicultural groups* independent of issues of client-therapist racial and ethnic differences or similarities" (Paniagua, 1998, p. 7; italics added), given the following stipulations: The therapist must demonstrate that he or she is both *culturally sensitive* (aware of cultural variations across groups that may affect the assessment and treatment of the case) and *culturally competent* (with the clinical skills to translate this awareness into actual practice leading to effective diagnosis and treatment of a given culturally diverse group).

The Case of Long
Nga Anh Nguyen, MD

Long, a six-year-old Vietnamese American boy, was referred by his English teacher because of his aggressive behavior toward his white friends and his inability, after 1 year, to learn a single English word (in spite of average intelligence). Three years prior to that time, Long had been tricked into coming to the United States with his father. The father had told Long to say goodbye to his mother and their little South Vietnamese rural town before a short trip to Saigon. In the mental status examination, it became obvious to the therapist that Long was still very attached to his mother and felt very angry and sad because of his traumatic loss of her. Significantly, Long preserved his mother's rural South Vietnamese dialect in its purest form, in spite of his constant exposure to his father's North Vietnamese accent over the past 3 years. His stubborn holding on to his mother's South Vietnamese dialect coupled with his reluctance (or even unwillingness?) to pick up either his father's North Vietnamese accent or English and his aggression toward American children created a metaphoric picture aimed at conveying Long's feelings of anger at his father and at America for having traumatically severed him from his mother. In this case, the therapist's ability to read the transcultural metaphoric communication was far more vital to the understanding of his symptoms than her knowledge of the Vietnamese language.

Discussion of the Case of Long
Freddy A. Paniagua

General Discussion

Long's pattern of aggressive behavior is clearly in violation of school rules, suggesting early development of Conduct Disorder (APA, 1994, p. 91). Long appears to be underachieved in school and with adjustment difficulty to American classrooms, suggesting the inclusion of two V-Codes in Axis IV, namely, V62.3: Academic Problem and V62.4: Acculturation Problem, respectively (APA, 1994, p. 685). The focus of clinical attention, however, appears to be Long's development of symptoms for Conduct Disorder and not these V-Codes. Long's aggressive acts (his aggression toward white students) appear to be a reaction to a particular social context, and he immigrated from a war-ravaged country (Vietnam) "with a history of aggressive behaviors that may have been necessary for [survival] in that context" (APA, 1994, p. 88). Under these two circumstances (evidence of a social context leading to symptoms and immigrant status from that country), the *DSM-IV* suggests that a diagnosis of Conduct Disorder should be considered carefully. Long, however, immigrated to the United States at the age of 3, and it is not likely that he had to display aggressive acts in his own country to survive, which eliminates the possibility that he is aggressive in American classrooms because of a prior history of aggression in Vietnam. Long's aggressive acts toward American children (particularly white students) appears to indicate his difficulty in dealing with a social context threatening his cultural identity, but these acts are clearly culturally unacceptable in American classrooms. Therefore, although cultural variables might have played a role in Long's display of aggressive acts, his maladaptive behaviors were clinically significant to deserve psychiatric treatment.

Cultural Formulation

Among all elements of the *DSM-IV* cultural formulation, the assessment of Long's cultural identity appears to be the critical issue to address in the treatment plan. He is Vietnamese and apparently is afraid of losing his racial and ethnic identity by being forced to adapt to values and norms of the dominant culture. For example, Long refused to learn English and another Vietnamese dialect other than his mother's South Vietnamese dialect. Long's aggressive acts against American children were probably a reaction to the social stressor he was experiencing in school, in terms of being forced to adapt to cultural patterns imposed on him through the tricking manipulation of his father, which also led to Long's expression of anger toward his father. Long's strong attachment to his mother should also be assessed around his perception of the cultural value of familism and how he interprets this value, in terms of the delivery of emotional support toward his struggle in maintaining his Vietnamese cultural identity.

The Case of Dien Wong
Nga Anh Nguyen, MD

Dien Wong, a seven-year-old Chinese American boy born to Taiwanese immigrant parents, was evaluated for "identity confusion." Although fluent in both Chinese and English, like his parents, Dien refused to speak Chinese with his mother. Dien also "talked back" to his mother and became, as she said, "as disobedient and selfish as the American kids." He defied his mother's order to play piano for Chinese relatives, although he enthusiastically performed piano recitals for American audiences. The onset of Dien's symptoms had coincided with his father's departure from home to attend law school in a nearby state 6 months earlier. Since then, Dien's father had not been home except during his monthly weekend visits. At the same time, Dien's mother started working full time while attending a graduate night class.

In her psychotherapeutic work with Dien, a white child [therapist] (supervised by the author) lent herself as a "mother of symbiosis," helping him to accurately identify the inner source of his identity confusion and to uncover why his mother was chosen to be the target of his power struggle around cultural issues. Through play and talk therapy, Dien became aware that his needs for attention and love were thwarted by what he perceived as a physically and emotionally unavailable father and an altogether too busy mother. Thus, Dien's behavioral transgression of Chinese ethics was his unconscious revenge on his mother, the only parent physically available as a target for his anger. He also reported his reluctance to face and to direct his anger at his father "because Dad may leave me for real." Like a good "mother of postsymbiosis," the child therapist conveyed to Dien her congenial acceptance of his individual needs for love and attention from his parents (and from herself, via transference, within the therapeutic boundaries). She also used communicative matching to praise the courage he exemplified in exploring the threatening and painful feelings of ambivalence he felt toward his parents.

Relieved by the therapist's empathetic understanding and acceptance, Dien became freer to explore more adaptive ways to get his parents to meet his needs; for instance, he "nicely and politely" (as well-behaved Chinese children do) asked his mother to take him for a walk to the park one day. This accomplishment represented the first step toward the therapeutic goal of restoring the sense of familial affiliation between Dien and his parents. This goal was also achieved through casework with the parents. The child therapist encouraged Mr. Wong to rearrange his schedule to make more frequent home visits and thus to spend more time with Dien. She advised Mrs. Wong to decrease her night school hours and to give her son more quality time. She also taught Mrs. Wong to emphasize positive rewards for Dien's adaptive behavior, while deemphasizing the mother-child power struggle over cultural issues.

Although object-relations-based individual therapy helped to bolster Dien's individual self, casework with the parents restored Dien's sense of familial affiliation and relatedness. Dien's "I-self" could grow stronger because it was reconnected with the "familial-self."

Dien's parents were strikingly polarized between Americanization and Chinese traditionalism. Mrs. Wong bitterly complained of her son's adoption of the American children's "decadent code of conduct," whereas Mr. Wong advocated his son's need to adapt to the American way of life. Thus, this appeared to be a classic case of parental cultural conflict that filtered down to their son, creating in him an "identity confusion."

However, during the course of marital therapy, instituted to alleviate the parents' cultural conflict, the following dynamics started to unfold. It became obvious that underneath the cultural conflict lay a severe, long-term marital discord, due to the parents' unresolved separation-individualization from their families of origin.

Mrs. Wong angrily blamed Mr. Wong for having always sided with his mother against her, for instance, by preventing Mrs. Wong from visiting her own mother back in Taiwan. A year ago, when Mrs. Wong's mother died, Mr. Wong had not allowed her to send enough money to Taiwan to provide her mother with a big funeral. Mrs. Wong also expressed rage at discovering, through friends and relatives, that Mr. Wong had secretly smuggled his mother out of Taiwan. Mr. Wong's side of the story was as follows: Mrs. Wong had always looked down on his mother and his family because his family was poorer than hers. He had sent some money to Taiwan for Mrs. Wong's mother's funeral but not as much as his wife had requested because of the couple's financial constraints. He had hidden his mother's arrival in the United States from his wife because he had known all along that his mother's presence would infuriate Mrs. Wong.

The marital therapy helped Mr. and Mrs. Wong to understand how these earlier unresolved developmental issues were reactivated by the couple's immigration to the United States and, inflamed by recent stressors, resurfaced under the more culturally acceptable pretense of cultural discord. Thus, the process of the marital therapy paralleled the process of Dien's individual therapy—both addressed the superficial layer of cultural conflict and the deeper layer of intrapsychic conflict.

Discussion of the Case of Dien Wong
Freddy A. Paniagua

General Discussion

The term *identity* is generally used in the *DSM-IV* in three ways. First, in the case of Dissociative Identity Disorder (formerly known as Multiple Personality Disorder; APA, 1994, pp. 484-487), in the diagnosis of Gender Identity Disorder (APA, 1994, pp. 532-538), and in the V-Code "Identity Problem" (APA, 1994, p. 685). Dien's "identity confusion" did not deal with these disorders but with a cultural identity problem, which would be a focus of clinical attention. Dien's symptoms as perceived by his mother suggest early development of Oppositional Defiant Disorder (ODD) (APA, 1994, pp. 91-94), and his struggle to deal with his apparent cultural identity problem was probably related to this disorder. Therefore, the V-code Identity Problem would also be considered in Axis IV (APA, 1994). The mother's perception of Dien as a kid behaving "like the American kids" and discrepancies between mother and father regarding the need for Dien to adapt to the "American way of life" point to three additional V-Codes to be considered in the overall diagnosis: Acculturation Problem (APA, 1994, p. 685), Partner Relational Problem (APA, 1994, p. 681), and Parent-Child Relational Problem (APA, 1994, p. 681). These V-Codes would be the focus of clinical attention but in relation to the mental problem Dien is experiencing (ODD).

Cultural Formulation

This is a case in which clinicians would have a difficult time determining whether the patient has a mental problem that is related to the mentioned V-Codes (particularly an identity problem in cultural terms) or whether such V-Codes are the focus of clinical attention and the patient does not have a mental disorder (see Chapter 2 for specific guidelines suggested in the *DSM-IV* regarding the use of V-Codes in the *Manual*). In this case, the conclusion is that Dien had a mental problem that was related to all of the mentioned V-Codes, particularly the V-Code Identity Problem. It appears that Dien's symptoms went beyond those expected by many Asian families when cultural variables are implicated. That is, despite Dien's intention to behave like American children, he would still to be expected to be extremely respectful to his mother rather than being oppositional in the presence of his mother's requests to perform certain behavior, such as speaking Chinese with his mother or playing the piano for Chinese relatives.

Dien's behaviors in this case were not examples of what would be expected among many Asians, who place heavy emphasis on familism and reject individualism in matters involving family affairs. That is, Dien's mother would expect that the family is first and then Dien's intention to behave according to the dominant culture would follow (see Paniagua, 1998, pp. 58-59). Dien's refusal to play the piano for his relatives was an example of his departure from his mother's acceptance of the extended family as more important than the individual (e.g., Dien). As noted by Ho (1992) and D. W. Sue and D. Sue (1999), Asian children are expected to be obedient in the presence of adults' requests to perform activities considered appropriate for the welfare of the family, be helpers, and respect the authority of their parents and, particularly, the elderly. Dien showed the opposite of these culturally expected characteristics among Asian children.

His mother perceived Dien's behaviors as different from other Asian children but similar to American children, and this led to her decision to report symptoms suggesting early development of ODD. Therefore, in the treatment, the cultural identity of Dien would be explored further, but the emphasis would be placed on the management of symptoms leading to the development of a mental disorder. For example, the therapist made sure that Dien would display behaviors culturally expected by his Chinese mother and that he would be able to understand the importance of the value of familism and the extended family in his relationships with his parents and relatives. This was achieved without confronting Dien with his intention to culturally identify himself with behaviors expected among American children.

The programming of marital therapy was also a culturally sensitive approach in this case. This approach involved assisting Dien's parents in exploring their differences regarding "Americanization and Chinese traditionalism" with regard to children's socialization in the dominant culture, as opposed to socialization in their own culture, as well as the parents' long-term marital discord around the father's apparent lack of support for Mrs. Wong's extended family.

The Case of Maria
Ian A. Canino, MD, and Jeanne Spurlock, MD

Maria, a 13-year-old Latino girl, was referred to the clinic for disrespectful behavior at home. Described by her parents as confrontational, assertive, and too autonomous, Maria demanded more freedom and openly talked about boys and sex. Her parents' traditional beliefs and childrearing attitudes were in direct opposition to their child's behavior. The differences in her parents' and teachers' perceptions of Maria were clear. Her teachers perceived her as an assertive and independent young woman who felt comfortable exploring difficult issues. They regarded her behavior as an indication of strength. Maria's parents, on the other hand, viewed her behavior as deviant. During the history taking, the clinician learned that the parents had sent Maria to a progressive liberal school to achieve their goal of a good education for their daughter. At school Maria had been told to speak up, know her own mind, question what she heard, and be independent. The evaluating clinician arranged a meeting between the teachers and the parents to clarify the mixed messages given to Maria. After a series of meetings directed by the biculturally sensitive clinician, misunderstandings were resolved and the family felt better able to direct their daughter through a healthy adolescence. For their part, the teachers became more aware of the family's cultural beliefs and values and helped Maria integrate both philosophies.

SOURCE: "Maria" from *Culturally Diverse Children and Adolescents: Assessment, Diagnosis, and Treatment,* (pp. 46-47) by Ian A. Canino and Jeanne Spurlock. Copyright © 1994 by Guilford Press, reprinted by permission of the publisher.

Discussion of the Case of Maria
Freddy A. Paniagua

General Discussion

Maria's symptoms present to clinicians a dilemma similar to that described in the case of Dien. Should Maria be diagnosed with a mental disorder? Should other conditions unrelated to that disorder be considered as the focus of clinical attention? Again, the critical issue is to determine whether Maria's symptoms are not culturally accepted by members of her own culture (Hispanics) and whether one or more of such "other conditions" are related with these symptoms and "sufficiently severe to warrant independent clinical attention" (APA, 1994, p. 675). Maria's parents did not consider her confrontational, assertive, and independent behaviors as acceptable among Hispanic children and adolescents. (Talking openly about sex in the presence of Hispanic parents is not generally expected among Hispanic children and adolescents. Talking about sex is not in itself considered being oppositional, but refusing to stop talking about sex when instructed to do so is, which was probably the issue in this case.) Maria's symptoms suggest the development of ODD (APA, 1994, pp. 91-94), and two V-Codes likely related with this disorder and severe enough to warrant clinical attention are "Parent-Child Relational Problem" (APA, 1994, p. 681) and "Acculturation Problem" (APA, 1994, p. 685).

The fact that Maria was told to be independent, question other people's opinion, and speak up does not necessarily mean that she would be expected to behave this way in the presence of her traditional Hispanic parents. Maria, however, probably displayed these assertive behaviors at home because of the mixed message given to Maria by her teachers; and this is why her parents were correct in their decision to bring Maria's symptoms to the attention of mental health professionals who most likely would diagnose Maria with ODD and then apply culturally sensitive strategies to manage these symptoms at home and in school (which was precisely what these clinicians did in this case).

Cultural Formulation

The most important issue of the cultural formulation applied to the treatment of this case is counseling Maria about her adopting a pattern of behavior from the dominant culture and the generalization of this pattern in the presence of her traditional Hispanic parents. Maria's intention to be assertive and autonomous is not the critical issue but her parents' rejection of these characteristics because they are not culturally accepted among members of their community, particularly their extended family and other Hispanic parents.

The Case of Enrique
Ian A. Canino, MD, & Jeanne Spurlock, MD

Enrique, a 7-year-old Latino child from a recently immigrated family, was referred to the clinic with symptoms of separation anxiety disorder and immature behavior. When the clinician elicited a history, it was learned that the child still slept with his parents and was not yet weaned from the mother. The parents came from a rural Central American town and informed the clinician that in their culture the decision to leave the parental bed and to be weaned was always made by the child. In further questioning it was learned that the older children in the family had made this decision at much earlier ages. Prior to the birth of Enrique the mother had lost two infant children. On arriving in this country the parents were still mourning these losses and in addition had to mourn the loss of their community of family and friends. Enrique had been born soon after their arrival. The parents had become overly attached to the child and in their overprotection of him had exaggerated cultural norms. They had been unable to cue into Enrique's earlier readiness to become more independent.

SOURCE: "Enrique" from *Culturally Diverse Children and Adolescents: Assessment, Diagnosis, and Treatment,* (pp. 46-47) by Ian A. Canino and Jeanne Spurlock. Copyright © 1994 by Guilford Press, reprinted by permission of the publisher.

Discussion of the Case of Enrique
Freddy A. Paniagua

General Discussion

Enrique's symptoms suggested to the diagnostic team one of the Other Disorders of Infancy, Childhood, or Adolescents in the *DSM-IV,* namely Separation Anxiety Disorder (APA, 1994, p. 113). Reactive Attachment Disorder (APA, 1994, pp. 116-118) should be ruled out in further assessment of the case. In the case of Separation Anxiety Disorder, in some cultures, "strong interdependence among family members" (APA, 1994, p. 111) is acceptable. In the particular case of children, symptoms for Separation Anxiety Disorder (e.g., fears of threats to parents, themselves, home) may not suggest a psychiatric disorder per se but children's difficulty in understanding why their culturally tolerated child-parents interdependence in the past is being threatened by individuals outside the family (e.g., mental health professionals counseling the family with the goal to make a child less dependent on his or her parents). Other cultural variables that should be considered when making this diagnosis include refugee or immigrant status in which children are suddenly separated from their parents and placing recent immigrant children in a school environment in which only English is allowed. The *DSM-IV* did not discuss potential cultural variants that clinicians should consider when diagnosing children with Reactive Attachment Disorder. As noted earlier, however, Cervantes and Arroyo (1995) pointed out that symptoms suggesting this disorder may be common among immigrant children who may not be allowed by their parents to socialize with individuals beyond the household because of fear for the child's safety.

Cultural Formulation

This case shows the possibility of "exaggerated cultural norms" in developing a mental disorder in children and adolescents and, as noted by the authors of this case, the imposition of these norms on Enrique's overall behaviors, preventing him from becoming an independent individual from his parents. Although the case does not provide materials to determine the therapeutic approach used to manage Enrique's symptoms, the programming of family therapy with emphasis on cultural variables leading to such symptoms would be the first treatment choice.

The Case of Marcia
Jewelle Taylor Gibbs, PhD

Thirteen-year-old Marcia, born out of wedlock to a white mother and a black father, was referred by her white adoptive parents because of rebellious behavior, truancy, and stealing from family members. The parents also suspected she was sexually active and using drugs. In individual sessions, Marcia, who had very light skin but black facial features and hair, spoke of always feeling inferior to her younger sister, who was part Asian and had always been favored by the adoptive parents. Her behavioral problems had surfaced when she entered junior high school, and she felt she did not belong with any of the cliques, was rejected by her former white neighborhood friends, and drifted into a group of "dopers" who were alienated from school and society. In family sessions, it was clear that Marcia had assumed the role of the "bad child," identifying with the negative stories she had been told about the African American father, who had been imprisoned for drugs and burglary, and playing out an unspoken script to fulfill the negative expectations communicated to her by her parents. Marcia tried to resolve her racial identity conflict through assuming a negative identity and seeking out deviate peers whose antisocial behaviors reinforced that identity. By "acting just like my dad," Marcia was identifying with her natural black parent while punishing her adoptive white parents for their ambivalence toward her blackness.

SOURCE: From "Biracial Adolescents," by Jewelle Taylor Gibbs, in J. T. Gibbs and L. N. Huang (Eds.), *Children of Color: Psychological Interventions with Culturally Diverse Youth* (pp. 305-332). Copyright 1998 © by Jossey-Bass Publishers, reprinted by permission.

Discussion of the Case of Marcia
Freddy A. Paniagua

General Discussion

The most likely diagnosis in this case is Conduct Disorder, adolescent-onset type (APA, 1994, pp. 85-91). Marcia's symptoms appear to be related to her racial identity conflict and her feeling that her adopted parents considered her as "inferior to her younger sister" who is part Asian. Therefore, in Axis IV, three V-Codes to consider as the focus of clinical attention during the treatment of this mental disorder are V61.20: Parent-Child Relational Problem, V61.8: Sibling Relational Problem (APA, 1994, p. 681), and 313.89: Identity Problem (APA, 1994, p. 685).

Cultural Formulation

As noted by Gibbs (1998b), in the assessment of biracial adolescents, "racial identity is the most widespread conflict encountered by clinicians when treating adolescents" (p. 315). In addition, Gibbs added that "adolescent females are more likely than males to feel ashamed of their black physical traits" (1998,

p. 315), including their facial features, curly hair, and dark skin. Marcia is a biracial female adolescent, and it is evident that the most important element of the cultural formulation in the treatment of her symptoms is an emphasis on her struggle to deal with her cultural identity. Individual psychotherapy with emphasis on problem solving and social skills training would be recommended (see Chapter 4 and Paniagua, 1998, pp. 34-35), which could help Marcia to explore alternative (adaptive) behaviors in her ways to deal with conflicts around her cultural identity (feeling rejected by neighborhood white friends, feeling inferior to her sister, and her maladaptive identification with negative histories she learned about her African American father). During this treatment modality, Marcia should be told that she is having a mental disorder but that it appears to be related with her struggle in dealing with those conflicts and their affect on her own cultural identity.

Family therapy would be recommended, to explore Marcia's relational problems with her sister and parents from a cultural perspective (see Paniagua, 1998, pp. 35-36). Prior to family therapy, it would be important to meet individually with Marcia's sister and parents to go over specific cultural variables and determine whether they understand how these variables might be affecting Marcia's overall emotional state. For example, her adoptive parents are both white, and the question is, do they understand potential cultural identity problems biracial adolescents often encounter when they are adopted by non-biracial parents? In the case of Marcia's sister, she is also biracial (she is part Asian, but her other racial identity is unknown in the current presentation of the case). It is also important to explore how her sister is dealing with her cultural identity and whether she is actually behaving as being "superior" to Marcia or being "always favored by the adoptive parents." Once these cultural issues are explored, the next step would be the programming of family therapy in which these and other cultural variables would be considered, using culturally sensitive treatment strategies recommended with African American clients (Boyd-Franklin, 1989; Gibbs, 1998a, 1998b; Paniagua, 1998).

The Case of Ron
Man Keung Ho, PhD

Ron, a 13-year-old American Indian boy, was referred to the therapist by a school counselor who claimed that Ron had been a quiet, "well-behaved" student until recently. He now attended school irregularly, wore dirty clothes, exhibited destructive behavior in class, and refused to speak to anybody.

When Ron showed up in the office, the therapist immediately told him that he had wanted to come by his school to visit with him but changed his mind, because he did not want Ron's classmates to think that he was in trouble (conveys interest and respect). Ron glanced at the therapist and said nothing. He then glanced at some Indian art and craft work in the office (create comfortable environment for clients). These had been given to the therapist by his former clients. The therapist asked him to feel free to take time to look at them (conveys Indian time orientation). Ron was also interested in the wall poster with pictures of Navajo Indians. The therapist asked Ron to explain to him what the symbols on the picture meant (to shift power position and to help client feel relaxed). Ron smiled and said that he wishes he knew. Then, hesitantly, Ron asked if the therapist was Indian (client showed beginning trust). The therapist replied, smiling, "No, but I feel we are cousins, for history tells us that thousands of years ago, Indians migrated from China" (to establish mutuality and ties). Ron was very interested in the therapist's explanation and his ethnic background.

Discussion of the Case of Ron
Freddy A. Paniagua

General Discussion

Ron's sudden change in behaviors suggest the development of Conduct Disorder (APA, 1994, pp. 85-91) and Oppositional Defiant Disorder (APA, 1994, pp. 91-94). The case does not provide enough details regarding risk factors (e.g., sudden environmental changes around Ron's style of living) leading to these sudden changes in Ron's adaptive behavior. For this reason, the possibility of an Adjustment Disorder should be ruled out in further explorations of variables leading to these changes in a similar case, most likely Adjustment Disorder with Disturbance of Conduct or Adjustment Disorder with Mixed Disturbance of Emotion and Conduct (APA, 1994, p. 624). Ron's refusal to speak to anybody (Ho, 1992, p. 134) suggests the development of a relational problem involving both teachers and peers, and under this possibility, the V-Code "Relational Problem Not Otherwise Specified" would be considered in Axis IV (APA, 1994, pp. 681-682).

Cultural Formulation

This case shows the importance of considering cultural variables at earlier stages in the evaluation of the case in the prevention of mental disorders generally developed in childhood and adolescence. For example, instead of visiting Ron's school, the therapist decided to invite Ron to his office, which Ron perceived as a sign of the therapist's interest in understanding Ron's problems as well as the sense of respect he (Ron) felt he should deserve. As noted by Dana (1993b) and LaFromboise, Dauphinais, and Rowe (1980), meeting an American Indian client outside the therapist's office is considered a critical precondition for the development of a trusting therapist-client relationship, and this culturally sensitive service delivery approach is particularly important to use in the assessment and treatment of American Indian high school students (LaFromboise et al., 1980).

In addition, visiting Ron's school would prevent Ron from openly discussing his problems with the therapist because many American Indian clients do not generally answer questions dealing with their private life during the first encounter with people who do not share their cultural and ethnic background (see Paniagua, 1998, p. 85, and Thompson et al., 1993). The display of Indian art and craft work not only created a comfortable environment for Ron (Dana, 1993a, 1993b), but it also indicated to Ron that the therapist appreciated the traditions of American Indian culture and that Ron should be proud of belonging to this culture (see Paniagua, 1998, pp. 83-84). Among many American Indians, the task under consideration is more important than the time (as a measurement tool in hours, minutes, and seconds) imposed on that task (see Paniagua, 1998, p. 82, and Thompson et al., 1993, p. 231). Therefore, allowing Ron to look at the Indian art (the task) was in accord with what he would expect during this portion of the client-therapist relationship.

Last, the therapist in this case was a Chinese but rather than perceiving his racial and ethnic differences relative to Ron's race and ethnic background as a negative cultural variable in the therapeutic process, the therapist emphasized cultural commonalities (the observation that many years ago, Indians migrated from China). Ron's interest in knowing more about this historical connection between the American Indian and the Chinese cultures not only suggested to the therapist that he was on the right track in developing a good therapeutic relationship with Ron (he needed to learn more about events leading to Ron's sudden changes in behavior), but it also suggested that Ron wanted to know more about the therapist's perception of Ron's group and personal cultural identity (Dana, 1993b).

Future Cases

This chapter described the clinical applications of cultural variables in examples of psychiatric disorders often developed in childhood and adolescence (APA, 1994). For future editions of the *Casebook,* the editor invites clinicians to submit cases illustrating these variables with disorders not covered in the present chapter. Please submit new cases to Dr. Freddy A. Paniagua, Sage Publications, 2455 Teller Road, Thousand Oaks, CA 91320. Examples of these disorders will be briefly discussed in terms of cultural considerations.

Mental Retardation, Learning Disorders, and Communication Disorders

In the case of Mental Retardation and Learning Disorders (e.g., reading disorder) the *DSM-IV* (APA, 1994) recommends that the individual's ethnic or cultural background should be taken into consideration during intellectual-testing procedures (Cervantes & Arroyo, 1995). Tests in which the person's relevant characteristics are represented in the standardization sample of the test should be considered. Similarly, examiners should be familiar with aspects of the individual ethnic or cultural background (APA, 1994, p. 44). For example, the Wechsler Intelligence Scales are recommended to assess IQ levels and learning problems in children and adults. As noted by Golden (1990), however, these scales are "heavily influenced by cultural and language concepts that reflect the life of the average American, but not that of most [multicultural] groups" (p. 46). This observation is particularly true in the performance of members of these groups on the Information, Comprehension, Vocabulary, Picture Completion, and Picture Arrangement subtests, which are associated with alternate cultural background.

For example, a Hispanic client may receive a very low score on the Information subtest (e.g., below 5, where a mean is 10 and the standard deviation is 3), not because the client is not intelligent but because he or she lacks information regarding the total population, height of women, number of senators, and other items of so-called general knowledge expected from the average American in the United States. A similar point could be made in the interpretation of the scores with the Comprehension (the client may not be able to understand basic U.S. customs and situation), Vocabulary (the client cannot define a word using Standard American English), Picture Completion (the client cannot complete the picture because he or she is not familiar with the objects pictured in the American culture), and Picture Arrangement subtests (the client cannot arrange the pictures to tell a logical and coherent story, because the social sequence required on the test is not part of the client's cultural background).

In the case of Communication Disorders (i.e., expressive language disorder), the *DSM-IV* (APA, 1994) suggests that the individual's cultural language context must be taken into consideration during the assessment of the development of communication abilities, particularly for persons growing up in bilingual settings. The standardized measures of language development and of nonverbal intellectual capacity must be relevant for the culture.

Pervasive Developmental Disorders

The *DSM-IV* (1994) did not include a discussion of potential cultural variables that clinicians should consider when diagnosing children with Pervasive Developmental Disorders (i.e., Autism, Rett's Disorder, Childhood Disintegrative Disorder, and Asperger's Disorder). Examples of *DSM-IV* criteria suggesting these disorders include difficulties in expressive and receptive language; social relationships; and repetitive, restricted, and stereotyped behaviors. Cervantes and Arroyo (1995) suggested that behavioral difficulties suggesting Pervasive Developmental Disorders could be significantly influenced by culture. For example, Cervantes and Arroyo (1995) pointed out that "some Hispanic children may be judged as being impaired if comparing above behaviors to non-Hispanic behavioral norms" (p. 143).

Pica and Selective Mutism

Regarding pica, the *DSM-IV* suggests that eating nonnutritive substances could be culturally accepted in some cultures (APA, 1994, p. 95). Selective mutism may be the result of unfamiliarity with the dominant language or a feeling of being not comfortable using this language. This is particularly true in the case of immigrant children (APA, 1994, p. 114).

The *DSM-IV* did not include a discussion of cultural variables for Rumination Disorder, Feeding Disorder of Infancy or Early Childhood, Tic Disorder, Tourette's Disorder, Chronic Motor or Vocal Tic Disorder, Transient Tic Disorder, Encopresis, Enuresis, Reactive Attachment Disorder (see "Enrique" in this Chapter), and Stereotypic Movement Disorder (see APA, 1994, pp. 96-121). New cases illustrating cultural variables with these disorders are welcomed for consideration in future editions of *Casebook.*

6

———
———
——

Applications of Cultural Variables
With Other Psychiatric Disorders
in Children, Adolescents, and Adults

The following cases illustrate the applicability of cultural variations with another set of examples of mental disorders in the *DSM-IV* (APA, 1994). The previous chapter emphasized mental disorders generally experienced by infants, children, and adolescents. The following set of disorders are not unique to a given age group; in the *DSM-IV* (APA, 1994), children, adolescents, and adults can be diagnosed with these (e.g., Adjustment Disorders). As noted in the Preface, the two-part discussion (general and cultural formulation) is provided by the editor, Dr. Freddy A. Paniagua, to ensure the commonality of the discussion across cases around specific cultural issues. The following list of disorders discussed in this chapter could assist clinicians with quick identification of specific disorders pertinent to their clinical practice:

Adjustment Disorders

Anxiety Disorders

Delusional Disorders

Dissociative Disorders

Mood Disorders

Personality Disorders

Schizophrenia and Other Psychotic Disorders

Somatoform Disorders

Substance Related Disorders

Psychiatric Disorders, Clinical Cases, and Discussion

Adjustment Disorders

With all forms of Adjustment Disorders, the client's cultural setting should be explored to determine whether the client's response to the stressor is either inappropriate or in excess of what would be expected in his or her culture. Variability exists across cultures with respect to the nature, meaning, and experience of the stressor and the evaluation of the response to the stressor (APA, 1994, p. 625).

The Case of Twe
Man Keung Ho, PhD

Twe, a 14-year-old Vietnamese American female student, was referred by a school counselor for depression. Throughout the interview session, Twe was extremely reluctant to talk about her depression. After she was assured confidentiality, Twe mentioned the discomfort she experienced when her Anglo classmates teased her, saying that despite her being a teenager, she still was "tied to her parents' apron strings." Twe explained that she was born in this country [U.S.A.] one year after her parents escaped from Saigon. Her parents owned a restaurant. Being the oldest of four children, Twe was expected to help out daily in the restaurant after school. Because of her heavy work involvement and diligent study habits, Twe had practically no time for a social life. Her isolation from her friends bothered her more when she turned fourteen. For financial reasons, and in order to provide a good role example for her younger siblings, Twe deferred to her parents. She never complained, but she suffered quietly and became increasingly depressed.

The therapist's knowledge of Twe's culture, which emphasizes filial piety, self-control, and collectivism, helped him to be empathic toward Twe's dilemma. Instead of encouraging Twe to individuate and to do her own thing, the therapist commended her for fulfilling her dutiful obligations to her parents and her younger siblings. However, the therapist also empathized by letting Twe know he understood how much she wanted to be accepted and to be with her friends. Twe responded by saying that this was the dilemma that drove her "crazy" or "depressed."

When Twe was asked the possible solution for this dilemma, she replied, "Some compromises have to be made." She later suggested, "If I could just have Friday evening off from work and be with my friends, I would be very happy." The therapist asked Twe if she had ever approached her parents about this problem and her desire to have one evening off from work. Twe replied, "I dare not, and besides my parents will never let me for they themselves have to work all the time." The therapist encouraged her to relate her desire to her parents and at the same time reminded her that she could not honor her family if she was physically and mentally sick and "imbalanced."

SOURCE: "Twe—Vietnamese American Female Student." From Man Keung Ho, *Minority Children and Adolescents in Therapy* (p. 143). Copyright © 1992 by Sage Publications, Inc.

Discussion of the Case of Twe
Freddy A. Paniagua

General Discussion

The fact that the counselor referred Twe for an assessment of depression suggests that her emotional responses to specific stressful events was probably seen by the counselor to be "in excess of what would be expected from exposure to the stressor," resulting in "significant impairment in social or occupational (academic) functioning" (APA, 1994, p. 626). This suggests Adjustment Disorder with Depressed Mood (APA, 1994, p. 623); Dysthymic Disorder should also be ruled out. In this case, the "identifiable psychosocial stressor or stressors" (APA, 1994, p. 623) centered around Twe's difficulty in adjusting her social life to cultural norms expected by her Anglo classmates (e.g., adolescents' independence from their parents) and her parents' expectations of filial piety, self-control, and collectivism, traditional among Asian children (D. W. Sue & D. Sue, 1999).

Cultural Formulation

Twe's decision to keep her parents uninformed about the social stressor leading to her depression is a clear sign of her strong cultural identity with the Vietnamese community and her acceptance of cultural values expected to be honored by members of this community (e.g., a sense of collectivism and helping behavior toward specific family goals instead of individual goals). The therapist demonstrated cultural sensitivity by encouraging Twe to fulfill her obligation to her parents and to explore culturally appropriate strategies in handling her dilemma (i.e., her desire to spend time with her friends vs. helping her parents in the restaurant). Encouraging Twe to relate her desire to her parents could be achieved through social skills training but without an emphasis on the assertive element of this training (teaching Twe to be assertive in violation of norms in the Asian community would not be a good strategy). Another alternative would be to plan family therapy sessions in which Twe and her parents would discuss the importance of Twe's individual needs to adjust to her Anglo classmates' expectations of social relationships without the need for Twe to move away from fulfilling her parents' own cultural norms.

Twe's parents immigrated to the United States and Twe was born in this country 1 year later. This suggests an acculturation problem (V-Code 62.4 in the *DSM-IV*, APA, 1994, p. 685) that should also be explored in the treatment plan. In regard to Twe's parents, communication family therapy would emphasize norms in this society regarding expectation of adolescents' independence from their parents, including adolescents' decision to deal with certain aspects of their social life. It would be important to discuss with Twe the fact that many Anglo American adolescents are not aware of cultural values in the Vietnamese community (e.g., an emphasis on familism rather than on individualism when dealing with family affairs) and that this lack of awareness could explain Anglo classmates' difficulty in understanding why Twe was "tied to her parents' apron strings" at her age.

The Case of Randy
Freddy A. Paniagua, PhD

Randy is a 13-year-old African American boy who was brought to the clinic by his African American mother because he gets "very angry and out of control" when other children in school tease him and say "bad things" about him. His mother reported that she had observed in the past 6 months that Randy appears "sad" and with "lack of interest" in having friends from school visit him at home. The mother also reported that Randy fights almost two times per month in school as a way to deal with the way other students treat him. Randy's engagement in arguments and fights with other students resulted in him being taken to the principal's office many times, which often led to verbal reprimands from the principal and notification to parents. The mother reported that Randy is a different person at home; with the exception of minor arguments between mother and Randy, he appears to follow mother's instructions at home, has never displayed physical aggression toward his mother, and does not argue a lot with mother. The mother reported that Randy is not "doing well in three subjects" (math, reading, and English, in all of which he was receiving Fs). The mother, however, reported that this was not the reason why she "is here today . . . I want my son to stop arguing and fighting in school." Mother reported that these arguments and fights have intensified in the past 4 months and that they are becoming "really bad" recently (increasing from the beginning of the school year to the present).

Randy was interviewed alone. He reported that it was true that he engages in arguments and fights in school. He explained these maladaptive behaviors by saying that "students always tease [him] and say negative things [about him]." He reported that all students teasing [him] were white students. Randy was asked to report how he identifies his own race, and he said that he is "African American." He was then asked if he thinks that these teasing and negative comments involve the fact that his skin color is different from those children, and his answer was "Yes." He said that when he is in the cafeteria, playground, and so on, those white children always remind him that he should be "with the bunch of Negroes." He reported that those white students also call black students "faggot" and "byatch" (meaning "homosexual" and "bitch," respectively, according to Randy). Randy said that when he listens to these words directed against him, he gets very angry, including verbal and physical fights leading to his removal from the classroom and visits to the principal's office. Randy also reported that several students have told him, "You're homosexual . . . you sleep with men" and that these accusations also led to similar negative responses in the way Randy handled the situation. During these reports, Randy appeared sad and cried when reporting the reasons why he engaged in maladaptive behaviors. He was not psychotic, and his thoughts were coherent and in accord with the topic (racism) he identified as the main source of maladaptive behaviors. His depressed mood and tearfulness did not appear predominant during this evaluation, and Randy reported that he is "happy with [his] life" except when he is exposed to those teasing situations and negative (racial) remarks.

Randy was asked to provide examples of alternative behaviors he could display to deal with those racist remarks and teasing situations. He said that he would (a) walk away and (b) tell the principal. He was told that these are excellent alternatives, and that two additional alternatives would be (c) to ignore these children and (d) to systematically (meaning all the time) ask those children why they could not say something positive about him instead of making those racist remarks. Randy was told that this approach is called "problem solving," in which he could make the effort to find an alternative solution to a specific problem, but in positive terms. Role-playing was used to teach Randy how to apply this technique, with emphasis on the second two alternatives. Randy was told that the first two alternatives are good, but that he might not want to move from the setting (e.g., the cafeteria) in which teasing and negative remarks against him occur, and he might not have the chance to tell the principal about each instance of teasing and negative remarks against him. Randy was told that the second two are more practical because he could always use them. He was told that if he does not pay attention to these teasing situations and racist remarks, he would stop children behaving that way against him. He was further told that if he *repeatedly* asked these children why they can't say something positive about him (this was role-played during this session), this repetition of the same statement would become aversive to these children, and the only way for those children to escape from Randy's repetition of that question would be for them to stop teasing and saying negative things about him. These things were explained to Randy in terms he could understand; for example, he was told,

> Randy, if you repeat the same question many, many times during the day, each time those children tease you or say something negative about your race, *they will get tired* of listening to you saying the same thing to them . . . and this is why I think those children will stop saying those bad things to you.

Randy was also provided with a brief explanation (in terms he could understand) about the problem of racism and how it is very difficult to stop those children from being racist against him because this is part of the belief system of those children.

The mother was interviewed alone. She reported that she suspected that racial remarks against Randy were a central issue in his display of maladaptive behaviors in school. The problem-solving approach was described to her, and she was told that this approach could teach Randy self-control skills and ways of displaying adaptive behaviors in the presence of teasing situations and negative racial remarks. The mother received a brief parent training session during which she role-played about the approach and was instructed to apply the same technique at home to encourage Randy's application of the technique in school.

Discussion of the Case of Randy
Freddy A. Paniagua

General Discussion

Randy's symptoms suggest either mood (e.g., Major Depressive Disorder) or disruptive behavior disorders (e.g., Conduct Disorder). However, Randy identified a significant stressor, namely, racist remarks directed against him by white students in school. In the presence of these remarks, Randy experienced depression and displayed behaviors characteristic of a disruptive behavior disorder but without sufficient *DSM-IV* criteria for either Major Depression or Conduct Disorder (APA, 1994). An alternative diagnosis for Randy's symptoms is Adjustment Disorder with Mixed Disturbance of Emotions and Conduct, which is used in those cases when "the predominant manifestations are both emotional (e.g., depression, anxiety) and disturbance of conduct [e.g., fighting]" (APA, 1994, p. 624) "in response to an identifiable psychosocial stressor or stressors (APA, 1994, p. 623). With Randy, racist remarks were the predominant stressor leading to symptoms.

Cultural Formulation

In terms of cultural identity, Randy clearly identified himself as an African American and appeared happy to be a member of this racial group. Randy's identification with this cultural reference group should be reinforced in the treatment plan. In terms of the cultural explanation of symptoms, it is clear that racism is the central topic to explore with Randy. In the treatment plan, the emphasis should be placed on the identification of adaptive behaviors Randy could use to deal with his perception of racial discrimination toward him by white students in school. A problem-solving approach was used to assist Randy with the development of self-control (adaptive) skills and their use when exposed to those racist remarks. To promote the practice of this approach at home, parent training was also used, and his mother was instructed to assist Randy with this practice. Last, the V-Code "Identity Problem" (APA, 1994, p. 685) could be considered in the treatment plan, *not as the central focus of clinical attention* but as a reminder to the clinical staff that it is important to include culturally appropriate interventions in the treatment plan to prevent the potential development of a racial identity problem during Randy's stage of adolescence.

The Case of Sylvia
Derald Wing Sue, PhD, and David Sue, PhD

Sylvia Echohawk is a 29-year-old American Indian woman who works for one of the major automobile manufacturing companies in the United States. The company has recently implemented an affirmative action program designed to open up jobs for minorities. The personnel director, a White male counseling psychologist, is in charge of it. Sylvia, who was hired under the affirmative action program, is referred to him by her immediate supervisor because of "frequent tardiness." Also, the supervisor informs the psychologist that other employees take advantage of Sylvia. She goes out of her way to help them, shares her lunches with them, and even lends them money. Several times during the lunch hours, other employees have borrowed her car to run errands. The supervisor feels that Sylvia needs to actively deal with her passive-aggressive means of handling anger (tardiness), to set limits on others, and to be able to assert her rights.

In an interview with Sylvia, the psychologist notices several things about her behavior. She is low-keyed, restrained in behavior, avoids eye contact, and finds it difficult to verbalize her thoughts and feelings. After several meetings, the psychologist concluded that Sylvia would benefit from assertion training. She is placed in such a group during regular working hours but fails to show up for meetings after attending the first one. Additionally, Sylvia's supervisor informs the psychologist that she has turned in a two-week resignation notice.

Discussion of the Case of Sylvia
Freddy A. Paniagua

General Discussion

Initially, the presentation of this case would suggest a Dependent Personality Disorder (APA, 1994, pp. 665-669). However, placing Sylvia in a working environment where sharing and helping behavior beyond expected levels is seen as possibly "maladaptive" was probably a stressful situation that Sylvia did not know how to deal with. If true, a more plausible diagnosis would be Adjustment Disorder, Unspecified (APA, 1994, p. 624). Sylvia's response to that stressor was her frequent tardiness, but the supervisor interpreted this response as an example of Sylvia's passive-aggressive means of handling anger, rather than Sylvia's only way to escape temporarily from that stressor. As noted in Chapter 4, the scheduling of assertion training (or social-skills training) should be considered carefully when treating culturally diverse clients. This is particularly true in the present case. In this training, Sylvia was asked to perform a behavior that is not culturally accepted among many American Indians (to be less cooperative, to stop sharing her things, and to assert her rights in a manner that she would perceive as rude or impolite in her own culture). This training was also another stressful event imposed on Sylvia, and her solution to this second stressor was to quit her job.

Cultural Formulation

Sylvia's helping behavior was in accord with what would be expected in her cultural reference group (e.g., sharing, low-keyed general behavior). This element of Sylvia's cultural identity would be a critical issue in the treatment plan. Another important variable is that the supervisor did not seek consultation from other American Indian coworkers before concluding that Sylvia's behaviors required counseling, and the white male counseling psychologist assigned to Sylvia apparently did not feel that such a consultation was necessary prior to the decision to schedule assertion training for her to be more assertive in the working environment.

The issue is not that Sylvia should have been evaluated and treated by an American Indian counseling psychologist but that both the supervisor and the psychologist were not culturally sensitive to Sylvia's difficulty in adjusting her cultural values to those expected by both the supervisor and the counseling psychologist. This issue deals with the "cultural elements of the relationship between the individual [client] and the clinician " in the cultural formulation suggested in the *DSM-IV* (APA, 1994, p. 844). In the assessment and treatment of Sylvia, the critical issue is not the fact that Sylvia's cultural background was different from the white male counselor (or supervisor) but that both the counselor and the supervisor lacked cultural sensitivity (an understanding of cultural variables that could have explained Sylvia's overall behaviors) and cultural competence (the ability to translate cultural sensitivity into behaviors leading to effective assessment and treatment of Sylvia's difficulties dealing with her stressors). This is the crux of the universalistic argument in the assessment and treatment of culturally diverse clients in mental health practice (Dana 1993b; Paniagua, 1996, 1998; Tharp, 1991), which, as noted earlier, states that the clinician-client racial and ethnic similarity or difference is not the critical element in securing affective assessment and treatment of such clients but whether providers from any race or ethnic background are culturally sensitive and competent when serving these clients.

The Case of Roland
Freddy A. Paniagua, PhD

Roland, an 11-year-old African American male, reported, "I wanted to kill myself," because he was having "a lot of problems" at home and in school. Roland said that on the day he intended to hang himself with a rope placed around two sections of the fence in the backyard, he was angry because he did not win a game in which students had to provide correct answers to questions around several school subjects; he also had a test schedule for the next day and was "afraid" that he did not study enough to pass the test. Roland also reported that on that day, he had a "big argument" with his mother because she wanted him to spend time doing schoolwork unrelated to that test. Roland said that because of these stressors, he decided to kill himself. Roland's father was present during the initial evaluation and reported that this was the first time that Roland tried to kill himself and added that another significant event was that Roland had just moved to a different school and in which he did not have his "old friends." The father was asked why he did not bring Roland to the emergency service, and he replied that Roland was just having "too much stress" on that day and that Roland did not have a "real intention" to kill himself because Roland was "too heavy" to be supported by that rope and Roland had told his father that he changed his mind because "If I kill myself, I won't go to heaven." When asked what the family did after that incident, the father replied that Roland and his parents spent approximately 2 hours praying and that at the end of this prayer session, the father contacted his minister to report what happened to the family on that day.

After the mental status exam to assess Roland's current state of mind (he was not suicidal, was alert, oriented, and without psychotic symptoms), the therapist encouraged the father and Roland in a further discussion of the role of religion in their family. The father appeared extremely pleased when the therapist said,

Mr.___, it appears that Roland was experiencing several stressful events on that day and that he did not have the intention to take his own life. I wonder if you and Roland would like to explore how your devotion to God helped the family to deal with that incident.

Roland's father reported that he, his wife, and Roland (the only child in the family) attend Sunday service each week of the year and they are engaged in many church activities. Roland's parents also consult with the minister about any problem the family encounters, including medical and emotional difficulties. The therapist listened and provided additional encouragement to indicate to Roland and his father that it was acceptable to continue with this topic. At the end of the session, the father asked for permission to pray, and the therapist agreed. The father asked Roland to lead the prayer, who said, "Thank you, God, for having Freddy today with me to help me with my problems. I promise I won't do that again. Thank you, God, for having my parents with me when I need help."

The treatment plan includes three elements. First, problem-solving strategies were implemented to teach Roland alternative, more acceptable responses to deal with similar stressful events. Second, the family was encouraged to assist Roland with the use of these strategies at home during a period of 15 minutes daily and to spend time praying at the end of this period. Third, parents were encouraged to continue consulting with their minister and to discuss with him the present treatment plan. Subsequent sessions in the clinic involved the programming of problem-solving strategies and praying (scheduled at the end of each session) in which the therapist also participated by saying his own prayer (e.g., "I thank God for helping Roland to learn better behaviors to deal with things that bother him . . . I thank God for everything Roland's parents are doing to help me with the treatment of Roland"). During the course of treatment, Roland learned skills to deal with similar stressful events, and his family appeared pleased with the opportunity they had had to include their religious beliefs in the treatment plan.

Discussion of the Case of Roland
Freddy A. Paniagua

General Discussion

Roland's case clearly showed symptoms in response to identifiable stressors, and these symptoms did not persist once these stressors were explored and terminated. This interpretation suggests a diagnosis of Adjustment Disorder with Depressed Mood (APA, 1994, p. 623). This case emphasizes the importance of integrating religious beliefs as a critical element in the treatment plan. Problem-solving strategies in combination with prayer sessions constituted the treatment to assist Roland with his adjustment to similar stressors in the absence of suicidal ideation or attempts. In this approach, the therapist should not only encourage the family to use religion as an alternative treatment modality, but it is also important for the therapist to be an active participant in this element of the treatment plan (e.g., praying with the family during family therapy sessions). It should be noted that in the multiaxial classification of this case (Axes I-V in the *DSM-IV*), the V-Code "Religious and Spiritual" issues (APA, 1994, p. 685) would be listed in Axis IV. In this case, however, these issues appear unrelated to the mental problem listed in Axis I (Adjustment Disorder with Depressed Mood).

Cultural Formulation

Roland and his parents are members of one of the church denominations (Baptist) generally reported by African American families (see Paniagua, 1998, p. 22 for a summary of major church denominations in this cultural group), in which the role of the minister is critical in those instances when the family experiences economical, emotional, or medical difficulties. For this reason, the third element of the treatment plan recognized the importance of including the minister in this plan. In terms of the "cultural elements of the relationship between the individual and the clinician" (APA, 1994, p. 844), Roland was assessed and treated by a Hispanic therapist, but they shared one important element: a recognition that religion could be a critical element in helping people deal with emotional disorders. This shared belief in religious matters was perceived by Roland's parents as a critical element in the treatment plan. This is another example of the applicability of the universalistic argument in the assessment and treatment of culturally diverse clients, when a client-therapist racial difference does exist but cultural values are shared that could enhance the client-therapist relationship (see Paniagua, 1998, pp. 7-8).

The Case of Carlos
Rita Sommers-Flanagan, PhD

Carlos, a 27-year-old Hispanic male, sought counseling at a community mental health center because his wife had moved out and was threatening divorce. He stated that he believed she might move back in if he got help with his problems. Carlos began work with a female intern who was bi-lingual to some extent. Counseling was conducted in English, but Carlos appreciated the fact that his counselor understood him when he needed to use his native Spanish occasionally. Over the course of the first four sessions, Carlos indicated his wife had left him due to his uncontrollable temper and his intermittent "inability to perform as a husband." He agreed to get a medical examination, but no physical reasons were found for his erectile dysfunction. At this examination, it was suggested that he try taking a selective serotonin reuptake inhibitor (SSRI) to address his overall distress, and he agreed to do so. [SSRIs are used to treat psychiatric disorders, e.g., depression, panic disorders, obsessive compulsive disorder.]

Carlos and his wife, Terry, had met in Carlos's home country, Costa Rica, where Terry was on extended vacation. Terry was born and raised in California and was 10 years older than Carlos. Their romance had been intense, and they decided to marry after knowing each other only 6 weeks. The couple moved to a state in the Northwest where Terry found work in her field and Carlos began attending college. The marriage began to deteriorate during the second year, but Terry didn't move out until just after their third anniversary.

Carlos reported that he began to lose his temper, which involved yelling, throwing things, and then refusing to speak to Terry for up to 3 or 4 days, during the first year of marriage. He stated that he did not wish to be an angry man who lost his temper so often but that Terry's ways of putting him down made him crazy. He had wanted Terry to try and have children right away, given her age. She was not willing. He wanted to find work so he could contribute more to the family income but had found that quite difficult due to immigration restrictions. He had tried to convince Terry to move back to Costa Rica, but she didn't feel that was feasible.

Carlos came faithfully to counseling, worked through an anger management sequence, and seemed to respond well to the SSRI. He was able to convince Terry to begin couples counseling with another counselor, so he suspended his individual work. The couples counseling was short-lived, with the couple deciding to proceed with a divorce. Carlos came back to individual counseling for five more sessions. He had elected to stay in school for the rest of the academic year but planned to return to his home in Costa Rica over the summer break. He wasn't sure if he would try to return for his final year of college or not. Carlos ended his counseling as a much calmer and more reflective individual. He had stopped taking the SSRI, was doing well in school, and reported no difficulties with either out-of-control anger or sexual functioning.

Discussion of the Case of Carlos
Freddy A. Paniagua

General Discussion

Carlos's symptoms suggest Adjustment Disorder with Mixed Anxiety and Depressed Mood (APA, 1994, p. 624). Sexual Dysfunctions, particularly Male Erectile Disorder (APA, 1994, pp. 502-504), and Intermittent Explosive Disorder (APA, 1994, pp. 609-612) should also be ruled out, but given the substantial impact of marriage and relocation within the context of Carlos's cultural background, an adjustment reaction seemed most likely.

Are Carlos's symptoms the result of his wife's decision to move out of the house or because his sense of masculinity was questioned by his wife? As noted in Chapter 1, the role of the male in Hispanic cultures includes the concept of machismo, and one important aspect of this cultural role is the expectation of masculinity among Hispanic males. Additional characteristics of machismo include a sense of physical strength, sexual attractiveness, aggressiveness, ability to impregnate women, and consumption of alcohol without getting drunk (Boyd-Franklin et al., 1995; Paniagua, 1998). It is likely that Carlos felt that he lost his masculinity and sexually dominant role in his marital relationship, which then led to the displayed symptoms. Another factor contributing to Carlos's sense of losing his "machista" role included his wife's choice to work, thereby making more money than he and giving her more freedom to be independent from Carlos's sense of machismo. Last, his wife's reluctance to consider having children and her decision not to return to Carlos's home country could have been perceived by Carlos as examples of his inability to impregnate his wife and his wife's lack of *respeto* (respect), respectively, also minimizing his sense of machismo in this context.

Cultural Formulation

The treatment plan for this case should include an assessment of the cultural identities of Carlos and his wife. Terry was born in California, was 10 years older than Carlos, and had met him in Costa Rica at the time she was on an extended vacation. Carlos was born in Costa Rica, and he married Terry 6 months after they met in Costa Rica. Therefore, whereas Terry was an American citizen,

Carlos was an immigrant in the United States. Carlos's cultural reference group was his own country (Costa Rica), and his wife apparently did not perceive herself culturally related to the expected norms and values (e.g., the machismo vs. *marianismo* cultural values described in Chapter 1) in Carlos's country, which probably prompted her to reject Carlos's request to move back to Costa Rica with him. Carlos did not provide a cultural explanation for the presenting symptoms. In the treatment plan, however, Carlos should be encouraged to talk about his feelings regarding the characteristics of machismo and his wife's apparent decision to reject Carlos's dominant role and his expectation of *marianismo* in the marital relationship (Terry's expected dependence, obedience, and submissive attitude in the presence of Carlos).

Another important aspect of the cultural formulation for this case is that Carlos was given the opportunity to speak his own language (Spanish) when he could not articulate his thoughts in English. In addition, Carlos agreed to attend several individual psychotherapy sessions with positive outcomes, suggesting that the therapist was culturally sensitive to Carlos's social stressors resulting from his immigrant status and his cultural identity conflicts with his wife. (It should be noted that the therapist was born to parents with mixed racial background, was raised primarily on an American Indian reservation, and spent part of her childhood in Los Angeles, California, where she lived with a Spanish-speaking family.) Last, many Hispanic clients expect medication during the treatment of their mental disorders or emotional difficulties (see Paniagua, 1998, pp. 54-56, and Chapter 1). The use of the SSRI not only assisted with the management of Carlos's symptoms, but the inclusion of the treatment modality in the treatment plan was in accordance with what would be expected by many Hispanic clients seeking counseling to deal with emotional problems.

Anxiety Disorders

Panic Disorder

Panic attacks could be seen in cultures where members strongly believe in evil spirit attacks and witchcraft (Castillo, 1997; Kirmayer, Young, & Hayton, 1995). For example, fear of dying, chest pain, palpitations, trembling and shaking, and other symptoms for Panic Disorder are generally reported by Hispanic clients with intense fears of evil spirit attacks, malign magic, or malevolent attacks by witchcraft. The culture-bound syndrome known as *ataques de nervios* among Hispanics is often used in the cultural interpretation of these symptoms (APA, 1994; Kirmayer et al., 1995; see Chapter 2, Table 2.3). As noted in the *DSM-IV* (APA, 1994), however, the "association of most *ataques* with a precipitating event and the frequent absence of the hallmark symptoms of acute fear or apprehensions distinguish [these *ataques*] from Panic Disorder" (p. 845). The culture-bound syndrome termed *ode-ori* (see Chapter 2, Table 2.3) is also used in the cultural interpretation of symptoms suggesting Panic Disorder. This syndrome is often reported among the Nigerian culture and is characterized by sensations of feelings of heat in the head and parasites crawling in the head. As noted by Kirmayer et al. (1995), these culture-bound syndromes should not be considered as "indicative of psychopathology" (p. 509). In addition, the *DSM-IV* pointed out that the participation of women in public life is sometimes restricted in some ethnic and cultural groups (e.g., Arabic countries), and this condition should be differentiated from Agoraphobia (APA, 1994, p. 399).

Specific Phobia

This type of phobia has been documented across different cultures. The DSM-IV (APA, 1994), however, advises clinicians to diagnose a client with this disorder "only if the fear is excessive in the context of that culture and causes significant impairment or distress" (p. 407). For example, fear of spirits, ghosts, and witches is often experienced by many members of the Hispanic community. In this situation, if anxiety states resulting from that fear do not exceed the expected level of anxiety in that community and the individual is able to control his or her emotions, that diagnosis should not be applied.

Social Phobia

Social demands may lead to symptoms of Social Phobia in some cultures. For example, Japanese and Korean clients may report excessive and persistent fears of giving offense to others in social situations, instead of being embarrassed (APA, 1994, p. 413). These clients may express these fears in terms of extreme anxiety states, which results from the belief that one's body odor, facial expression, or eye contact will be offensive to others. In Table 2.3 (Chapter 2), these symptoms resemble *taijin kyofusho* (APA, 1994, p. 849; Schneider et al., 1999).

Obsessive-Compulsive Disorder

In the *DSM-IV* (APA, 1994), behaviors that are culturally prescribed should be distinguished from symptoms suggesting Obsessive-Compulsive Disorder (OCD). Exceptions to this guideline include those behaviors that exceed cultural norms, occur at times and places judged inappropriate by other members of the same culture, and interfere with the client's social role and functioning in the community (APA, 1994, p. 420). Cultural beliefs around spiritual themes are sometimes used to explain the origin of symptoms for OCD (Bernstein, 1997; Castillo, 1997). For example, repetitive washing, checking and ordering objects, praying, repetition of words or phrases silently, and other religious rituals are expected in many cultures (Castillo, 1997; Kirmayer et al. 1995). Among strict

Egyptian Moslems, compulsive praying (praying five times per day) associated with obsessive rules (repetition of the same words many times during prayer) are expected among members of this cultural group (Bernstein, 1997; Castillo, 1997). Clinicians unfamiliar with this cultural group could consider these rituals pathological. Other cultures in which similar obsessive and compulsive behaviors have been observed include Israel, India, Taiwan, and Latin American countries (e.g., Cuba, Colombia, Dominican Republic, Mexico, Puerto Rico, Venezuela, etc.).

Posttraumatic Stress Disorder and Acute Stress Disorder

Immigrants from countries with a history of civil conflicts, wars, and social unrest may display symptoms suggesting PTSD during the initial evaluation of the case (Boehnlein & Kinzie, 1995). Because of political immigrant status (see APA, 1994, p. 426), however, these clients may not divulge experience of torture and trauma during the first session (the clinical intake interview with emphasis on a general screening of symptoms prior to making a diagnosis). Specifically with American Indians and Alaska Natives, McNeil, Kee, and Zvolensky (1999) recommended an assessment of historical events leading to discrimination and cultural abuses against these groups (see Paniagua, 1998, pp. 77-81) as well as an assessment of the role of these historical (aversive) events leading "to intergenerational Posttraumatic Stress Disorder [among members of these groups]" (McNeil et al., 1999, p. 62). In the case of Acute Stress Disorder, the severity of symptoms may be a function of cultural differences among cultural groups in the presence of loss; coping behaviors used to deal with this loss may also be culturally determined. Many Hispanic clients, for example, are expected to show symptoms resembling Acute Stress Disorder when they are exposed to stressful events associated with the family (e.g., separation and divorce and the death of a close relative). The culture-bound syndromes known as *ataques de nervios* and *susto* (see Table 2.3, Chapter 2) may resemble symptoms indicative of Posttraumatic Stress Disorder and Acute Stress Disorder (APA, 1994, p. 849; Castillo, 1997).

Generalized Anxiety Disorder

Variables in the expression of this disorder exist across cultures. In some cultures, anxiety is expressed predominantly through cognitive symptoms, in others, through somatic symptoms. In the evaluation of worries about certain conditions as excessive, the cultural context in which these worries occur should be considered (APA, 1994, pp. 433-434). Similar to Panic Disorder, symptoms of Generalized Anxiety Disorder may also resemble the culture-bound syndrome termed *odi-ori* (Table 2.3, Chapter 2; Castillo, 1997).

The Case of the Hex
Cervando Martinez, Jr., MD

A 19-year-old single Mexican-American woman had gradually become withdrawn, quieter, and begun talking to herself. The parents were older and more traditional. She had tended to be shy and "stay-at-home." About a year previously she had felt rejected by a boyfriend. When the family noted these changes and other peculiarities of behavior, such as excessive hand washing and long periods in the bathroom, they wondered whether she might have a hex (*mal puesto*) and on several occasions took her to *curanderas* to have it removed. The *curandera* performed religious rituals, said prayers, and prescribed teas. There were brief periods of improvement but the changes in behavior continued. Last, at the urging of an older sister, she was taken to a mental health clinic. She described multiple psychiatric symptoms and was admitted to the hospital for full evaluation.

SOURCE: From Cervando Martinez, Jr., "Mexican-Americans." In L. Comas-Díaz & E. E. H. Griffith (Eds.), *Clinical Guidelines in Cross-Cultural Mental Health* (p. 194). Copyright © 1988 by John Wiley & Sons, Inc. Reprinted by permission of the publisher.

Discussion of the Case of the Hex
Freddy A. Paniagua

General Discussion

Initial symptoms would suggest a mood disorder (e.g., early development of Dysthymic Disorder, APA, 1994, p. 345). The symptoms that prompted the family to bring the girl to the clinic, however, pointed to a current case of OCD (APA, 1994, pp. 422-423). The fact that the client's parents were more traditional than the client (in the acceptance of cultural norms and beliefs) would suggest an acculturation problem, such as the V-code 62.4 in the *DSM-IV* (APA, 1994, p. 685). This V-code, however, would not be the "focus of clinical attention" (APA, 1994, p. 685); the focus would be the symptoms of OCD (and other "multiple psychiatric symptoms") reported by the parents, which led to the hospitalization of the client for further evaluation.

Cultural Formulation

In terms of the cultural identity of the client, the treatment plan should emphasize an assessment of the level of acculturation among all family members (see Paniagua, 1998, pp. 10-11). For example, the parents were more traditional than the client, and her older sister apparently realized that embracing folk beliefs was not the best way to handle the symptoms the client was experiencing. The parents' cultural explanation of their daughter's symptoms is another critical variable to consider in the treatment plan. Among many traditional Hispanic families, the *mal puesto* (hex) is a cultural phenomenon used to explain emotional, family, economic, or social difficulties experienced by individual members or by the entire family; this cultural belief is often accompanied by the belief in the role of the *curandero(a)* (folk healer) who is the person with the spiritual power to "treat" the symptoms resulting from the hex.

In most cases in which the curandero(a) is consulted, accidental (chance) relationships between the healing process and improvement in symptoms might happen. These accidental relationships serve to reinforce people's beliefs about the role of the curandero(a) in dealing with such difficulties. In the present case, a brief period of improvement was noted by parents, and the question is, should the clinician encourage the parents to seek the assistant of the curandero(a) to deal with similar situations in the future? According to Martinez (1988), the answer to this question is "No" for two reasons: (a) Families who believe in *curanderismo* (folk healing) have consulted the curandero(a) many times without success and (b) "powerful psychological reasons that aren't easy to resolve" (Martinez, 1988, p. 194) prevent those families from accepting the fact that beliefs such as *mal puesto* (hex), *susto* (magical fright or soul loss), *mal de ojo* (evil eye), and other culture-bound syndromes listed in Table 2.3 are *not* the real causes of emotional, family, economic, or social difficulties.

Martinez's recommendation should be considered seriously, because it points to the prevention of a given mental disorder from becoming chronic due to a long period of services provided by healers rather than by mental health professionals. In the present case, the severity of symptoms apparently increased over time because the parents elected to seek the help of folk healers before consulting with a mental health professional. The current cross-cultural literature in mental health, however, suggests that not encouraging these families to talk about such beliefs *during the evaluation and treatment* of the case might enhance attrition or refusal to continue in therapy (Garza-Trevino, Ruiz, & Venegas-Samuels, 1997; Paniagua, 1998). Therefore, although it might be a good tactic to discourage these families from seeking the help of folk healers to prevent the problem becoming chronic over the years in the absence of professional assistance, it appears important to encourage such families to talk about their folk beliefs and supernatural or spiritual explanations during the assessment and treatment of the case. This recommendation is an example of the application of the fourth component of the cultural formulation in the *DSM-IV* (APA, 1994, p. 844), namely, the cultural elements of the relationship between the client and the clinician, in which the therapist would be culturally sensitive to the client's belief system and include it in the clinical assessment and treatment of the mental disorder under consideration.

The Case of C.C.
Richard F. Mollica, MD, and James P. Lavelle, MSW

C.C. is a 40-year-old Cambodian male with a negative past medical-psychiatry history. He was referred to IPC [Indochinese Psychiatry Clinic] by the primary care clinic in January 1983 for an evaluation of depression since a medical basis could not be determined for his chronic headaches, dizziness, chest pain, blurred vision, and motion sickness.

C.C. was the fourth child born to a poor rural Cambodian family, whose father was murdered when the patient was 10 months old. Unable to educate him or provide for his physical needs, the mother gave him to a monk to serve as an apprentice at an area temple. He remained at the temple for 10 years until he joined the army after the Communist invasion. He was subsequently captured and escaped from a Communist prison four times. During one of his imprisonments, his mother suffered a fatal heart attack. His only sister died of starvation in his presence, after his frantic but futile attempts to find food for her.

C.C. was married twice. These unions produced three children. In addition, the patient raised his sister's son with whom he felt a special connection. All were lost in the war. The patient does not know whether they died or remain alive. C.C. has married a third time, living in the Boston area with his wife (a marriage arranged by the Pol Pot regime) and her 11-year-old daughter. Recently, a pregnancy from this union was terminated because of severe financial constraints upon the family.

C.C. presented with numerous somatic complaints, including headaches, chest pain, weakness, poor appetite, and motion sickness. C.C.'s depression is severe with major neurovegetative[ness] including severe psychomotor retardation, diminished appetite (C.C. has lost 30 pounds), difficulty sleeping, and frequent awakening. One and a half years of treatment including many drug trials has resulted in only slight decreases in his depressive symptoms.

Discussion of the Case of C.C.
Freddy A. Paniagua

General Discussion

This case illustrates three clinical issues to consider in a treatment plan designed for Southeast Asian refugees. First, as noted in Chapter 1, because of the shame, humiliation, and guilt resulting from making psychological or emotional disorders public, many Asian clients tend to express these disorders in somatic terms (Paniagua, 1998). Therefore, a thorough medical (physical) examination of symptoms reported by the client (e.g., headaches, chest pain, blurred vision) should be conducted before concluding that these symptoms are the result of an underlying psychological or emotional disorder that the patient does not want to reveal during the initial evaluation. Second, reports of somatic manifestations suggesting a given psychological disorder among many Asian clients could lead to a diagnosis involving a Mood Disorder, more than likely, Major Depressive Disorder (APA, 1994, p. 327) or Mood Disorder Due to a General Medical Condition (APA, 1994, pp. 366-370). In the particular case of Southeast Asian refugees, however, the underlying psychiatric disorder leading to symptoms resembling a Mood Disorder is often associated with Posttraumatic Stress Disorder (APA, 1994, pp. 424-429). Therefore, although the treatment plan for C.C. emphasized the management of his depression, in the discussion for this case, Mollica and Lavelle (1988, see pp. 290-291) pointed out that the goal of this intervention was to assist C. C. in dealing with those traumatic experiences. Third, the *DSM-IV* (APA, 1994) pointed out that "immigrants from areas of considerable social unrest and civil conflicts . . . may be especially reluctant to divulge experiences of torture and trauma due to their vulnerable political immigrant status" (p. 426). For this reason, clinicians are advised not to force these clients to report about such traumatic events during the first session and instead wait until "the patient is ready to tell the trauma story" (Mollica & Lavelle, 1988, p. 289; see also Paniagua, 1998, p. 67).

Cultural Formulation

In general, three critical components of the cultural formulation to include in the treatment plan are (a) the cultural identity of the client, (b) cultural factors related to psychosocial environment and level of functioning, and (c) cultural elements of the relationship between the client and the clinician. In the first case, C.C. clearly identified himself with his racial-ethnic group (born and raised in Cambodia). In the second component, a careful exploration of social and family support should be considered. Many Southeast Asian refugees lack the support of the extended family because most members of the family were arrested and killed during the war (Mollica & Lavelle, 1988). In addition, many of these refugees lack experiences in seeking community and social services (e.g., available mental health services for refugees or housing and vocational resources). For C.C., the Indochinese Psychiatry Clinic was the only available resource for the services needed (Mollica & Lavelle, 1988). Last, services provided by clinicians sharing racial or ethnic similarities with these refugees would greatly enhance the goal of the treatment plan (e.g., reduction of symptoms, adapting the client to a different cultural context, etc.).

The Case of Miss D.
David M. Bernstein, MD

Miss D., a 28-year-old single African-American female, presented to an outpatient mental health clinic with complaints of anxiety and depression. She had been assigned to Hawaii to complete her final few months of active duty as a computer operator with the United States Army. Although she initially enjoyed her assignment, she noted that she "never really fit in because there are almost no Blacks in Hawaii except in the military." After her discharge from the Army, she decided to stay in Hawaii, and obtain a computer-related job in the civilian sector.

On presentation to the VA Mental Health Clinic, she had been out of the Army for two months and was still unemployed. She angrily described how prejudice against African Americans, which was magnified in the Asian-influenced culture of Hawaii, was responsible for her unemployment and anxiety in public. She reported that shortly after her discharge from the army, while standing in line to purchase an item at a convenience store, she felt "like everybody was staring at me as if I was the first Black person they had ever seen." She became anxious and left the store without completing her purchase. Miss D. noted that while still on active duty she did her shopping at the PX, "where there were plenty of other Black people around and I never had a problem." Approximately two weeks later, while eating with a friend in a fast-food restaurant, she felt as though other patrons were staring at her, "like I didn't belong there. I've experienced prejudice before, and I recognize it when I see it." She expressed her discomfort to her friend, who was also African-American, but was annoyed when he told her that "it was all in her head. He felt perfectly comfortable." Despite feeling anxious, she finished her meal, and afterwards came to the conclusion that "compared to all these skinny little Japanese girls, I must look like some kind of giant Black freak. Back home nobody would care what I ate." Miss D. began to have frequent thoughts that when around Asians she had to carefully self-monitor her etiquette and food intake to avoid negative stereotyping of African-Americans as "uncivilized." She reported being extremely self-conscious in restaurants, and carried extra napkins with her to ensure that she could adequately wipe her face and hands. She stated that "all these Oriental people here are neat-freaks, and I am already discriminated against because I'm Black. I don't want to be sloppy, too."

Miss D. began to notice that she no longer felt comfortable eating on base or in other military settings, including parties at the homes of friends, even though her friends were almost exclusively African-American. She began to wonder "if I am going crazy. Why can't I just eat without thinking about it, like a normal person?" She began to experience feelings of depression, accompanied by crying spells. She rearranged her schedule so that she could eat meals alone, and avoided social events where she would be expected to eat in front of others. Her friends commented that she seemed depressed and withdrawn. One joked, "maybe you should see a psychiatrist." After much rumination, she presented to the VA Mental Health clinic, complaining of anxiety and depression, which she attributed to "too much prejudice against Blacks in Hawaii."

A diagnosis of Social Phobia was made, and Miss D. was started on phenelzine. After approximately six weeks, she reported a significant decrease in phobic symptoms, and felt that she was "adjusting better to civilian life thanks to the medicine."

SOURCE: "Case 2" from "Anxiety Disorders" by David M. Bernstein (pp. 48-49), in Wen-Shing Tseng & Jon Streltzer (Eds.), *Culture and Psychopathology: A Guide to Clinical Assessment* (pp. 46-66). Copyright © 1997 by Brunner/Mazel, reprinted by permission of the publisher.

Discussion of the Case of Miss D.
Freddy A. Paniagua

General Discussion

In this case, in addition to a diagnosis of Social Phobia (APA, 1994, pp. 411-417), it is important to rule out Major Depressive Disorder with Psychotic Features (APA, 1994, pp. 339-345) and Adjustment Disorder with Anxiety and Depressed Mood (APA, 1994, p. 624). In support of the first alternative, Miss D. reported depression in response to her difficulty dealing with racism in a setting with few African Americans. Reporting that she *felt* "like everybody was staring at me as if I was the first Black person they had ever seen. . . . Like I didn't belong there" points to the possibility of psychotic features. Further assessment with culturally sensitive tests (see Paniagua, 1998, p. 122) should be used to rule out psychotic features resembling the healthy paranoid phenomenon among many African Americans (see Chapter 1), in which some members of this racial group present "themselves as highly suspicious of others with different color and values" (Paniagua, 1998, p. 23). In support of the second alternative, Miss D.'s anxiety and depressive symptoms were related to a significant stressor: moving to a setting in which she felt that she could not "fit in because there are almost no Blacks in Hawaii except in the military" (Bernstein, 1997, p. 48). Therefore, Miss D.'s responses to this stressor included not only significant emotional symptoms, but such responses were in "excess of what would be expected given the nature of the stressor, or by significant impairment in social or occupational . . . functioning" (APA, 1994, p. 623), which is Criterion A for Adjustment Disorder. In addition, Miss D.'s symptoms developed after she was "assigned to Hawaii to complete her final few months of active duty as a computer systems operator" (Bernstein, 1997, p. 48), which corresponds to Criterion B in a diagnosis of Adjustment Disorder (APA, 1994, p. 623). Because Miss D.'s difficulty in adjusting to that stressor was accompanied by predominant anxiety and depressive symptoms, the possibility of an Adjustment Disorder with Anxiety and Depressed Mood should be carefully considered in the overall assessment of the case.

Cultural Formulation

In the management of Miss D.'s symptoms, a critical element in the cultural formulation is to validate Miss D.'s strong cultural identity with the African American community and her sense of prejudice against members of this racial group. Miss D.'s explanation of the origin of these symptoms is around racially discriminatory behaviors against her from members of a different cultural group (the Asian community of Hawaii). The goal of treatment would be to assist Miss D. in distinguishing racial discrimination, as a real phenomenon experienced by many members of the African American community, from reports about this phenomenon resembling psychotic features. For example, an African American friend of Miss D. told her that he did not experience racial discrimination in Hawaii and that "it was all in [Miss D.'s] head." (Bernstein, 1997, p. 49). Miss D. became very upset because that friend was probably questioning the reality of Miss D.'s interpretation of racial discrimination against her. Last, the availability of social support (e.g., other African Americans residing in Hawaii) should be explored and discussed with Miss D.

The Case of Thuy
Larke Nahme Huang, PhD

Thuy, a 12-year-old Vietnamese girl, was referred to the child and adolescent unit of a community mental health center by her teacher and counselor. Her teacher had noticed a marked deterioration in her academic performance and that she frequently complained of headaches and asked to leave the class, seemed to lack energy, showed a loss of appetite, and nonverbally conveyed a general feeling of hopelessness. During the previous six months she had changed from a good student, actively involved with peers, to a withdrawn, depressed preadolescent. More recently, for days at a time she would not talk unless pressured to, and frequently stared off into space.

Thuy was from a middle-class family in Saigon, where until the downfall of South Vietnam her father had been a lower-level clerk with the army. He fled Saigon with his family, a wife and three children, in 1978; however, during the escape, the family became separated and the wife and two younger children remained in Vietnam. Thuy and her father escaped by boat. Their boat was intercepted by Thai pirates, and Thuy's father was beaten and several women were raped. Although Thuy observed this, she herself was not physically assaulted. Eventually Thuy and her father reached Malaysia, where they remained in a refugee camp for nearly a year until they located relatives in the United States. They have been in the United States for two years and reside in a small apartment with a cousin's family of five in the inner city of a West Coast metropolitan area.

Thuy's father has had a particularly difficult time adjusting to the United States. He struggles with English classes and has been unable to maintain several jobs as a waiter. He attributes these difficulties to the assault during his escape, saying blows to the head impaired his memory and crippled him physically.

Just before onset of Thuy's problems, she received a letter from her mother informing them of the death of her five-year-old brother. Complications from a childhood disease combined with malnutrition had contributed to his death. Thuy remained impassive on receiving this news, while her father wept uncontrollably, mourning the loss of his only son. Soon after that, her father was fired from yet another job, seemed to lose interest in English classes, and just languished around the small apartment.

At the insistence of the school and accompanied by her father, Thuy came to the clinic most reluctantly. She was reticent and scowling. Her father immediately began to plead with the therapist to help Thuy because she was all he had and he depended on her to make it in this country. He vacillated between sadness and anger toward Thuy. The therapist decided that father and daughter needed to be seen separately and arranged for the father to see another therapist ostensibly to deal with Thuy's problems, but also to address his own issues.

Discussion of the Case of Thuy
Freddy A. Paniagua

General Discussion

The initial evaluation of Thuy's symptoms would suggest Major Depressive Disorder (APA, 1994, pp. 320-327). Symptoms for depression, however, are most likely associated with five traumatic experiences. First, she was exposed to the Vietnam War. Second, when the entire family escaped from Saigon, the escaping situation was not only traumatic in itself, but Thuy also experienced the traumatic separation from her mother and two younger children who were forced to remain in Vietnam. Third, Thuy observed Thai pirates beating her father when they escaped by boat heading to Malaysia. Fourth, in Malaysia, Thuy was placed (with her father) in a refugee camp, which was in itself a traumatic situation; and fifth, she learned that one brother who tried to escape with her from Vietnam had died, which intensified depressive symptoms she had already been experiencing for many years before her mother's notification of the death of her brother. These traumatic events suggest the development of PTSD (APA, 1994, pp. 424-429). As noted in the *DSM-IV* (see APA, 1994, p. 425), PTSD is a risk for the development of Major Depressive Disorder. Assuming that symptoms for depression resulted from Thuy's exposure to these traumatic events, the treatment plan would emphasis further exploration of these events with the goal being to minimize their impact on Thuy's handling of these events with the presentation of depressive symptoms. This was precisely the approach Dr. Huang followed in the treatment of this case. In terms of other "conditions that may be a focus of clinical attention" (APA, 1994, p. 675), the following V-Codes would be considered in Axis IV: V62.3: Academic Problem and V62.4: Acculturation Problem (APA, 1994, p. 685).

Cultural Formulation

Prior exposure to the Vietnam War and the severe traumatic events experienced by Thuy during her escaping from Saigon were two critical variables explaining the presenting symptoms. In general, it is extremely difficult for Vietnamese refugees to talk openly about traumatic events they experienced in the past (Paniagua, 1998). In the discussion of this case, however, Dr. Huang employed the "tell their story" strategy to encourage Thuy to talk about these events (see Huang, 1998, pp. 293-294). This culturally sensitive strategy is based on the assumption that allowing refugee children to report about these events, using their own words and minimal verbal intervention from the therapist, could greatly enhance the building of trust (Huang, 1998, p. 294) between the client and the therapist, which is in itself a critical variable in the therapist's goal toward the gathering of an accurate clinical history leading to an accurate diagnosis and effective management of symptoms.

As suggested by Huang (1998), the issue is not that these children do not want to tell their story in their own words but that

> refugee youth rarely have the *opportunity* to do this, because family rules implicitly advocate "Don't talk about it." Community pressure to keep the "secrets" hidden and not incur shame for unavoidable events similarly inhibit disclosure about the migration." (p. 294, italics added)

Therefore, these social pressures might explain why refugee children are generally reluctant to talk about such traumatic events openly during the first therapy session, particularly in those cases when the therapist's statements, questions, or commentaries about these events appear to be a way of "forcing" the child to talk about these events (see Paniagua, 1998, p. 67, for more details on this point). Allowing those children to tell their story is a more culturally sensitive strategy because it would minimize anxiety resulting from the violation of those family rules, as well as enhancing the trusting therapist-client relationship necessary for the understanding of specific variables leading to symptoms and the exploration of culturally sensitive treatment strategy (see Huang, 1998, pp. 293-296, for an extensive discussion of this case, with emphasis on cultural variables, including many features of the "cultural elements of the relationship between the individual and the clinician" considered in the cultural formulation; see also APA, 1994, p. 844).

Last, the decision to arrange individual psychotherapy for the father and Thuy separately was also culturally appropriate for three reasons. First, although family therapy is often recommended with Asian clients, this form of therapy is not often feasible to implement with Southeast Asian refugees because all family members affected by those traumatic events might not be available, which was the case of Thuy (see Paniagua, 1998, p. 73). Second, Thuy was in need of intensive individual psychotherapy to allow her the opportunity to tell her story in the absence of her father (who would probably prevent her from talking about these events in public). Third, the therapist rightly assumed that Thuy's father also experienced depression resulting from those traumatic events and that he also needed individual psychotherapy to allow him to deal with his own symptoms. Encouraging the father to tell his own story would also be recommended because similar community pressure would prevent him from talking about these events in public.

Delusional Disorders

The individual's religious and cultural background should be considered in the assessment of Delusional Disorders. As noted in the *DSM-IV* (see APA, 1994, p. 298), cultural variability in the expression of these disorders exists across cultural groups. For example, a strong belief in the machismo cultural variant might suggest a Jealous Type delusion in a Hispanic male who feels uneasy with the way his wife begins to show behavioral changes after a number of years of residing in the United States. Unfamiliarity with that variant would lead to the conclusion that the case is an example of Delusional Disorder (Jealous Type), rather than an example of the impact of cultural variables (e.g., acculturation of the wife to new styles of dressing in this country and the husband's refusal to accept the assimilation of styles by his wife). The culture-bound syndrome termed "koro" (see Chapter 2, Table 2.3, and Bernstein & Gaw, 1990) might also resemble symptoms for the Somatic Type of delusion. The following cases illustrate the importance of considering cultural variations when diagnosing these two types of delusions. These cases, however, also show that the fact that cultural variables may explain the presence of nonbizarre delusions does not necessarily suggest that the client is not experiencing a mental disorder (i.e., a delusion in the present context).

The Case of Mr. Bienvenido
Freddy A. Paniagua, PhD

Mr. Bienvenido is a 52-year-old man from Mexico. He asked to be interviewed in Spanish because *"Yo no hablo o entiendo Ingles"* ("I cannot speak or understand English"). He reported that he married his current wife 20 years ago at the age of 32; she was 18 years old at the time of their marriage, and she is now 38 years old. Mr. Bienvenido reported that during the earlier years of the marriage, his wife used to do "everything [he] asked her to do" and that he "always told her how to dress" and the "type of makeup" she was allowed to use, without asking her husband the reasons for his requests. The patient reported that his wife would "never use makeup or wear a dress" without asking him for his "opinion." He reported that over the years, his wife has "changed" and "does not listen" to him. For example, according to Mr. Bienvenido, his wife stopped asking "permission" regarding which dress to wear, what makeup to use, and with whom she should "associate."

Mr. Bienvenido reported that he and his wife moved from Mexico to the United States 10 years after their marriage and that this was the time when he first started noticing that his wife was changing. He decided to move to a different city because he thought that this move could help his wife to "listen [to him] again." His wife, however, apparently did not return to her pattern of listening behaviors she had displayed in Mexico. The patient reported that most recently, he has "noticed" that his wife is "more independent" and that they engage in frequent verbal fights, which patient perceives as a lack of respect toward him (he said, *"Ella ya no me respeta,"*

"She does not respect me anymore"). He said that such independence has led to his wife's engagement in a job he does not like because it keeps his wife out of the house for "a long time" and particularly at night. This job involves selling jewelry during the evening hours. His wife is working for a man who owns this business, and Mr. Bienvenido came to the "conclusion that [his wife] is doing something very wrong with that man." He said that this explains why she "is wearing those dress and makeup" each time she goes out to work.

Mr. Bienvenido reported that his wife's behavioral changes over the years have resulted in many "emotional problems." When asked to be more specific, he said that he feels "depressed" many times during the day, thinking about answers for his wife's changes in behavior. He denied suicidal ideation or attempts but reported most symptoms suggesting Major Depressive and Dysthymic Disorders. The patient has three children (2-year-old boy, 14-year-old boy, and 17-year-old girl), and he said that he is very happy with his family; his only problem is that his wife does not want to listen to him as she used to do when they married 20 years ago.

Mr. Bienvenido was asked why he decided to come to the clinic today. He replied that his wife told him that she wants to separate from him (not to divorce him) and that this situation made him even more "depressed" in the last several weeks. He said that he wants to bring his wife to the clinic because he wants her to understand that he always wants to do "the best thing" for her. He said that he cannot understand why his wife wants to separate from him and explicitly requested that the therapist contact his wife to invite her to participate in the next meeting. Mr. Bienvenido was told that this was a good idea, because it is possible that after several years of living in this country, his wife is probably experiencing cultural changes and that these changes do not mean that she is not respecting him. Mr. Bienvenido appeared reluctant to agree with this explanation and returned to his own explanation of why his wife is changing, namely, that she is wearing certain types of dress and makeup without his permission because she is doing "something wrong" each time she goes out to work.

During the second meeting, Mr. Bienvenido and his wife were present. Mr. Bienvenido was asked for permission to talk to his wife alone, and he agreed. His wife reported that her husband "cannot understand" that she still loves him but that she wants him to stop "telling" her how to dress, what "type of shoe" to wear, and how to do her "hairstyle." She said that her husband has became so "controlling" that he even asked her several times recently that she should not buy "my private clothes without his permission" (she did not mention the name of these clothes, but apparently she was referring to her underwear). She said that they need money to support the family (he is a janitor) and that this is why she decided to work after many years "taking care of the children at home." She recognized that she has changed "a lot" after their arrival in the United States, but she cannot understand why her husband is so "jealous about these changes." She then revealed that her husband is "getting into the habit of smelling my clothes when I return from work" and is "now telling me that I cannot wash my clothes without his permission." She considered her husband's behavior very "weird" and asked why he is doing "those crazy things."

In subsequent sessions, individual and family therapy were programmed, with emphasis on three cultural variables: acculturation, machismo, and *marianismo*. Because of the strong cultural identity difference between Mr. Bienvenido and his wife, social skills training strategies (e.g., teaching his wife to be more assertive) were not programmed. Instead, the emphasis was placed on both partners understanding how these variables could lead to marital difficulties, in language they were able to understand. Cognitive-behavioral strategies (e.g., identification of negative thoughts and replacing them with more acceptable and realistic thoughts) were programmed with Mr. Bienvenido. In subsequent sessions, Mr. Bienvenido appeared more receptive to discussions involving these variables (understanding the difficulty in extrapolating cultural values in Mexico into social norms in the United States regulating marital relationship patterns) and became less delusional around his wife's overall changing patterns.

Discussion of the Case of Mr. Bienvenido
Freddy A. Paniagua

General Discussion

Mr. Bienvenido was clearly experiencing symptoms of depression, but the core symptoms are most likely associated with a Delusional Disorder, Jealous Type (APA, 1994, pp. 297-298). The phenomenon of jealousy among married people (or in other relationships) is not necessarily an abnormal situation. Actually, among many couples, the absence of some degree of jealousy could be interpreted as disinterest in the partner (Berg-Cross, 1997). This phenomenon becomes an indication of a mental disorder when behaviors leading to jealousy are beyond what would be expected in the particular cultural group. For example, Mr. Bienvenido's wife felt that her husband's engagement in smelling her clothes was not a normal thing to do, among Hispanic men. In addition, Mr. Bienvenido's demand that his wife should not buy "private clothes" was also something outside what most Hispanic men would do to show the type of controlling behavior expected when the phenomenon of machismo is suspected in the interpretation of the case. His wife reported her reason for her decision to have a job (to bring more money to the family), but her husband interpreted her reason in a different way (that this was a way for her to "do something wrong" and to disrespect his authority); his delusional state over the years did not permit Mr. Bienvenido to understand the main reason for his wife's behavioral changes.

Cultural Formulation

An assessment of the cultural identity of Mr. Bienvenido and his wife should be considered in the treatment plan before suggesting specific ways to handle his symptoms and their marital difficulties. For example, Mr. Bienvenido and his wife are from Mexico (not Mexican American, because they were not born in the United States). During their early marriage, his wife did not see a problem in following Mr. Bienvenido's requests regarding the way she should present herself in public (e.g., dressing, makeup, and hairstyle); she probably perceived these requests as culturally accepted in her community at the time they were living in Mexico. His wife started showing signs of lack of "respect" toward Mr. Bienvenido when they moved to the United States. At this moment, a cultural identity conflict emerged between the patient and his wife that was probably the result of his wife getting acculturated to new cultural norms, whereas the impact of acculturation was less dramatic over the years for her husband.

Another important element of the cultural formulation is to avoid explaining current symptoms in terms of cultural variables when, indeed, this is a case pointing to a mental disorder (i.e., Delusional Disorder). One could argue that Mr. Bienvenido's intention to control his wife, in terms described earlier, is an example of the phenomenon of machismo among many Hispanic men. As noted in Chapter 1, the spouse would accept this cultural phenomenon (i.e., a sense of *marianismo*) when she shows respect to the authority of the husband (or any Hispanic man in position of authority in the family, e.g., brothers, uncles, etc.) in terms of listening to and following the man's wishes without verbal confrontation. In general, Mr. Bienvenido's behavior toward his wife could be seen as a case of machismo, but his pattern of behaviors over the years went beyond what would be expected among Hispanic men. This is why his wife felt that it was very unusual for Mr. Bienvenido to smell her clothes and order her not to buy "private clothes" without his permission.

Last, the discussions of the potential impact of specific cultural variables on the couple's relationship during individual and family therapy sessions, as well as the programming of cognitive-behavioral strategies, were culturally appropriate. Rather than emphasizing who was "right" or "wrong" in that relationship, the emphasis was placed on variables that were out of the control of both partners (e.g., different levels of acculturation). In addition, instead of blaming Mr. Bienvenido for his problems, the programming of cognitive-behavioral strategies allowed him to explore his own negative thoughts about external events leading to symptoms as well as the replacement of these thoughts with more positive and productive thoughts, which resulted in the solution of marital conflicts and substantial reduction in his delusional states (see Paniagua, 1998, p. 56).

The Case of Koro
Ruth Levine, MD, and Albert Gaw, MD

The patient is a 25-year-old single male of Cantonese origin, seen in Boston, MA, beginning in 1972. His problems began approximately 1 month after visiting a prostitute. He began to experience a periodic burning pain in his penis and the perception that his penis was retracting into his abdomen. He became frightened that this was happening to him and went repeatedly to the bathroom to pull on his penis and make sure it didn't shrink.

His fear about the problem he was experiencing led to significant anxiety and insomnia. He became preoccupied with the size of his penis, and would masturbate frequently to reassure himself that he was capable of an erection. On one occasion, he was unable to achieve an erection, and this led to a feeling of panic. He experienced chest pain, palpitations, and pallor.

He became concerned that he had lost too much "vital energy" through his masturbation. He consulted some Chinese elders, and was told that he had "Suk-yeong" or "Koro" and that he was in danger of dying because this is a condition in which pain in the penis could lead to retraction into the abdomen and eventual death. This reinforced his anxiety and led to further insomnia, depression, and suicidal ideation.

He sought consultation with physicians at a local emergency room. Though physical and laboratory findings were unremarkable, he was treated with antibiotics, analgesics, and tranquilizers. These interventions did not relieve his symptoms, and increasing distress prompted referral to a psychiatrist.

On initial psychiatric evaluation he was interviewed with his younger brother, who acted as an interpreter. He appeared disheveled, fatigued, agitated, and anxious. He had difficulty sitting still in his chair. He spoke in a loud voice and used excessive foul language. While couched in a chair, with both legs spread out, he would repeatedly point to his penis and say ". . . my penis is pain . . . go inside, the man die. . . ." When asked about his inner thoughts and feelings, he offered little information. His thought processes were coherent, and there was no evidence of psychotic disorganization. He was oriented, and appeared cognitively intact. He did not appear to be particularly depressed. He did express a desire for medication to help him sleep.

He denied any previous history of medical or emotional problems, and had never seen a psychiatrist before. Personal history revealed that he had been born in China, the second of three children. His mother recalled that he had been a shy but amiable child with few friends, who [she] kept home most of the time to assist in housework. His family moved to Hong Kong when he was ten years old, and he attended school through the 7th grade. He immigrated again to Boston at age 19, and shortly thereafter his father died of tuberculosis at age 57. To help support the family, he worked as a cook in Chinese restaurants. He remained a loner, and his primary hobbies consisted of seeing Chinese movies and occasionally gambling. He began masturbating regularly at age 13, but denied having any sexual intercourse until the encounter that preceded the onset of his illness. He described a fear of being infected with a sexually transmitted disease as the reason had avoided sexual intercourse. At the time of the evaluation he was living with his 59-year-old mother and his younger brother.

After an intensive clinical interview, it appears that the patient was indeed experiencing "koro," which is one of the culture-bound syndromes listed in the *DSM-IV* (APA, 1994, Appendix I, p. 846). This syndrome has generally been reported in the Asian culture, and is characterized by acute anxiety associated with the fear of genital retraction (Bernstein & Gaw, 1990). Individuals afflicted with this disorder usually believe that complete disappearance of the organ into the abdomen will result in death. The patient was assured, along with his mother, that he did not have a fatal condition, but an illness that was "emotional" or "mental" in origin. He accepted this explanation, and was agreeable to treatment. He was started on Librium, 10 mg four times a day for anxiety, Chloral Hydrate, 1000 mg at night for insomnia, and supportive psychotherapy.

During the course of his therapy, he initially had considerable difficulty revealing his thoughts and feelings. Eventually he began to describe "bad dreams" of situations such as the communists taking over Hong Kong, being accused of killing Hitler, and his family members suffering broken limbs. He also described dreams of being dead and his fear of death. On two occasions, while describing his thoughts and feelings he experienced several minutes of numbness in his right foot. This numbness disappeared as the topic of conversation was directed away from discussing feelings. After six individual psychotherapy sessions, the patient described himself as feeling better and he returned to work. Treatment was terminated, but seven months later he returned with a recurrence of symptoms following a visit to a prostitute. He resumed his previous treatment and after three sessions his symptoms subsided.

SOURCE: An abbreviated description of this case was published by the authors in the following source: "Koro: Proposed Classification for *DSM-IV*" by Ruth Bernstein and Albert C. Gaw, *American Journal of Psychiatry,* Vol. 147, No. 2, p. 1670. Copyright © 1990 by the American Psychiatric Press. Materials from this abbreviated report of this case are reproduced with permission of the publisher.

Discussion of the Case of Koro
Freddy A. Paniagua

General Discussion

This is one of the classic cases of *koro* because when this case was seen in 1972 and a short version of the case published in 1990 (Bernstein & Gaw, 1990), discussion of culture-bound syndromes in psychiatry was not a standard practice among clinicians (including the present syndrome). In addition, these syndromes were not considered in the *DSM* until the fourth edition (APA, 1994). Therefore, the client in this case was fortunate to be evaluated and treated by two mental health professionals (one of them a Chinese psychiatrist) who were able to understand the context for the client's symptoms and treated him appropriately.

The inclusion of this culture-bound syndrome in Appendix I of the *DSM-IV* (APA, 1994) is an invitation to clinicians to consider this syndrome in the differential diagnosis of the case with emphasis on cultural variations. Therefore, an attempt to diagnosis this patient with a mental disorder without considering cultural guidelines for this syndrome in the *DSM-IV* (Appendix I) would indicate lack of cultural competency in the assessment and diagnosis of this case.

In terms of the *DSM-IV* Multiaxial Classification of mental disorders, the initial diagnosis for this case would be Delusional Disorder, Somatic Type, which is applied in those cases when "the central theme of the delusion involves bodily functions or sensations" (APA, 1994, p. 298). Patients who are not raised in a culture that believes in *koro* should probably be considered delusional if they expressed the conviction that they were dying from penile retraction. This patient, however, was clearly influenced by a culturally sanctioned belief involving this culture-bound syndrome, suggesting alternative diagnoses.

Another possible diagnosis would be Hypochondriasis because this client did appear to be afflicted with "preoccupation with fears of having, or the idea that one has, a serious disease based on the person's misinterpretation of bodily symptoms" (APA, 1994, pp. 462-463). The patient clearly believed that the pain in his penis was indicative of a fatal disease. He also was persistent in his preoccupation with a medical problem despite appropriate medical evaluation. In general, clients with a diagnosis of Hypochondriasis often resist psychological interpretations of their symptoms and are reluctant to see mental health practitioners. This client, however, accepted the possibility that the symptoms were psychological in nature.

Another alternative diagnosis is an Anxiety Disorder. This client reported excessive worry about sexual intercourse, avoiding sexual encounters primarily for fear of obtaining a sexually transmitted disease. In addition, he was afraid of masturbating for fear that he would deplete himself of vital energy. Symptoms of Panic Attack were probably experienced by this patient when he sensed that he was not able reach an erection.

Preoccupation with the negative thought involving the belief that the penis was shrinking might be interpreted as a case of Obsessive Compulsive Disorder. In the *DSM-IV,* (APA, 1994), an obsession is interpreted in terms of "persistent ideas, thoughts, impulses, or images that are experienced as intrusive and inappropriate and that cause marked anxiety or distress" (p. 418). Instances of masturbation might be considered a compulsion, which is defined in *DSM-IV* as "a repetitive behavior or mental act, the goal of which is to prevent or reduce anxiety or distress, not to provide pleasure or gratification" (p. 418). This client's response to benzoDíazepines and supportive psychotherapy, however, would minimize the assumption that he was experiencing true OCD symptoms, which often require intensive treatment beyond that provided in this case.

The treatment team clearly understood that this patient was afraid of experiencing a situation that was culturally accepted in his own culture. Therefore, it was particularly important to understand symptoms in relation to the client's culture and what symptoms beyond what was expected in that culture would suggest a psychiatric disorder. This level of understanding probably explains why the treatment team was able to educate this client regarding the possibility that he was experiencing a psychiatric disorder and not a medical problem and why this client responded to the treatment. One would argue that this client's decision to accept this psychiatric interpretation of his symptoms was the result of the availability of a Chinese physician during the evaluation and treatment of this case. Another variable that could have contributed to this patient's acceptance of this psychiatric interpretation of symptoms and psychological treatment was that the evaluation process included his family, as well as the explanation of symptoms to the patient and family in terms they understood without threatening their cultural assumptions regarding the present culture-bound syndrome. As noted in Chapter 1, in the Chinese culture, it is essential to appreciate the importance of including the family in all interventions, which was a culturally sensitive evaluation and treatment approach in this case.

Cultural Formulation

Clinicians may disagree with which specific psychiatric diagnosis should be applied to this case. Regardless of this disagreement, three elements of the cultural formulation (APA, 1994) should be considered when discussing the most appropriate treatment plan. First, the client learned from one of the most respected members of the Asian community (i.e., the elderly) that his symptoms were the result of *koro,* which suggested that he was not really experiencing a psychiatric disorder but a culture-bound syndrome specific to his racial group. In this circumstance, a treatment plan for this client would have to bring into the therapy process the "client's cultural explanation" of symptoms suggesting a given mental disorder (see Table 2.3). Second, the present symptoms pointed to the possibility of a psychiatric disorder, and the difficult task for the authors was to explore culturally sensitive strategies to convince this client that he needed psychiatric treatment rather than sending him to a folk healer because his symptoms were examples of a culture-bound syndrome. As noted by Paniagua (1998), "too much emphasis on culture-related syndromes may prevent practitioners from considering that many of these syndromes may actually include symptoms for severe psychiatric disorders" (p. 116). Thus, in terms of the "overall cultural assessment for diagnosis and care" (APA, 1994, p. 844) of the present mental disorder, the client received appropriate psychiatric treatment, despite the fact that *koro* is a condition specific to the client's culture. Third, in terms of the cultural elements of the relationship between the client and the clinician (see Table 2.4), the fact that the diagnostic and treatment team included a Chinese psychiatrist familiar with that culture-bound syndrome in his own culture was critical in this case, particularly with respect to enhancing this client's intention to report about symptoms. As noted in Chapter 1, shame and guilt are two mechanisms that prevent many Asians to publicly report their emotional problems to people outside this racial group (Paniagua, 1998; D. W. Sue & D. Sue, 1990, 1999). The enforcement of these mechanisms is more dramatic in those cases when the emotional problems involve sexual behavior, which is the case in *koro*.

The Case of Ms. A.
Xiao-yan He, MD

Ms. A. is a Chinese woman who was admitted to a psychiatric hospital in 1996. She was born in China and came to the United States to "look for a husband" in 1983. At age 35, she met an Anglo American man in California. They courted and married rather rapidly.

During the first 2 years of their marriage, they enjoyed traveling together, taking classes together. She did not have any problems in interacting with Mr. A.'s grown children by his first marriage. After 2 years of happy marriage, Ms. A. gradually became paranoid and began to "do weird things," which mainly involved her "wanting him totally to herself"; she allowed no one to come to their house, including Mr. A.'s children. She began to act suspicious and do things that "did not make any sense," such as turning on a burglar alarm, refusing to let Mr. A. to pick up his son from a hospital, threatening to jump out of a moving car if he took the son to their home. Mr. A. could not continue with his marriage; he decided to divorce Mrs. A., but she could not accept it. Mr. A. offered her a ticket to go back to her mother in China; she went and came back several months later. Mr. A. then arranged an apartment for her, but she moved out and came to his house. He took her to Salvation Army; she continued to come back to him. Although Mr. A. had completed their divorce proceedings, she kept telling him that she was his wife and she would come back to their house. She firmly believed that she was still married to him, and she broke into his house several times, cooked for him, and hid herself in the attic for periods of time. Mr. A. finally filed criminal charges against her after he failed to stop her from breaking in to his house. She was then arrested several times and spent 2 years in a local county jail. She sent numerous letters that all started with "my dearest husband" and ended with "your wife" to Mr. A., despite their final divorce, and promised that she would see him soon and spend the rest of her life with him.

Ms. A. was evaluated by a psychiatrist for competency to stand trial for multiple charges for entering her ex-husband's house without his permission. The psychiatrist concluded that she was suffering from a delusional disorder and not competent to stand trial. She was then admitted to a psychiatric hospital for treatment of her delusional disorder. During the hospitalization, she continued with the delusion that she remained married to Mr. A. She became easily agitated and frankly paranoid when this delusion was challenged, that she was no longer married. She refused court-ordered psychiatric medications in the hospital. She was transferred to a crisis resolution unit with a plan to secure a replacement passport for her to return to China. While in the program, she continued to vacillate between wishing to return to China or wishing to return, although illegally, to the home of her ex-husband. Ms. A. continued to refuse the medications and left the program without notifying staff. She later attempted to leave the program again. She was finally court committed to a state hospital for treatment.

Discussion of the Case of Ms. A.
Freddy A. Paniagua

General Discussion

Ms. A's nonbizarre delusions suggest a Delusional Disorder, Unspecified Type (APA, 1994, p. 298). Ms. A.'s relational problems with her husband would be noted in Axis IV with the V-Code V61.1: Partner Relational Problem (APA, 1994, p. 681), but these problems do not appear related to the present mental disorder. During the assessment of this case, clinicians should explore cultural variables that may explain Ms. A.'s continued efforts to keep her marriage intact in the presence of evidence that she was no longer married to Mr. A. In the Chinese culture (especially prior to the cultural revolution in 1966), marriage is traditionally a commitment for a lifetime, particularly for women. Among many Chinese families, it is expected that a Chinese woman would marry to serve her husband and to have children, and divorce is regarded by this society as a shameful failure for women. The client grew up in that culture (Ms. A. was already 18 years old at the beginning of the cultural revolution in 1966), and in her delusional state, remaining in her marriage was a logical thing to do.

Therefore, Ms. A.'s delusions could be partially explained in terms of her beliefs regarding marriage as a commitment for the life of husband and wife and the role she expected in this relationship. Many of her behaviors suggest her strong belief in the cultural value of marriage among traditional Chinese families, including her denial of the fact that her husband divorced her and her involvement in behaviors expected among married people (e.g., returning to Mr. A.'s house to cook for him). Ms. A.'s false belief regarding her "marriage" and the fact that she acted on these false beliefs with the display of nonbizarre behaviors, suggesting a delusional disorder, should also be considered carefully. This explains the need to hospitalize Ms. A. for the assessment and treatment of her nonbizarre delusions. To promote Ms. A.'s participation in treatment (she refused psychiatric interventions several times), an emphasis on her cultural background and the circumstances surrounding this cross-racial marriage should be considered.

Cultural Formulation

A significant feature of this case is that the client's cultural identity was different from her husband's. Ms. A. was Chinese, and she married an Anglo American man who could not understand Ms. A.'s strong feeling against divorce in her own culture. What would be the outcome of this case if Ms. A.'s ex-husband was educated regarding the strong cultural value Chinese families placed on marriage as something that should "last forever" in Ms. A.'s understanding of this value? For one thing, Mr. A. would probably not seek criminal charges against his ex-wife and instead assist with the psychiatric assessment and treatment of the case (in view of the fact that Ms. A.'s behaviors appeared to indicate symptoms for a Delusional Disorder). It should be noted that the therapist was Chinese and culturally competent to assist Ms. A. and Mr. A. with an understanding of cultural variables affecting their relationship. Ms. A. however, left the treatment program without permission from the staff, which prevented the therapist from exploring these cultural variables with Ms. A. and her ex-husband in the treatment plan. In a similar case, these variables should be discussed as soon as the client begins receiving treatment, to prevent termination of the case without a discussion of such variables with the client and significant others.

The Case of Rose
Larke Nahme Huang, PhD, and Yu-Wen Ying, PhD

Rose was an eighteen-year-old adolescent who had immigrated from China with her parents as a young child. She was brought to an inpatient mental health crisis unit by her mother and seventeen-year-old brother, with the assistance of a mental health outreach worker. At intake she was hostile and belligerent and needed to be restrained. She was disheveled and unkempt, was disoriented, and had delusions of meeting Chairman Mao in Chinatown. She was angry at her parents for "incarcerating" her, and she claimed that she had important appointments to keep.

Rose's mother spoke only Toishanese, so a history was obtained using the brother as translator. The mother noted a gradual deterioration in Rose's behavior following completion of high school about one and a half years earlier. At that time she had become sullen and withdrawn, had lost all her friendships, and had experienced difficulty maintaining a job in the family's small restaurant. She had begun using makeup in a garish fashion, staying out late at night, and verbally abusing her mother. The precipitating incident for admission to the crisis unit was increasingly bizarre behavior in the home followed by a physical assault on her mother.

During the first six months of Rose's deterioration, the mother had sought help from an acupuncturist, relatives, the family doctor, and a minister. When nothing seemed to relieve the problem, the family, very ashamed and desperate, began to lock Rose in her room. It was during this eight-month period that she would escape at night and wander the streets. Her brother would find her, usually quite delusional, and bring her home. Rose's mother was tearful as she provided this history; the brother seemed nonexpressive but tense. After completion of the intake procedure and medical exam, it was discovered that Rose was six to seven months pregnant. The mother and brother said they were totally unaware of this.

Discussion of the Case of Rose
Freddy A. Paniagua

General Discussion

Rose's symptoms suggest Delusional Disorder, Unspecified Type (APA, 1994, p. 298). Her symptoms, however, most likely suggest Grandiose Type (APA, 1994, p. 297) and Persecutory Type delusions (APA, 1994, p. 298). She reported meeting a prominent person, such as Chairman Mao, in Chinatown and having an important appointment to keep, which suggests Grandiose Type delusion; believing that her parents were incarcerating her, thus obstructing her in the pursuit of her delusional goals, points to a Persecutory Type delusion. The onset of symptoms were associated with unknown events Rose experienced "following completion of high school about one and a half years earlier" (Huang & Ying, 1998, p. 54), but these events did not appear to be culturally related.

This case, however, illustrates several cultural variations of importance in the cultural formulation applied to the treatment of Rose.

Cultural Formulation

Rose's parents waited for a long time before seeking help from mental health professionals. Initially, her parents kept Rose at home without any form of intervention, which increased the severity of Rose's symptoms over time. Then, Rose's parents decided to seek help from a healer (the acupuncturist) and members of the extended family (relatives and a minister). These efforts, however, were not effective. Her parents then decided to seek the assistance of mental health professionals. Rose's parents' decision to seek professional help very late after the onset of her symptoms is a function of a critical element of the cultural identity of Rose's parents (and many traditional Asians): the "[belief] that mental illness can bring shame and humiliation to the entire family" (Paniagua, 1998, p. 63; see also Chapter 1) when mental disorders are reported to the general public (Fujii et al., 1993; Gaw, 1993b; Huang & Ying, 1998, p. 55). The therapists, however, did not blame parents for making the "mistake" of waiting for a long time before seeking professional health but rather supported parents' decision in a culturally sensitive manner.

Another important element in the cultural formulation of this case is the cultural elements of the relationship between the client and the clinician. One critical "mismatching" element was language. The solution was to seek the help of Rose's bother as a translator. As noted by Huang and Ying (1998) in their discussion of this case, when family members are used as translators, "there is always a potential conflict of interest" (p. 55). Although the role of Rose's brother did not lead to a conflict of interest in this case, it is important to avoid relatives in the translation process and to "use interpreters experienced in psychological issues, because of the difficulty in translating English expressions or emotional terms into Chinese" (Huang & Ying, 1998, p. 55). Additional guidelines in the use of translators across culturally diverse clients can be found in Paniagua (1998, pp. 12-13).

Dissociative Disorders

Dissociative Identity Disorder

This disorder is considered a culture-specific syndrome because it occurs "primarily in persons holding a modern set of cultural schemas" (Castillo, 1997, p. 275). The *DSM-IV* (APA, 1994) suggested that in the United States, this disorder might be an example of culture-specific syndromes because of the "recent relatively high rates of the disorder reported [in this country]" (p. 485).

Dissociative Fugue

The sudden and unexpected travel away from home and work, as well as the individual's inability to recall past events associated with this travel, is a condition commonly reported among people from the Arctic, Subarctic Eskimo, the Miskito Indians of Honduras and Nicaragua, and the Navajo Indians (APA, 1994, p. 842; Castillo, 1997). In Table 2.3 (Chapter 2), the culture-bound syndrome known as *pibloktoq* includes symptoms resembling this disorder. This syndrome is characterized by an episode involving an uncontrollable desire to leave one's home, tear off one's clothes, and submit oneself to the Arctic winter; excitement; convulsive seizures; and coma, which is observed primarily in Alaska, the Canadian Arctic, and Greenland (APA, 1994, p. 482; Berry, Poortinga, Segall, & Dasen, 1992).

Depersonalization Disorder and Dissociative Amnesia

In many religions and cultures, induced experiences of depersonalization have been reported. These experiences should not be confused with Depersonalization Disorder (APA, 1994, p. 488). In the case of Dissociative Amnesia, the *DSM-IV* (APA, 1994) did not provide a discussion of cultural variations.

The Case of Mrs. Lee
Richard J. Castillo, PhD

Mrs. Lee, a 35-year-old Taiwanese housewife and the mother of three children, was brought by her family to see a psychiatrist. She had been a successful spirit medium, practicing for two years since the delivery of her second child. However, one month before, following the delivery of her third child, she began to lose her self-control. She would speak in tongues and go into possession trances, even when she was not being consulted by a client. She became hyperaroused, talked all day, and was unable to sleep at night. Because of her overtalkativeness and excitement, and her inability to extract herself from her possession trance, her family decided to bring her to the hospital for treatment.

Mrs. Lee's history revealed that she was born to a very poor family. As a young girl she deeply regretted her family's poverty and fervently wished to someday become rich and successful. When she grew up she entered into an arranged marriage, but was disappointed with her husband, who was unsuccessful and unambitious. Shortly after the birth of her first baby she had a mental breakdown. She became excited and talked a great deal, saying that she was going to start an international business, and singing songs all day. Her mental condition returned to normal within a couple of weeks. However, two years later, shortly after the birth of her second child, she experienced a second mental breakdown. This time she experienced drowsiness, feelings of personal strangeness, and auditory hallucinations in the form of a god's voice speaking to her. Against her own will she began to speak with a masculine voice. At this point, she realized that she was possessed by the "thief-god" she had worshipped since she was a little girl. According to local belief, there once was a thief who stole from the rich and gave to the poor. After his death, this thief was worshipped as a god by the local people. It was this thief-god who possessed her.

As a result of her experience, she realized that the thief-god wanted her to become a spirit medium, allowing him to serve the poor people through her.

Without further training she began to practice as a spirit medium at home. Soon she was known in her neighborhood as a spirit medium who could help poor people become rich. During her consultations, she would go into trances in which she became "possessed," speaking and behaving as the thief-god. In her practice she often saw five to ten clients in an evening, which did not interfere with her daytime duties as a housewife and mother. She practiced in this way for almost two years, until the birth of her third child.

Discussion of the Case of Mrs. Lee
Freddy A. Paniagua

General Discussion

At a first glance at symptoms, this case would be considered an example of Schizotypical Personality Disorder (APA, 1994, pp. 641-645). In general, two critical diagnostic features for this disorder include (a) a "pervasive pattern of social and interpersonal deficits" and (b) "cognitive or perceptual distortions and eccentricities of behavior" (APA, 1994, p. 641). The first feature is not evident in this case. Mrs. Lee's cognitive and perceptual distortions are exemplified by her spiritual medium practices, including speaking in tongues and feeling that a thief-god possessed her. As noted in the *DSM-IV*, these "cognitive and perceptual distortions must be evaluated in the context of the individual's cultural milieu" (APA, 1994, p. 643). Voodoo, speaking in tongues, and magical beliefs are culturally accepted practices in many cultures, and these practices "can appear to be schizotypical to the uninformed outsider" (APA, 1994, p. 643).

When these practices are not accepted by the individual's culture either because they do not conform with what is expected in a given culture or lead to significant functional impairment and distress, the possibility of a mental disorder should be considered. This was precisely the strategy the author of this case followed with the exception that the author concluded (rightly) that Mrs. Lee was experiencing a Dissociative Disorder and *not* a Schizotypical Personality Disorder.

In general, Mrs. Lee's symptoms point to two dissociative disorders in the *DSM-IV:* Dissociative Identity Disorder (formerly termed "Multiple Personality Disorder") and Depersonalization Disorder (APA, 1994, pp. 484-487 and pp. 488-490, respectively). In the first case, an identified personality took control of Mrs. Lee's overall behaviors but only during her state of possession trances during which she behaved as the thief-god. Under this circumstance, *DSM-IV* recommends the diagnosis of Dissociative Disorder Not Otherwise Specified instead of a diagnosis of Dissociative Identity Disorder because individuals "with trance and possession trance symptoms typically describe external spirits or entities that have entered their bodies and take control" (APA, 1994, p. 487). Until the birth of her third child, Mrs. Lee's spirit medium practices were examples of "voluntarily induced experiences of depersonalization" (APA, 1994, p. 488), which were culturally accepted in her culture.

Following the delivery of her third child, however, "she began to lose her self-control . . . [and went] into possession trances, even when she was not being consulted by a client" (Castillo, 1997, p. 101). These possession trances did not appear voluntarily induced and were outside the range of culturally accepted spirit medium practices in the minds of family members who brought Mrs. Lee to the clinic for a psychiatric evaluation of her symptoms. Under these circumstances, the *DSM-IV* recommends the diagnosis of Depersonalization Disorder (APA, 1994, pp. 488-490), which is the most likely diagnosis in the present case. Mrs. Lee not only showed symptoms suggesting that she was involuntarily detached from herself, with lack of control of her own actions (including speaking in tongues), and aware of significant changes in her previous spirit medium practices (inferred from the fact that she apparently agreed to come to the clinic for a psychiatric evaluation), but her symptoms were also "sufficiently severe to cause marked distress [and] impairment in functioning" (APA, 1994, p. 488).

It should be noted that *DSM-IV* proposed (not yet accepted) an alternative psychiatric diagnosis to cover those cases resembling Mrs. Lee's: *Dissociative Trance Disorder* (APA, 1994, pp. 726-729). Clinicians cannot use this diagnosis because it was included in Appendix B as an example of "criteria sets and axes provided for further study" (APA, 1994, p. 703). The main proposed feature of this alternative diagnosis "is an involuntary state of trance that is not accepted by the person's culture as a normal part of a collective culture or religious practice and that causes clinically significant distress or functional impairment" (APA, 1994, p. 727). In addition, the *DSM-IV* recommends that the proposed Dissociative Trance Disorder "should not be considered in individuals who enter trance or possession states voluntarily and without distress in the context of cultural and religious practices that are broadly accepted by the person's cultural group" (APA, 1994, p. 727).

In future editions of the *DSM,* the inclusion of a Dissociative Trance Disorder in the Multiaxial Classification (i.e., *DSM-V*) would constitute a significant contribution in cross-cultural assessment and diagnostic practices for three reasons. First, it would prevent clinicians from misdiagnosing individuals experiencing such trance or possession trances in those cases when symptoms are just what is expected in "a collective cultural or religious practice" (APA, 1994, p. 727). Second, this proposed diagnosis would prevent underdiagnosis of a mental disorder (i.e., failure to diagnose a true case of mental disorder) simply because the client reports symptoms resembling culturally accepted behaviors. Regarding this specific scenario, the *DSM-IV* proposed that this alternative diagnosis should be seriously considered in those cases when "some individuals undergoing culturally normative trance or possession trance states may [also] develop symptoms that cause distress or impairment" (APA, 1994, p. 727). Last, this proposed diagnosis would assist clinicians in differentiating many culture-bound syndromes (see APA, 1994, pp. 844-849, and Table 2.3 in this text) from symptoms pointing to a clear case of Dissociative Trance Disorder (Mrs. Lee's case could be a candidate for this disorder).

In future studies researching this proposed diagnosis, the *DSM* task forces should particularly consider (a) results from studies clearly *categorizing* the criteria and *differential diagnostic* features of the proposed diagnosis against other, established (approved) disorders in the *DSM* having closely resembling symptoms (e.g. Depersonalization Disorder) and (b) the possibility of excluding the section dealing with *dissociative trance disorder* (see APA, 1994, p. 490, example number four) from the Dissociative Disorder Not Otherwise Specified (NOS) category. That is, if the proposed Dissociative Trance Disorder is accepted for inclusion in the Multiaxial Classification of mental disorders, materials in the current Dissociative Disorder NOS would constitute the main features for a diagnosis of Dissociative Trance Disorder. The inclusion of this proposed dissociative disorder will increase the list of such disorders to five (amnesia, fugue, identity, depersonalization, and (the added) trance dissociative disorders). In the case of the proposed disorder, clinical guidelines to deal with the insufficient number of criteria to make this proposed diagnosis would need to be developed to differentiate it from a Dissociative Disorder NOS (see APA, 1994, p. 490, examples 1-3).

Cultural Formulation

A critical element of this formulation to consider in treatment planning is the fact that Mrs. Lee's family recognized that this client engaged in spirit medium practices outside the range of culturally accepted practice in the Taiwan culture. For example, Mrs. Lee spoke in tongues and experienced possession trances even when she was alone and without being consulted by a client. Therefore, although Mrs. Lee's family shared the same cultural reference group, they did not explain her symptoms in cultural terms and instead decided to seek help from a mental health professional. During the assessment and treatment of this case (and similar cases), the therapist should provide evidence to the family that he or she respects their belief system in spirit medium practice and at the same time socially reinforce (Skinner, 1953) the family for seeking professional mental health in those cases when they feel that their loved one's spirit medium practice is outside cultural norms in the community.

Other important factors to consider in the treatment plan are the role of Mrs. Lee's extended family in the assessment and treatment of this case, as well as what exactly her extended family expects after the completion of treatment. For example, one would not expect the family to agree with a therapist's recommendation to *withdraw social attention* in the presence of Mrs. Lee's spirit medium practices, with the explicit goal of decreasing the probability that Mrs. Lee would engage in such practice in the future. (In the paradigm of behavioral psychology, *social attention* is considered a powerful reinforcing event that could establish new behavior and maintain it over time. If this social reinforcer [attention] is not available, the resulting process is termed *extinction,* in which the probability of occurrence of that behavior could be decreased in the future; see Skinner, 1953, pp. 78-79.) The reason for this family's probable rejection of this recommendation is that they observed Mrs. Lee functioning as a spirit medium to help poor people in the community in the past. Under this circumstance, Mrs. Lee's family could rather expect a treatment with emphasis on returning Mrs. Lee's spirit medium practices to a context considered normal by members of the community.

Mood Disorders

Major Depressive Disorder

In some cultures, symptoms of depression are not generally recognized as a case for a mental disorder. Furthermore, symptoms of depression might be expressed in somatic terms rather than sadness or guilt (Castillo, 1997). In Mediterranean and Latin American cultures, depressive experiences might be manifested in terms of complaints of "nerves" and headaches; Asians may show similar experiences in terms of weakness, tiredness, or "imbalance," whereas among people from the Middle East and American Indian tribes, these experiences might be shown in terms of difficulties with the "heart" or being "heartbroken," respectively (see APA, 1994, pp. 324-325). The severity of the depression might also be evaluated differently across cultures (e.g., sadness may lead to more irritability than concern in some cultures). Hallucinations and delusions, which are sometimes part of Major Depressive Disorder, should be differentiated from cultural hallucinations and delusions (e.g., fear of being hexed, feeling of being visited by those who have died). In Chapter 2, Table 2.3, the culture-bound syndromes "brain fag" and "susto" may resemble symptoms suggesting Major Depressive Disorder (APA, 1994, p. 486, p. 849). Symptoms for depression could also be triggered by a racial identity crisis experienced by individuals who feel rejected by a different racial group.

Bipolar I and II, Dysthymic, and Cyclothymic Disorders

Differential incidence of Bipolar Disorder I associated with race or ethnicity has not been reported (APA, 1994, p. 352). Some evidence exists suggesting that clinicians may overdiagnose Schizophrenia rather than Bipolar Disorder I in some ethnic groups (APA, 1994, pp. 352-353). The *DSM-IV* (APA, 1994) did not provide a description of cultural variants for Bipolar II, Dysthymic, and Cyclothymic Disorders. A major characteristic of Bipolar II and Cyclothymic Disorders is the presence of hypomanic symptoms. As noted by Castillo (1997), these symptoms are accepted in some cultural contexts. For example, members of the Hindu culture generally engage in "meditative trances to achieve a permanent hypomanic state [during their religious practices]" (Castillo, 1997, p. 219). In the case of Dysthymic Disorder, being depressed most of the time over at least 2 years could be the result of specific cultural variables, such as racial discrimination and severe poverty (Castillo, 1997; Weiss, 1995). Difficulty in adjustment to the acculturation level of a partner in a marital relationship could also trigger a mood disorder (particularly Major Depressive and Dysthymic Disorders).

The Case of Janet T.
Derald Wing Sue, PhD, and David Sue, PhD

Janet T. is a 21-year-old senior, majoring in sociology. She was born and raised in Portland, Oregon, where she had limited contact with members of her own race. Her father, a second generation Chinese American, is a 53-year-old doctor. Her mother, age 44, is a housewife. Janet is the second oldest of three children and has an older brother (currently in medical school) and a younger brother, age 17.

Janet came for therapy suffering from a severe depressive reaction manifested by feelings of worthlessness, by suicidal ideation, and by inability to concentrate. She was unable to recognize the cause of her depression throughout the initial interviews. However, much light was shed on problems when the therapist noticed an inordinate amount of hostility directed toward him.

When inquiries were made about the hostility, it became apparent that Janet greatly resented being seen by a Chinese psychologist. Janet suspected that she had been assigned to a Chinese therapist because of her own race. When confronted with this fact, Janet openly expressed scorn for "anything which reminds me of Chinese." Apparently, she felt very hostile towards Chinese customs and especially the Chinese male, whom she described as introverted, passive, and sexually unattractive. Further exploration revealed a long-standing history of attempts to deny her Chinese ancestry by associating only with Caucasians. When in high school, Janet would frequently bring home White boyfriends, which greatly upset her parents. It was as though she blamed her parents for being a Chinese, and used this method to hurt them.

During her college career Janet became involved in two love affairs with Caucasians, both ending unsatisfactorily and abruptly. The last breakup occurred four months ago when the boy's parents threatened to cut off financial support for their son unless he ended the relationship. Apparently, objections arose because of Janet's race.

Although not completely consciously, Janet was having increasing difficulty with denying her racial heritage. The breakup of her last torrid love affair made her realize that she was Chinese and not fully accepted by all segments of society. At first she vehemently and bitterly denounced the Chinese for her present dilemma. Later, much of her hostility was turned inward against herself. Feeling alienated from her own subculture and not fully accepted by American Society, she experienced an identity crisis. This resulted in feelings of worthlessness and depression. It was at this point that Janet came for therapy.

SOURCE: "Janet T." From *Counseling the Culturally Different: Theory and Practice, Second Edition* (pp. 202-203) by Derald W. Sue and David Sue. Copyright © 1990 by John Wiley & Sons, reprinted by permission of the publisher.

Discussion of the Case of Janet T.
Freddy A. Paniagua

General Discussion

This case illustrates those situations in which the client has a mental disorder, and a given V-Code with cultural implications is clearly related with the disorder. Janet's symptoms appear to suggest a mood disorder. Additional information would be needed to determine which specific mood disorder Janet was experiencing. Two candidates are Major Depressive Disorder, if Janet's symptoms were present "most of the day, nearly every day, for a period of at least two weeks" (APA, 1994, p. 343), or Dysthymic Disorder, if her symptoms were "present for more days than not over a period of at least 2 years" (APA, 1994, p. 343). It is clear, however, that Janet experienced an identity problem (V-Code 313.82, APA, 1994, p. 685) regarding her efforts to associate with individuals from a different race, her parents' strong disagreement with this association, and her feeling of being rejected by members of the race she wanted to associate with (the Caucasian father who rejected her relationship with the last boyfriend because she was Chinese). Therefore, the treatment plan for this case would have to include a discussion of individual and cultural racism and their impact on the present case (see Chapter 1 and "The Case of Clarence" in Chapter 5). In addition, her parents' disapproval of Caucasian boyfriends points to a Parent-Child Relational problem (V-Code 61.20, APA, 1994, p. 681), which is probably related to different levels of acculturation among family members, including Janet's brothers.

Cultural Formulation

In this case, client-therapist racial similarity is an important variable to consider in the treatment plan. Janet is an Asian American, Chinese descended, and apparently she did not like the fact that her case was assigned to a Chinese psychologist. Her negative feeling toward Chinese people could have prevented her from receiving treatment from a Chinese psychologist who may have a good understanding of racism against people by other cultural groups and clinical training in the management of Janet's difficulties with her racial identity problem. Under this circumstance, however, it may be necessary to initially offer to Janet the opportunity to enter treatment for her mental disorder with a therapist from a different race or ethnic background but with an understanding of cultural values in the Asian community, a therapist culturally competent in terms of parameters suggested in the universalistic approach when assessing and treating clients from the racial groups discussed in this text (see Paniagua, 1998, pp. 7-8; Tharp, 1991).

Other significant elements of the cultural formulation framework relevant to this case are Janet's cultural explanation of symptoms and her difficulty in accepting the fact that her cultural reference group is still Chinese. She may have a problem understanding that her emotional responses are the product of her unrealistic manner of trying to fit into American society; this should be part of Janet's treatment during individual psychotherapy. Last, Janet's rejection of her parents is a critical issue to consider because this rejection is contrary to the role the extended family is expected to play in many Asian families. This issue should be discussed during family therapy sessions with Janet and her parents, with emphasis on the importance of the extended family among Chinese families in terms of providing social, instrumental, and emotional support to members of the family affected by the kind of problem confronted by Janet.

Individual psychotherapy with Janet would be the first choice to deal with her understanding of personal prejudice, individual and cultural racism in American society, and ways for her to develop both behavioral and cognitive skills to deal with these forms of racism, as well as the development of skills to minimize her emotional responses toward this cultural variable. The second treatment choice should be family therapy, in which acculturation issues would be explored. The

Brief Acculturation Scale (Paniagua, 1998) and more extensive scales in Table 3.1 should be considered to assess these levels of acculturation.

The Case of Dolores
Rita Sommers-Flanagan, PhD

Dolores was a 43-year-old American Indian woman who came to therapy with clear symptoms of depression. She reported sadness, inability to concentrate, changes in sleep patterns, loss of pleasure in activities that used to bring her joy, and an overall feeling of dread regarding the future. She adamantly refused to consider taking any form of psychotropic medication but was receiving adequate medical care through the tribal health service. She reported that Gabe, her husband of 23 years, had a serious gambling addiction for which he refused treatment. He could control himself for periods of years but would then begin again, causing the couple to lose much of their savings before he stopped. Dolores and her husband had one grown son. In addition, 5 years earlier, they had adopted a little girl who was a distant relative. The child was 3 at the time of the adoption. The adoption was a traditional arrangement within the tribe, but neither the child's biological mother nor Dolores and Gabe had pursued formal legal adoption.

Dolores reported that she had come to counseling because Gabe was gambling again, sneaking out, doing things, lying to her, and causing terrible financial hardship. The year before, Dolores had begun work on her master's degree in a social science. She felt she was going to have to give it up and go back to work full time. Dolores had also begun having serious fears that somehow, her adopted daughter would be taken away from her. Dolores stated that she had experienced depression on and off during her marriage and that she had been in counseling once before.

The therapy direction took three prongs. We began working on basic cognitive-behavioral strategies, changing the way Dolores thought about Gabe and the gambling. Dolores began to realize she could set limits, establish financial independence, and distance herself from some of the consequences of Gabe's addiction. Dolores also realized there were things she could do to get a realistic idea of the threats to her adoptive arrangement, and after consultation with a tribal attorney, proceeded with legal adoption of her daughter. Seeking dominant-culture adoption caused Dolores considerable discomfort because she felt she should be able to honor the tribal customs and not be afraid. The second prong of therapy involved encouraging Dolores to explore her tribal identity by connecting to other high-achieving but very traditional American Indian people in the community. Dolores began to take part in tribal ceremonies that she had stayed away from for years because of shame associated with Gabe's behaviors. Her sense of what it meant to be Indian, by her own report, deep-ened significantly. The third prong of therapy involved addressing Dolores's overall health care. After exploring how to set it up in therapy, Dolores put herself on an exercise plan and began eating a more balanced diet.

Dolores came to therapy somewhat sporadically over the course of 18 months. For another 2 years, she made occasional appointments, which she called "her tune-ups." She still struggled with bouts of "the blues" but did not ever deteriorate to the point of diagnosable depression again. She did not finish her master's degree, but the additional course work had made her eligible for a well-paid job with the tribe, which she took and was still doing the last time I saw her.

Discussion of the Case of Dolores
Freddy A. Paniagua

General Discussion

Dolores's symptoms suggest Major Depressive Disorder, Recurrent (APA, 1994, pp. 320-326). Another possible diagnosis is Dysthymic Disorder (APA, 1994, pp. 345-349). These symptoms were related to two identified stressors: her husband's gambling addiction and her fears that her adoptive daughter could be taken away from her. A negative consequence of pathological gambling is the disruption of the family and, as noted in Chapter 1, many American Indians would expect members of this group to emphasize familism rather than the self. Dolores's feeling of inadequacy in terms of preventing her husband to move away from this tradition probably led to Dolores's decision to seek professional mental health help. Dolores, however, experienced these symptoms for several years before she decided to seek mental health services. The author of this case pointed out that a strong protective ethic within many American Indian tribal members probably prevented Dolores from seeking professional assistance when she initially noticed that her husband's gambling activities were nega-tively affecting her sense of familism. Among American Indians, it is consid-ered disloyal to speak negatively of another family member's troubles. Fears of contributing to old stereotypes about "Indian inadequacy" when dealing with their problems could also prevent members of this group from seeking profes-sional help. This fear and the stress it causes probably led to the exacerbation of symptoms in the case of Dolores.

Dolores's fear involving the potential removal of her stepdaughter from the family should also be considered in cultural terms, to prevent misdiagnosing Dolores with a mood disorder. To minimize Dolores's fear regarding this issue, the first thing a clinician should do is to be familiar with the Indian Child Welfare Act (O'Brien, 1989, see also Paniagua, 1998, pp. 90-91), which, among other important points, provides that American Indian families must have preference in making decisions regarding foster care or adoption of American Indian children. Dolores adopted her stepdaughter following a traditional arrangement within the tribe, which probably included criteria recommended in that act. Making Dolores aware of this act could greatly reduce her symptoms associated with the fear that her daughter could be removed from her family. The clinician, however, should also consider historical variables associated with Dolores's fear in this particular context. Because of governmental interventions, American Indians have experienced loss of control of the lives and destinies of their children (Paniagua, 1998; Walker & LaDue, 1986). Dolores's fears regarding losing custody of her adoptive daughter might be seen as irrational or overblown, but historic precedent exists for this happening in American Indian families (O'Brien, 1989). This historical fact should be discussed with Dolores, with emphasis on current guidelines established in that Act and how they could affect Dolores at the present moment.

Cultural Formulation

Dolores's cultural identity with her reference group changed over time, probably because of her feeling of shame associated with her husband's pathological gambling. The treatment plan helped Dolores explore her tribal identity, including participation in tribal ceremonies and a self-assessment of what it meant to her to be Indian. In terms of the client's cultural explanation of symptoms, the experience of mood disorders (e.g., Major Depressive and Dysthymic Disorders in this case) are considered real disorders in the American Indian communities. With Dolores, however, it appears that these symptoms resulted from her feelings of shame involving making public her husband's condition to other tribal members, her efforts to maintain her cultural identity around many cultural values in her tribe (e.g., embracing familism rather than the self), and her fear that the dominant-culture adoption practice (which emphasizes formal legal adoption) would deny her the right of adoption she received through the traditional arrangement within the tribe. These potential cultural variables were appropriately addressed in the treatment plan, including a consultation with a tribal attorney, who apparently convinced Dolores that she could proceed with the legal adoption of her daughter and still honor the tribal customs in the matter of adoption of Indian children by traditional arrangement in the tribe. This intervention significantly decreased the negative impact of these cultural variables on Dolores's symptoms, and her level of functioning was reestablished over time (e.g., she took a well-paid job in her tribe).

Last, in terms of cultural elements of the relationship between Dolores and her therapist, Dolores clearly benefited from having a clinician culturally sensitive to her needs. For example, cognitive-behavioral interventions are recommended with American Indian clients (see Chapter 4); decisions to seek consultation from a tribal attorney met Dolores's expectancy in terms of being assisted in legal matters from someone from her own culture. Encouraging Dolores to explore her tribal identity and engage in tribal ceremonies enhanced her self-esteem and sense of being in control of her life to the point of regaining her level of functioning at the end of therapy. Dolores needed help understanding that she could choose to think differently about her life and about her husband without necessarily putting him down. In addition, rather than stereotyping any of her fears or experiences, she was encouraged to delve deeper into traditional cultural practices, and at the same time, address her fears of the dominant culture intervening in her parenting arrangement.

The Case of Carol
Angela S. Lew, PhD

Carol is a 21-year-old Chinese American female. Based on the hierarchical structure in Asian families, which prescribes respectful behavior toward elders, the therapist decided to interview the mother first during the intake session. The mother reported that the problem started when Carol moved away from home to attend college. Carol returned home from college after failing all her classes. The mother described Carol as exhibiting inappropriate giggling and laughing, frequent crying bouts, withdrawn behavior, intrusive thoughts, and talking to herself. Carol presented an increased appetite, depressed mood, difficulty falling asleep, anhedonia, impaired concentration, suicidal ideation, and difficulty in establishing social relationships with new friends. Carol reported that her depression started during adolescence and intensified during periods of interpersonal conflict, particularly between her parents or with friends. Her past psychiatric history revealed that she had been diagnosed with Major Depressive Disorder with psychotic features, in partial remission, and at the time of this intake, she was given a similar diagnosis and antipsychotic medication by a psychiatrist. No other diagnosis and treatment history was reported.

During the first few months of weekly, individual psychotherapy, Carol appeared anxious, guarded, and spoke only in responses to inquiries from the therapist, and then only minimally. Carol alternated between long periods of silence and a recitation of her daily activities, devoid of any affect. A shift occurred in the course of treatment when the meaning of her silence was explored. Carol disclosed that she was complying with her mother's admonishments regarding the dangers involved in revealing her internal world to anyone. She expressed her anger and frustration concerning mother's controlling behavior toward her. Carol reported that mother would control how much money she would give her, what she could wear, when she could go out, and who she could affiliate with. As a result, Carol felt helpless, depressed, angry, and resentful. However, Carol could not outwardly verbalize these feelings to her mother. The mother seemed anxious about Carol's display of emotions, especially her anger toward her, and agreed to increases in the medication dosage to suppress her daughter's emotional problems.

During individual psychotherapy sessions, it was evident that Carol was caught in a dilemma. She found it difficult to express her feelings and thoughts openly to her mother but at the same time, had problems in separating herself from her mother within the context of cultural values determining Asian children's dependence on their parents. The core of individual psychotherapy was in understanding Carol's dilemma and its impact on her depression, feelings of emptiness, and anger within the context of her family system, including cultural factors that may affect family functioning. Carol was encouraged to talk about her understanding of her mother's behavior on a cultural level. Carol's cultural identity with the Asian community allowed her to understand that in this culture, the elders are regarded with reverence, respect, and authority powers and that her mother was probably acting in accord with this cultural belief system and probably using her expected authoritative role in the Asian culture to ensure Carol's well-being. For example, during the course of treatment the mother reported that Carol was unable to function without her and that it was dangerous for Carol to move away from her and to establish her own separateness. Carol, however, perceived this message as something that could prevent her from achieving her own identity and reported that her depression was the result of her difficulty in dealing with that cultural belief system and how her mother was using it to justify her controlling behaviors toward Carol.

During the course of treatment, it was apparent that Carol also experienced significant stressors resulting from multiple losses in the family due to illnesses. Carol and her mother did not want to talk about these losses, and Carol appeared to internalize these losses in her dreams, with adversity content around her family. For example, Carol reported seeing a "ghost" twice when she was falling asleep at the time a family member was hospitalized and again when this individual died. She also reported significant symptoms for depression at that time. The therapist knew that the theme of ghosts is common in Chinese folklore to explain tragic or unhappy events, but it is not common for a Chinese to actually report *seeing* ghosts. Carol's belief system in this context, however, was not challenged by the therapist, and instead, emphasis was placed on the possibility that Carol's reports involving seeing ghosts were the result of such stressful events in her life.

During the course of treatment, Carol's depression slowly lifted, her range of affect was broader, and her anger at her mother appeared more apparent. Carol was able to identify feelings, thoughts, and experiences preventing her from openly expressing her concern to her mother without sensing a lack of respect to the expected authority of the mother in the Asian culture. She began to articulate these feelings, thoughts, and experiences in a cultural context and was less overwhelmed or guilty for doing so. Carol disentangled and distinguished her own feelings and needs from those of her mother, began to explore career goals, and enrolled in a college of her interest with a sense that she was making independent decisions regarding her future without violating her mother's culturally expected norms as a member of the Asian community.

Discussion of the Case of Carol
Freddy A. Paniagua

General Discussion

Carol's symptoms suggest Major Depressive Disorder (APA, 1994, p. 327), but psychotic features are not apparent in the present vignette. Leaving the mother to go to college and her negative experience in college should be considered, to rule out Adjustment Disorder with Depressed Mood (APA, 1993, p. 623). Further exploration of Carol's experiences in college would be needed to determine the potential impact of an acculturation problem explaining her potential difficulty in getting adjusted to college. In this case, the V-Code "Acculturation Problem" (APA, 1994, p. 685) should be included in Axis IV (*DSM-IV*, APA, 1994). Two additional V-Codes to consider prior to diagnosing Carol with a mental disorder are "Parent-Child Relational Problem" (APA, 1994, p. 681) and "Identity Problem" (APA, 1994, p. 685). In the first case, it is evident that Carol appeared less traditional than her mother in terms of accepting a submissive role toward her mother as expected in the Asian community (D. W. Sue & D. Sue, 1990, 1999). In the second case, Carol struggled to keep her Chinese identity, whereas at the same time, she explored alternatives to deal with her mother's controlling behavior, which is perceived as culturally accepted among many members of the Chinese community (D. W. Sue & D. Sue, 1990). In this case, Carol's symptoms point to a mental disorder, and these problems (e.g., identity problems) appear "sufficiently severe to warrant independent clinical attention" (APA, 1994, p. 675), which is the approach the therapist employed in treating Carol's symptoms with individual psychotherapy (and apparently, family therapy) in combination with psychotropic medication.

Cultural Formulation

In the treatment plan, Carol's cultural identity with the Chinese community should be explored further, with emphasis on the fact that *tangential* separation from cultural values expected in this community does not necessarily imply that the individual is moving away from his or her cultural identity. Implicit in the description of this case is Carol's desire to become independent from her mother and at the same time remain loyal to her Asian values and heritage. This points to a difference in acculturation levels between Carol and her mother, leading to interpersonal conflicts. Carol's mother represented the Asian view that optimal health involves rigorous control of feelings and impulses, such that open expression of emotions is seen as a taboo and a reflection of maladjustment. Like many Asian Americans experiencing acculturation difficulties in the United States, Carol was faced with the struggle to mix two different cultures to form a bicultural identity (shared values and norms from both the dominant culture and her own). The individual psychotherapy process suggests that the therapist was able to show to Carol that she could achieve this level of bicultural identity in the absence of emotional difficulties.

In a cultural explanation of Carol's emotional difficulties (second element of the cultural formulation in the *DSM-IV*, APA, 1994, p. 843), the therapist realized that despite the impact of cultural variations on the development of symptoms Carol was indeed experiencing a mental disorder and treated it using Western treatment modalities (e.g., medication, psychotherapy). Another important element of the cultural formulation is the fact that the present therapist was extremely sensitive to critical cultural values and norms shared by members of the Chinese community. For example, Carol's mother was interviewed first. This approach was a way to prevent embarrassing the mother in front of her daughter as well as to protect the dignity of the mother. This approach is termed *saving face* in the assessment and treatment of Asian clients (D. W. Sue & D. Sue, 1990, 1999; see also Paniagua, 1998, pp. 71-72). In addition, during early treatment sessions, the therapist did not force Carol to openly confront her mother's controlling behavior because to do so would be the opposite of the culturally expected respectful behavior toward Chinese elders. The therapist, a clinical psychologist, not a psychiatrist, agreed with the medication management of Carol in combination with individual psychotherapy (and probably family therapy), because this therapist was aware that many Asian clients expect medication in the management of their psychological or psychiatric disorders (see Paniagua, 1998, pp. 69-70). This approach was not only therapeutically appropriate (that combination of treatments is often recommended in clinical practice), but it was also a culturally sensitive approach in this case.

The Case of Felicia Marquez
Virginia S. Burlingame, MSW, PhD

Felicia Marquez, age 76, is the oldest of five children of rich Cuban entrepreneurs. After attending the university, she married. Her husband, Arnoldo, was a physician. They had three children. Their life in Cuba was - affluent and happy until the Communist Revolution in 1959; they fled in 1962. Arnoldo Marquez set up practice in Miami, and they maintained an upper-class Cuban lifestyle, though their children became decubanized.

Felicia Marquez's siblings had stayed in Cuba to care for her ailing father and to save the family business. Guilty about leaving, she worked for a family reunion in 1972. By then, however, her father, the business, and the money were gone. Instead of a happy reunion, the next 25 years brought dissension and blaming. Often, the most heated arguments were political.

Mrs. Marquez felt that she had failed her family and tried, literally, to work herself out of her suffering. Priding herself on being a good daughter, wife, mother, grandmother, and housekeeper—but most of all a good Catholic—she tripled her efforts in each area. She and her siblings competed over being the mother's caregiver.

In confession, she told her priest that she believed she was paying for her sins. (Perhaps a santeria god was angry at her.) Her own well being was unimportant. Nobody appreciated her, and her own children paid more attention to their children than to her. The priest recognized that Mrs. Marquez was depressed. She admitted she was not sleeping and had lost 25 pounds in the past 3 months. But she said she was not suicidal—suicide "was a sin." The priest suggested prayers, a novena, and the Stations of the Cross. When these helped only partially, he advised her to consult her physician. She refused. She felt ashamed, and she wanted help from family or not at all.

SOURCE: From *Ethnogerocounseling: Counseling Ethnic Elders and Their Families,* by Virginia S. Burlingame. Copyright 1999 © by Springer Publishing Company, reprinted by permission of the publishers.

Discussion of the Case of Felicia Marquez
Freddy A. Paniagua

General Discussion

Mrs. Marquez's symptoms suggest a Mood Disorder NOS (APA, 1994, p. 375). She probably began experiencing these symptoms 25 years before her priest noted that she was depressed and advised her to consult a physician. This would suggest Dysthymic Disorder (APA, 1994, pp. 345-349), but the Mood Disorder NOS is the best diagnostic choice in this case. The V-Code 62.89, "Religious or Spiritual Problem," should be considered in Axis IV. Early symptoms were likely associated with Mrs. Marquez's sense of guilt resulting from her decision to immigrate to the United States and leaving many of her relatives behind in Cuba.

Cultural Formulation

In terms of the cultural identity of the client, critical issues to consider in the treatment plan include further exploration of Mrs. Marquez's sense of guilt about leaving Cuba and whether she perceives that this move from Cuba led to a denial of values and norms expected by members of her culture. For example, the fact that she perceived that she "failed her family and tried, literally, to work herself out of her suffering" (Burlingame, 1999, p. 98) would suggest her struggle to reestablish a sense of *familismo* (familism) and a recognition of social, emotional, or instrumental supports expected from members of the extended family among many Hispanics (Paniagua, 1998).

The treatment plan for this case should also include discussions around potential cultural explanations of Mrs. Marquez's symptoms. These discussions should be conducted without confronting Mrs. Marquez's overall belief system (e.g., her perceived violation of the familismo cultural value). The role of religion and the extended family "in providing emotional, instrumental, and informational support" (APA, 1994, p. 844) should be delineated in the cultural formulation of the plan dealing with "cultural factors related to psychosocial environment and levels of functioning" (APA, 1994, p. 844). For example, Mrs. Marquez's beliefs in "sins" and rituals (e.g., prayers, novena, and the Stations of the Cross) and her decision to seek help from her priest should be validated during individual psychotherapy, including giving her the opportunity to continue consulting with her priest during the psychotherapy process. Mrs. Marquez obviously considered the priest a member of her extended family (see Paniagua, 1998, pp. 14-16) who provided both emotional (e.g., listening to her problems and counseling her with the use of such rituals) and informational (e.g., advising her to consult her physician) supports.

Last, although the programming of family therapy is often recommended as the first therapeutic approach with Hispanic clients (Paniagua, 1998), in this particular case, it would be more appropriate to initially schedule individual psychotherapy and to explore the belief system of the husband and children to determine the timing for the schedule of family therapy sessions. The reason for this recommendation is that it appears that Mrs. Marquez's husband and her children were more acculturated to the American culture (e.g., her children were "decubanized") relative to Mrs. Marquez's level of acculturation. This difference in level of acculturation could create problems during the discussion of events leading to Mrs. Marquez's symptoms, with all family members present. The Brief Acculturation Scale (Paniagua, 1998) could be used to assess these levels of acculturation before the programming of family therapy.

The Case of Tony Mulos
Virginia S. Burlingame, MSW, PhD

Tony Mulos is age 76. At age 29, as a veteran, he qualified to immigrate to the United States from the northern Philippines. A high school graduate, he spoke both English and Ilocano. Mr. Mulos found work in the service industry, married, divorced, and then settled south of Market Street in San Francisco—alone, until he remarried in 1965. He and his second wife,

Dolores, were childless. She died of cancer when he was 70. He had lovingly nursed her through her illness, but the stress aggravated his hypertension and his tendency to isolate himself.

Neighbors expected Mr. Mulos to be depressed when his wife died; but when he did not improve after 2 years, they were concerned. He had become emaciated and lifeless-looking. One neighbor discussed her concerns with her own case manager, and Peter F. from the Philippine Outreach Program of the Department of Mental Health was called in.

Peter F. was sensitive to Mr. Mulos's pride and to his other ethnic customs. He did not speak in terms of mental illness but simply said that such a shy, quiet, and now sad man perhaps needed some medicine to give him more energy to do things. (The word "depression" was never used.) Mr. Mulos agreed, for the sake of increasing his energy.

Once Mr. Mulos was on an antidepressant medication, Peter F. called weekly, speaking in the Ilocano dialect. Mr. Mulos imagined that these were just friendly calls, but actually they were a form of therapy. He told the counselor about his homeland, the army, his hardships in the United States, and now his loneliness. The counselor supported him and suggested that he attend the Philippine Senior Center to play cards and bingo, and to dance. Mr. Mulos refused initially, but with continued prompting, he agreed to go once with the counselor.

Mr. Mulos enjoyed the center, where he soon met Rose A., who also spoke the Ilocano dialect. She was a pleasant widow with five daughters and sixteen grandchildren. They eventually married, and now Mr. Mulos is the patriarch of a large family, like the one he had always dreamed about (even though his wife indirectly runs the show).

SOURCE: From *Ethnogerocounseling: Counseling Ethnic Elders and Their Families,*" by Virginia S. Burlingame. Copyright © 1999 by Springer Publishing Company, reprinted by permission of the publishers.

Discussion of the Case of Tony Mulos
Freddy A. Paniagua

General Discussion

This case also suggests a Mood Disorder NOS (APA, 1994, p. 375). Early onset of Mr. Mulos's symptoms of depression could be traced to the time when he took care of his wife, which resulted in a stressful situation worsening his hypertension. At that time, two possible diagnoses would have been Major Depressive Disorder (APA, 1994, pp. 339-345) and Mood Disorder Due to a General Medical Condition (APA, 1994, pp. 366-370). The fact that Mr. Mulos's symptoms continued over a period of 2 years after the death of his wife would suggest Dysthymic Disorder (APA, pp. 345-349). Because these symptoms were still present 2 years after the death of his wife, the V-Code "Bereavement" (APA, 1994, pp. 684-685) would not be applied in this case. The V-Code "Phase of Life Problem" (APA, 1994, pp. 685-686), however, would be appropriately considered.

Cultural Formulation

Considerations of cultural variables during the diagnosis of Mr. Mulos do not appear to be a critical issue in this case. The case was selected, however, because it provides an excellent example of the role of nonbiological extended family members in helping the elderly in need of emotional and instrumental supports, as well as the importance of using culturally sensitive treatment approaches that might differ from those often recommended with younger clients. For example, his neighbors did not see a problem with Mr. Mulos's depression when his wife died (a case for the V-Code "Bereavement" if Mr. Mulos sought professional counseling at that time). One of the neighbors became concerned when Mr. Mulos did not improve 2 years after the death of his wife and decided to consult with her own case manager (who shared Mr. Mulos's cultural background and ethnicity). This neighbor did two things to quickly assist Mr. Mulos with the management of symptoms: She decided to provide instrumental support (i.e., seeking professional assistance for Mr. Mulos) and selected a mental health professional who shared Mr. Mulos's cultural and ethnic background.

The counselor, Peter F., was aware that elderly clients might be more reluctant to seek mental health services, relative to younger clients (McCarthy, Katz, & Foa, 1991), and decided to talk to Mr. Mulos without labeling symptoms in terms of a mental problem. Mr. Mulos was told that he probably needed medicine to help him to increase his energy level and be involved in more social activities. In addition, when the case manager contacted Mr. Mulos by phone to assess the effects of the antidepressant medication, he made sure that they would be perceived as friendly calls by Mr. Mulos when, in fact, they were therapeutic, scheduled phone calls. During these phone calls, Peter F. engaged Mr. Mulos in conversations involving cultural issues they shared (e.g., customs), but the case manager also introduced topics around stressful events, such as Mr. Mulos's difficulty in adjusting to his long-time immigration status in the United States and his current loneliness.

Peter F.'s culturally sensitive approach allowed him to introduce Mr. Mulos to the idea that he should be involved in social activities by attending the Philippine Senior Center to socially relate to other individuals of his age and, more important, a setting in which Mr. Mulos could meet people who could speak his native dialect (Ilocano). Meeting new friends from his own country and having the opportunity to speak Ilocano were two critical variables in the counselor's efforts to reinforce the cultural identity of Mr. Mulos. Last, the counselor spoke Mr. Mulos's native language (Ilocano), which greatly enhanced the goal of the treatment plan (engaging Mr. Mulos in social activities, which resulted in his last marriage with a women sharing his cultural and ethnic background). In the treatment plan for this case, the counselor's ability to speak Ilocano (plus his culturally sensitive approach in the overall management of the case) would be included as part of the "cultural elements of the relationship between the individual and the clinician" in the cultural formulation of the treatment plan (APA, 1994, p. 844).

The Case of Ms. Chinchin
Michael M. O'Boyle, MD, PhD, and Lee E. Emory, MD

Ms. Chinchin, a 30-year-old Japanese woman, described herself as the black sheep of the family because she did not do well in school. She also had a pregnancy before marrying a white American serviceman at age 20; this further alienated her from her family. The couple moved to the United States that year. He was a truck driver who had been married previously. He did not want any more children, as a son from a prior marriage was involved with drugs. When Ms. Chinchin became pregnant after 4 years of marriage, the husband requested that she get an abortion, which she did not do. They had another child 2 years later. Ms. Chinchin was described by neighbors as a devoted mother who spent a lot of time teaching her children both Japanese and English and reading to them. She worked as an accountant, doing well at that job, until she had her first documented psychiatric episode at age 28. In January of that year, she had pressured her husband to get a vasectomy, but he refused, and she underwent a hysterectomy. Ms. Chinchin's husband later related that the patient had become paranoid early that summer, feeling that he was seeing another woman, which he denied. The husband said that she was angry, and he took this very hard. She also felt that he hated her father, because of prejudice against Japanese. The husband stated that the patient seemed to recover shortly thereafter. In July, however, she quit her job secondary to advances made by a male employee at the company where she worked.

In September, they went to visit relatives and argued on the trip. Ms. Chinchin stated that she became worried that her husband would speed to scare her, leading her to call a sheriff in a town along the way. Eventually, the husband stated that she got hysterical and said that he, the husband, was going to kill her. She was hospitalized briefly and released. On her release, she returned home. The husband reported that things seemed well until November, when the patient called a friend, saying that she was depressed and was thinking about shooting herself and the children. She was hospitalized at a community hospital and then transferred to the university hospital. Her diagnosis on discharge from the community hospital was psychotic depression. She was discharged on antipsychotic medication. At that time, it was reported that her husband abused alcohol and was away from home most of the time driving a truck. It was also reported that he was seeing another woman.

On admission to the university hospital, Ms. Chinchin was extremely worried that her husband would leave her. She said that she was anxious and not depressed and denied suicidal thoughts. She complained of sleep problems and had multiple somatic complaints. On interview, it was felt that she did not have major depression and was not psychotic. It was felt her presenting symptoms were due to overmedication, and all medications were discontinued. She gradually became more relaxed and participated in activities. Family therapy was recommended, but as her husband's job required him to be out of town for varying periods of time, it was felt that this would not be feasible. The diagnosis on discharge was adjustment disorder with mixed features.

She was then seen as an outpatient, but was readmitted in late December as her psychiatrist felt that he could not sort out her multitude of physical and marital complaints on an outpatient basis. At the time of this admission, she was constantly asking for reassurance, stating that she did not trust anyone talking to her husband, because one would believe him. One minute, she believed that he wanted to kill her; the next minute, she laughed this off. She complained of many physical problems, such as crying without tears, her hair falling out, her stool content changing from normal shape and consistency to stringy and chalky. She also complained of fatigue and of being unable to perform housework.

Ms. Chinchin considered returning to work and leaving her husband, who, she said, had gone to spend Christmas with a girlfriend. She vacillated about suicide and was very ambivalent about what she wanted to do with her life. She had recently tried to give the children up for adoption. During her 1-week admission, it was reported that initially she was very anxious and preoccupied with physical complaints. Later, she stated that her children were ill, for example, with tonsillitis and that there was nobody that she could rely on to take care of them. She mentioned being distressed at her marriage. On the day of discharge, the husband came to the hospital, saying that he had to take the patient home because he had to go back to work on his truck route and had no one to take care of the children. The husband stated that the children were drifting away from her because of her vacillating nature but that she was the only one he had to take care of the children. Given her request to leave, she was discharged with a diagnosis of psychotic depression. She was to be seen as an outpatient a week after admission. She did not keep the appointment and around the time of the appointment, shot and killed all 3 of her family members before killing herself. The bodies were discovered 1 week later.

Discussion of the Case of Ms. Chinchin
Freddy A. Paniagua

General Discussion

Ms. Chinchin's symptoms suggest Major Depressive Disorder with Psychotic Features (APA, 1994, pp. 339-345). The Diagnosis of Adjustment Disorder with Depressed Mood (APA, 1994, p. 624) would also be considered. One factor that might contribute to these alternative psychiatric diagnoses is related to her husband's behavior. If one assumed that he was faithful, then her reports of him seeing another woman and perhaps planning to hurt her could be viewed as psychotic, accompanied with depressive symptoms. On the other hand, if this were not the case, one could justify the diagnosis of Adjustment Disorder; that is, Ms. Chinchin developed emotional and behavioral symptoms in response to an identifiable stressor.

Cultural Formulation

This is the only case in this text in which the patient's emotional problems led to suicidal and homicidal behavior. This case was selected because it shows that despite efforts from clinicians to implement the most effective treatment plans, the occurrence of suicidal behaviors is an unfortunate possibility, regardless of the race of the client. In addition, many cultural variables could be identified, but none of them would necessarily indicate that such behaviors would occur in the near future or many years after the completion of treatment. For example, evidence exists suggesting that Japanese may be more likely to think that suicide is not always an abnormal behavior and perhaps permissible in some cases. In addition, in Japan, the term *shinju,* which initially indicated a mutual suicide agreement by lovers, has broadened over time to include murder-suicides (Takahashi & Berger, 1996). Ms. Chinchin's actions may reveal her belief that suicidal behavior and murder-suicides were normal ways to end her emotional difficulties. That is, for Ms. Chinchin, suicide may have been a permissible solution to an intolerable situation involving her fear of losing her husband and the problem of not knowing who would care for her children in the absence of support from her extended family.

In terms of the extreme importance of the mother-child bond in the Japanese culture (i.e., the recognition of familism as a critical cultural value in this culture), one could argue that Ms. Chinchin killed her children believing that they would be mistreated on her death because the only family she had was her husband and children. Her severe symptoms (including depression with psychotic features) probably prevented Ms. Chinchin to visualize a world for her children after her death. Another cultural variation to consider is that Ms. Chinchin realized that her extended family rejected her because she engaged in a biracial marriage. For example, when her father died, the family in Japan did not inform her about his death until he was buried. Ms. Chinchin's feeling that she was not part of the extended family (a fundamental cultural value among many Asians; D. W. Sue & D. Sue, 1990, 1999) probably became a severe social stressor for many years, and having this feeling in combination with her severe psychiatric symptoms could have contributed to her decision to kill her family.

Personality Disorders

Paranoid Personality Disorder

Patterns of behavior determined by sociocultural contexts or specific life circumstances may be erroneously labeled *paranoid*. Immigrants, political and economic refugees, and members of culturally diverse groups may show guarded or defensive behaviors either because of unfamiliarity with the language, rules, and regulations in the United States or because of the perceived neglect or indifference of the majority society (APA, 1994, p. 636). Castillo (1997) provided further illustration of this disorder in cultural terms in the case of men in Swat Pukhtun society (tribal people living in the mountains of northern Pakistan). All males in this society own guns, and "they trust no one and are constantly vigilant in protecting their honor and their personal interests. Pukhtun men distrust the sexual loyalty of all women to the extent of keeping them confined in their homes" (Castillo, 1997, p. 99). As noted by Castillo, these behavioral patterns among Pukhtun men are examples of normative personality development in this society, and it would be considered a maladaptive behavior "not to be constantly on guard and suspicious of everyone [in this society]" (p. 99). For this reason, the diagnosis of Paranoid Personality Disorder is not recommended in the case of the Swat Pukhtun (Castillo, 1997).

Schizoid and Schizotypal Personality Disorders

Restrictive range of emotions, defensive behaviors, and detachment from social activities displayed by individuals from different cultural backgrounds may be erroneously considered as *schizoid*. For example, individuals who have moved from rural to metropolitan areas may show "emotional freezing," as manifested by solitary activities and constricted affect. Immigrants may also be mistakenly perceived as cold, hostile, and indifferent (APA, 1994, p. 639). In his cross-cultural interpretation of personality disorders in India, Castillo (1997) reported that

> to be detached and unmoved by good or bad events is considered to be saintly in the Hindu culture. . . . This type of personality development would not be considered pathological in Hindu society. Schizoid personality disorder . . . would be an inappropriate diagnosis [in this society]. (p. 100)

Cognitive and perceptual distortions may be associated with religious beliefs and rituals, which may appear to be *schizotypal* to clinicians uninformed about these cultural variations (see APA, 1994, p. 643). Examples of these distortions include voodoo ceremonies, speaking in tongues, belief in life beyond death, mind reading, evil eye, and magical beliefs associated with health and illness (Campinha-Bacote, 1992).

Antisocial Personality Disorder

Clinicians should consider the social and economic context in which the behaviors occur. Many behaviors associated with this disorder also appear to be associated with low socioeconomic status, urban settings, and social contexts in which antisocial behavior functions as a protective survival strategy (APA, 1994, p. 647).

Borderline, Histrionic, and Narcissistic Personality Disorders

Regarding Borderline Personality Disorder, the *DSM-IV* suggests that this disorder might not represent a culture-specific disorder because " the pattern of behavior seen in [this disorder] has been identified in many settings around the world" (APA, 1994, p. 652). Regarding the Histrionic Personality Disorder, norms for personal appearance, emotional expressiveness, and interpersonal behavior vary widely across cultures. Symptoms associated with this disorder (e.g., emotionality, seductiveness, impressionability) may be culturally accepted by the community, and it is important to determine whether these symptoms cause clinically significant impairment or distress to the individual in comparison to what is culturally expected. Among Hispanics, this disorder might be confused with the cultural phenomenon of machismo, in which a Hispanic male would be sexually seductive, feel uncomfortable if he is not the center of attention, and show exaggerated expression of emotions (APA, 1994, p. 656; Castillo, 1997). The *DSM-IV* did not provide a description of cultural variables in the case of Narcissistic Personality Disorder. Several symptoms in this disorder, however, might suggest machismo in cultures that are hierarchical. For example, symptoms resembling Narcissistic Personality Disorder are common in the Swat Pukhtun culture (Castillo, 1997). These symptoms might also be seen among macho Hispanic males, including the need for excessive admiration and the belief that they have unlimited power over others (particularly females).

Avoidant and Dependent Personality Disorders

Cultural variations exist in the degree to which different cultures and ethnic groups regard avoidance as appropriate. Acculturation problems associated with immigration could also lead to symptoms suggesting an Avoidant Personality Disorder (APA, 1994, p. 663). The appropriateness of *dependent* behaviors varies across sociocultural groups. Behaviors associated with this disorder (e.g., passivity, difficulty in making everyday decisions) would be considered characteristic of this disorder only when they are clearly in excess of the individual's cultural norms or reflect unrealistic concerns. In addition, some cultures may differentially foster dependent behaviors in females (Paniagua, 1998). As mentioned, in the Hispanic culture, *marianismo* (the opposite of machismo) is a cultural value in which women are expected to be submissive, obedient, dependent, timid, docile, and gentle in the presence of Hispanic males, particularly the husband (see Chapter 1 and Paniagua, 1998). A Hispanic female with *marianismo* characteristics in therapy would most likely display a great deal of "dependent personality" difficulties because she probably would behave in terms of the expected *marianismo* in the Hispanic community. Among many Asian families, "passivity, politeness, and differential treatment" (APA, 1994, p. 667) in children are expected toward their parents, and this could be erroneously considered as symptoms of Dependent Personality Disorder.

Obsessive-Compulsive Personality Disorder

Habits, customs, or interpersonal styles culturally sanctioned by the individual's reference groups should not be included when making this diagnosis. The individual may place heavy emphasis on work and productivity because these behaviors are reinforced by the individual's reference group (APA, 1994, p. 671; Bernstein, 1997).

The Case of Ms. X.
Daphne C. Brazile, MD

Ms. X. is a middle-aged African American woman who has lived in the area all of her life. She began seeking treatment at our facility after her family members had noted that, to them, she was acting strangely. Ms. X. stated that she believed that her family members were out to make her crazy and convince her neighbors of the same. She stated the reason for this was because she was the "darkest one" in her family. Ms. X. was a fair-skinned black woman. She was born to a dark-skinned black mother and a white father. She was the darkest sibling of her family. Because of this, she felt that her family had treated her and her mother unjustly. She stated that as a child, she was instructed to look after her lighter-skinned older sisters, whom the family held in high regard. She stated that she did not complete high school because she had to care for her older sisters' children. She described that she would be instructed to "cook and clean" for them, as though she were their slave, and be available to them whenever they needed her. She stated that she did her job with pride because this was expected of her. Because of this, she was not able to have a social life. After Ms. X. married, she continued to receive the same treatment from her sisters. She stated that her children were treated unfairly because of their darker skin as well. She believed that her oldest child, who committed suicide while a teenager, did so because of the treatment received by her family. As she got older, Ms. X. stated that her sisters, who were part of the elite society, would "embarrass" her while around their socialite friends. She believed this to be due to her darker skin color. She stated that her sisters convinced her neighbors that she was a "bad" person, and because of this, her neighbors would do "evil" things to spite her. She described an incident where she asked a neighbor to help her to paint her porch. She stated that after the job was complete, the neighbor tried to charge more than what was originally discussed. She stated that they began to argue, ending in the neighbor leaving without being paid.

Ms. X. attributed the incident to her sisters' influence over this person. She believed this was done because she was darker than the rest of her family. Ms. X. met with her sisters to discuss this issue. When confronted, the sisters denied that they were treating her negatively. They acknowledged that their skin was fairer than hers but denied that they were treating her in such a way. They believed that their sister was "delusional." Ms. X. refused to believe her sisters, and when confronted with the idea that her family was not in any way harming her, she would shift the conversation to another topic. Ms. X. had visited a psychiatrist to help cope with these thoughts. She was given an antidepressant and antipsychotic medication. She refused to take the antipsychotic medication. She did, however, take the antidepressant at a very low dose.

Discussion of Ms. X.
Freddy A. Paniagua

General Discussion

The presenting symptoms of this case suggest the following disorders: (a) Delusional Disorder, Persecutory type (APA, 1994, p. 301), in view of the patient's belief that she was deceived by her family and that her family was responsible for her current state of mind; (b) Paranoid Personality Disorder (APA, 1994, pp. 637-638), reflecting the patient's distrust and suspiciousness toward her family, which appeared to indicate a pattern of behaviors with long-lasting effects; (c) Shared Psychotic Disorder (APA, 1994, p. 306)—it may be that her mother may have had these same thoughts and shared them with the patient. This patient, however, reported a "pattern of pervasive distrust and suspiciousness" (APA,

1994, p. 634) toward family members dating back to her early childhood. For this reason, among the alternative disorders mentioned, Paranoid Personality Disorder would be the first choice in the treatment plan. A critical issue to consider to avoid misdiagnosing this case is the patient's racial- and ethnic-identity conflicts she reported as the essential source for her symptoms (Helms, 1986, 1987). During the evaluation of this case, the clinician would have to determine whether the patient's ways of coping with these conflicts are within the normal cultural range or are clear indication of a paranoid state.

Cultural Formulation

The first goal of a treatment plan designed for this case would involve an assessment of the cultural identity of the client. It appears that this client's struggle to deal with her racial and ethnic identity over the course of many years led to her current symptoms, suggesting Personality Disorder, Paranoid Type. In this assessment, the V-Code "Identity Problem" (APA, 1994, p. 685) should be included in Axis IV as an essential element in the treatment plan. That is, this client appeared to be experiencing a mental disorder that is related to her struggle to deal with her racial and ethnic identity conflicts (see Chapter 7 for examples of clinical applications of V-Codes in those cases when the patient is not having a mental problem but the V-Code is the focus of clinical attention).

The next critical element of the cultural formulation is the client's cultural explanation of her symptoms. Her paranoid state appeared to be associated with one single theme, namely, her beliefs around the "unjust" treatment she received from her family over many years because she was the darkest one in a multiracial family (with a black mother and a white father), as well as her beliefs around a similar injustice her children experienced, which led to suicide in her oldest child. The family, however, *denied* that they were treating Ms. X. unjustly, and family members "noted that . . . she [patient] was acting strange," which resulted in Ms. X.'s family seeking psychiatric treatment for her. The goal of the treatment plan, however, should not be to determine whether Ms. X. is right and family members (particularly her sisters) are wrong, or vice versa, but to further explore Ms. X.'s paranoid state involving noncultural topics to determine if similar symptoms are noted. That is, telling Ms. X. that her cultural explanation of her symptoms does not appear reliable or valid would not help (confronting her with apparent false beliefs with cultural themes). The introduction of tasks involving noncultural themes and an assessment of Ms. X.'s responses in the presence of these tasks would be a more appropriate approach in the present context. An example of these tasks would be to evaluate Ms. X. with the MMPI (Golden, 1990) and determine her score on the Paranoid Scale. In this scale, a patient with a score exceeding 70 suggests paranoid delusions. Two additional issues to consider in the treatment emphasizing the cultural formulation are (a) the role of the extended family and (b) the client-clinician racial or ethnic differences or similarities. In the first, it is important to explore potential social and emotional support that members from the mother's side (who are African Americans) and members from the father's side (who are white) could provide during the treatment of this case. In the second issue, it is important to know whether Ms. X. would feel more comfortable being assessed and treated by a multiracial clinician who she might perceive as someone who had experienced similar racial and ethnic difficulties in the past but appears "adjusted" to these difficulties.

The Case of David
Derald Wing Sue, PhD, and David Sue, PhD

David Chan is a 21-year-old [Asian American] student majoring in electrical engineering. He first sought counseling because he was having increasing study problems and was receiving failing grades. These academic difficulties became apparent during the first quarter of his senior year and were accompanied by headaches, indigestion, and insomnia. Since he had been an excellent student in the past, David felt that his lower academic performance was caused by illness. However, a medical examination failed to reveal any organic disorder.

During the initial interview, David seemed depressed and anxious. He was difficult to counsel because he would respond to inquiries with short, polite statements and would seldom volunteer about himself. He avoided any statements that involved feelings and presented his problem as strictly an education one. Although he never expressed it directly, David seemed to doubt the value of counseling and needed much reassurance and feedback about his performance in the interview.

After several sessions, the counselor was able to discern one of David's major concerns. David did not like engineering and felt pressured by his parents to go into this field. Yet, he was unable to take responsibility for any of his own actions, was excessively dependent on his parents, and was afraid to express the anger he felt toward them. Using the Gestalt "empty chair" technique, the counselor had David pretend that his parents were seated in empty chairs opposite him. The counselor encouraged him to express his true feelings toward them. While initially he found it very difficult to do, David was able to ventilate some of his true feelings under constant encouragement by the counselor. Unfortunately, the following sessions with Dave proved unproductive in that he seemed more withdrawn and guilt-ridden than ever.

Discussion of the Case of David
Freddy A. Paniagua

General Discussion

The initial diagnosis for David would be Dependent Personality Disorder. In the *DSM-IV* (APA, 1994, p. 665), a client with this disorder would tend to be passive, allow others to assume responsibility for significant areas in his or her life, and would generally depend on a member of the family (e.g., parents) to make decisions involving social activities and goals (e.g., living arrangement, type of career choice). The authors of this case, however, asked "What cultural forces may be affecting David's manner of expressing psychological conflicts?" (D. W. Sue & D. Sue, 1990, p. 259). Among many Asians, filial piety and collectivism are two cultural values strongly emphasized among family members (Ho, 1992; D. W. Sue & D. Sue, 1990, 1999). This is particularly true in the case of children who are expected to fulfill their dutiful obligations to their parents because, in general, Asian parents are expected to make significant decisions regarding their children's personal desires and ambitions (D. W. Sue &. D. Sue, 1990). Asian children who violate this cultural norm in the Asian community would be considered threats to the parents' authority (Paniagua, 1998). David's inability to make decisions about critical areas of his life and his "excessively dependent" behaviors could be explained in terms of these cultural values.

This case also illustrates the tendency among many Asian clients to express their emotional disorders in somatic terms (see Chapter 1 and Gaw, 1993b). As noted earlier, this situation results from the belief of many Asian clients that making these disorders public would lead to shame and humiliation in the family. In this case, the counselor appropriately consulted with a medical doctor to rule out organic disorders to explain David's presentation of physical symptoms (e.g., indigestion).

A final issue has to do with the type of treatment the counselor used to encourage David to express his feelings to his parents. The "empty chair" technique resembles a role-playing situation in which a client would learn to practice social skills or assertive responses and then it is expected that this client would generalize learned skills across settings and people. The technique appeared to work when it was used in the individual psychotherapy situation under "constant encouragement by the counselor." Apparently, the positive effects of this technique did not generalize outside the clinic setting, and in subsequent sessions, David became more "withdrawn and guilt-ridden than ever." Encouraging a client to be assertive (see Chapter 4) and express his or her feelings openly to parents or other individuals with authority in the family would be problematic if that client was raised in a culture in which obedience, submissiveness, and respectful behaviors toward the authority of parents is expected. The present case indicates that David was raised in a culture that reinforces these cultural values, suggesting an explanation for David's inability to generalize skills he learned in the clinic across different settings and people (at home and in the presence of his parents).

Cultural Formulation

In the discussion of this case, the authors asked the following question: "If you were the counselor, what course of action would you take?" (D. W. Sue & D. Sue, 1990, p. 258). In a treatment plan, David's cultural identity would not be an issue (he did not question his racial identity). An area to consider in that plan, however, is a discussion of David's relational problem with his parents (V61.20, APA, 1994, p. 681) in terms of different levels of acculturation between himself and his parents. Individual sessions should be scheduled with David and parents alone, in which the potential role of acculturation would be discussed in terms they could understand. Family therapy sessions (see Chapter 4) would follow, during which David and his parents could explore alternative responses in dealing with this (assumed) acculturation problem. For example, David's intention to be independent from his parents does not necessarily mean that he had decided to make drastic changes around long-standing values he has learned to accept and respect in his culture; he simply wants to introduce flexibility in the way his apparently less acculturated parents believe such values should be used in the American culture.

The Case of Anita
Israel Cuéllar, PhD

Anita is a 30-year-old, Mexican American, unmarried female attending a day psychosocial program for the chronically mentally ill in the Lower Rio Grande Valley, which is a region in Texas with over 85% of residents from the Mexican American community. She was referred for reasons of agitation, suicidal threats in which she threatened to cut herself with a knife that she didn't have, and to take pills that she didn't have, either. She was also threatening to run into the street. She was intensely angry, irritable, and impulsive. Psychosocial program staff were exhausted in managing her behavioral reactions. Anita was referred specifically for development of a behavior program to manage behaviors. By the time the consultant was able to see her, staff reported that for the past 3 days, she had been doing very well and was no longer behaviorally acting out or disturbed. She was reported to be "back to her normal chronic depressed self."

A review of Anita's social history indicates that at the age of 12, she was at home while her migrant parents were working in the fields. Her brothers and sisters were with neighbors while she was left alone. An 18-year-old cousin entered the house through the window and raped her. Anita became pregnant from that rape. She recalls she had only experienced her menstrual period for a matter of 6 or 7 months before being raped. She held the rape secret, as the rapist threatened to kill her and her family members if she made it public. When Anita was no longer able to hide the pregnancy or her suffering, she told her mother about the rape. Her mother was supportive, but her father refused to press charges, with the explanation being, "What would extended family members, such as aunts, uncles, cousins, etc., think or say?" She eventually gave birth, and the child was given up for adoption. She does not know the child's gender or where the child lives or with whom.

Anita is still very angry with her parents, particularly her father, with whom she continues to live. She reports that several weeks ago, when she was threatening suicide, she had become upset because she had left instructions with her parents not to allow her brother to use her car. And on returning home, she found out that her brother had indeed taken the car with her parents' permission. She felt that her parents disrespected her opinion. As she put it, "Despite telling the rapist 'No!' many times, he continued to rape me!" She felt her father also ignored her statement of "No, do not let him borrow my car!" exactly as the rapist had, 18 years before. Incidentally, she managed to purchase her car from savings from her disability check that is used to help support her parents as well as herself.

Anita's diagnoses were Major Depression, Dissociative Disorder NOS, and Borderline Personality Disorder. She had been treated with numerous and multiple psychotropic medications over the past 18 years. Yet she reported that she has never been treated psychologically for her trauma. She reports having nightmares on a regular basis in which she reexperiences the rape, and she admits to harboring intense anger at the rapist. She would like to press charges against her rapist if she still could. She also harbors intense anger at her father for not pressing charges 18 years ago. In addition, she reports that she cannot stand to be touched by anyone, has never had a sexual relationship, and does not relate well with men in general. She reports that at the age of 12, she was an "A" student. Now she feels "stupid, ugly, fat, and useless," and thinks of herself as suffering a mental illness that is essentially incurable. She had never reported her history of rape, the unwanted pregnancy, or giving her child up for adoption to any previous therapist. At most, she would refer to it as "something confidential that happened to me when I was a young child." She has never been able to see herself in the mirror. She reports hating herself. She sees herself as a victim.

Discussion of the Case of Anita
Freddy A. Paniagua, PhD

General Discussion

The diagnoses of Major Depressive Disorder (APA, 1994, pp. 320-327), Dissociative Disorder NOS (APA, 1994, p. 490), and Borderline Personality Disorder (BPD) (APA, 1994, pp. 645-650) were initially considered in this case. Anita's overall symptoms, however, most likely point to BPD. As noted earlier, because this disorder can be found in many settings across cultures, clinicians should carefully consider whether symptoms for this disorder are transiently displayed by the client under clinical assessment or whether there are examples of an "enduring pattern of inner experience and behavior that deviates markedly from the expectations of the individual's culture" (APA, 1994, p. 629). In this case, Anita's symptoms were in accord with this stipulation in the *DSM-IV* (they were not transient and deviated markedly from expectations in her own culture). Once this conclusion is reached (i.e., the exclusion of cultural explanation for this disorder), the next step is to carefully document the *DSM-IV* criteria Anita meets for a diagnosis of BPD. In the *DSM-IV,* this disorder includes nine criteria and only five of them must be met for diagnosing the client with this disorder. Anita met the following criteria for BPD: (a) identity disturbance (e.g., she felt "stupid, ugly, and fat" and not able to see herself in the mirror); (b) recurrent suicidal behavior (e.g., threatening to cut herself with a knife), (c) inappropriate, intense anger or difficulty controlling anger (e.g., she displayed intense anger toward her father and brother), (d) affective instability due to a marked reactivity of mood (she was intensively irritable), (e) a chronic feeling of emptiness (e.g., she felt useless), and (f) an overall pattern of unstable and intense interpersonal relationships (e.g., she cannot stand to be touched by anyone, does not relate with men in general, and has a history of parent-child and sibling relational problems, i.e., two V-Codes in the *DSM-IV,* see APA, 1994, p. 681).

Cultural Formulation

The treatment of BPD is in itself a difficult task to accomplish; this task becomes even more difficult when cultural variables are involved. In this particular case, Anita felt that her parents "disrespected her opinion" when the parents probably would expect Anita to be the one to respect their opinion regarding their disagreement toward Anita's request. That is, among many Hispanics a sense of respect (*respeto*) toward the authority of parents is expected from their children, regardless of their age (Paniagua, 1998); Anita was 30 years old, and she would still be expected to show that sense of respect toward her parents. Another important element of the cultural formulation to be carefully considered in the treatment plan is the father's sense of future conflicts with the extended family if he would have elected to press charges against Anita's cousin (the rapist). Anita was 12 years old when she was raped by her cousin, and at that time,

Anita's father felt that he could not afford to lose instrumental (e.g., financial assistance) and emotional (e.g., counseling) supports he would expect to receive from his extended family in case of future family difficulties (see Paniagua, 1998, pp. 14-16). Although Anita's cultural identity is with the Mexican American community, it appears that she did not value the important role of the extended family as her father did, and this child-father discrepancy and its clinical significance would be an important variable to consider in the treatment plan. This issue would be noted in the V-Code "Parent-Child Relational Problem" (APA, 1994, p. 681), but it would not be the center of clinical attention—the focus would be Anita's symptoms pointing to a BPD.

Furthermore, this case also needs to be examined as an example of possible misdiagnosis by her treating clinicians. Her being raped at the age of 12, possibly and likely, precipitated all her symptoms and played a role in the development of her BPD. Her experience was never uncovered by her previous attending psychiatrists or psychologists over an 18-year period of time, during which she was supposedly treated. Was this failure to uncover the most important clinical fact of the case the result of cross-cultural mistrust by Anita? Or was the failure to uncover the rape a result of failure to probe by biologically oriented clinicians who were not interested in looking at contextual environmental and cultural variables? The answer to these questions should be considered in the overall cultural assessment for diagnosis and care of Anita (see APA, 1994, p. 844, last element in the cultural formulation suggested in the *DSM-IV*).

Schizophrenia and Other Psychotic Disorders

Auditory hallucinations (e.g., seeing the Virgin Mary or hearing God's voice) and delusional ideas (e.g., witchcraft) may be normal in one culture and abnormal in others (Castillo, 1997). For example, in the Nigerian culture, paranoid-like fears of evil attacks by spirits are part of the local beliefs (Kirmayer et al., 1995). These fears are examples of the culture-bound syndrome named "ode-ori" in Chapter 2, Table 2.3. As noted by Kirmayer et al. (1995), these paranoid fears "might be misdiagnosed as symptoms of psychosis by the uninformed clinician" (p. 509).

Variability across cultures in body language, style of emotional expressions, language, and eye contact should be considered when assessing symptoms of Schizophrenia. Brief Psychotic Disorder should be distinguished from culturally sanctioned response patterns. For example, in certain religious ceremonies, a person may report hearing voices, which is not considered abnormal by members of that religion and generally does not persist beyond the termination of such ceremonies (APA, 1994, p. 303). Temporal visual and auditory hallucinations reported by a client in therapy may also result from the recent death of a loved one. As noted earlier, Brief Psychotic Disorder episodes may resemble the culture-bound syndrome "boufee delirante" (*DSM-IV*, 1994, p. 845; see Table 2.3, Chapter 2).

The Case of the Haitian Woman
Junji Takeshita, MD

Within a year after immigrating to the United States, a 21-year-old Haitian woman was referred to a psychiatrist by her schoolteacher because of hallucinations and withdrawn behavior. The patient was fluent in English, although her first language was Creole. Her history revealed that she had seen an ear, nose, and throat specialist in Haiti after her family doctor could not find any medical pathology other than a mild sinus infection. No hearing problems were noted and no treatment was offered. Examination revealed extensive auditory hallucinations, flat affect, and peculiar delusional references to voodoo. The psychiatrist wondered if symptoms of hearing voices and references to voodoo could be explained by her Haitian background, although the negative symptoms seem unrelated. As a result, he consulted with a Creole-speaking, Haitian psychiatrist.

The Haitian psychiatrist interviewed the patient in English, French, and Creole. Communication was not a problem in any language. He discovered that in Haiti, the patient was considered "odd" by both peers and family, as she frequently talked to herself and did not work or participate in school activities. He felt that culture may have influenced the content of her hallucinations and delusions (i.e., references to voodoo) but that the bizarre content of the delusions, extensive hallucinations, and associated negative symptoms were consistent with the diagnosis of schizophrenia.

SOURCE: "Case 1" from "Psychosis" by Junji Takeshita, MD (pp. 124-125), in Wen-Shing Tseng & Jon Streltzer (Eds.), *Culture and Psychopathology: A Guide to Clinical Assessment* (pp. 124-138). Copyright 1997 © by Brunner/Mazel, reprinted by permission of the publisher.

Discussion of the Case of the Haitian Woman
Freddy A. Paniagua

General Discussion

In this case, a diagnosis of Schizophrenia is the most likely conclusion from current symptoms. The *DSM-IV* lists five types of schizophrenia: Paranoid, Disorganized, Catatonic, Undifferentiated, and Residual types (APA, 1994, p. 278). the Paranoid Type is the most likely diagnosis because this client showed (a) extensive auditory hallucinations (Criteria A, APA, 1994, p. 287), and (b) her flat or inappropriate affect was not prominent (Criteria B, APA, 1994, p. 287). The critical question prior to making this diagnosis, however, would be "What specific culturally appropriate strategies would a clinician consider to avoid misdiagnosing this case with Schizophrenia, Paranoid Type? In this specific case, the evaluation strategy used by the author of this case was in accord with specific recommendations provided in the *DSM-IV* in answering that question (see APA, 1994, p. 281). For example the therapist consulted with a Creole-speaking Haitian psychiatrist to assure himself that symptoms were not culturally related but clear signs pointing to schizophrenia as described in the *DSM-IV*. In addition, the consulting psychiatrist applied a *critical* recommendation in the *DSM-IV:* The interview during the consultation process was conducted in English, French, and Creole (see APA, 1994, p. 281) and "communication was not a problem in any language" (Takeshita, 1997, p. 125).

Cultural Formulation

This is another case in which members of a given culturally diverse group realize that something is "culturally" wrong with another member of the same group who displays behaviors that might be considered abnormal because they are outside the range of the belief system in the particular culture. In this case, the teacher recognized that this client did not appear "mentally normal," but the individual who actually determined that such symptoms were beyond what one would expect in the Haitian culture was the consulting Haitian psychiatrist. Hearing voices and reference to voodoo are common characteristics among many Haitians engaged in spirit medium practices; but the fact that the present client displayed behaviors culturally disapproved of by her peers and family members in combination with "the bizarre content of the delusions, extensive hallucinations and associated negative symptoms" (Takeshita, 1997, p. 125) led both the therapist and the consulting psychiatrist to conclude that this was a case of schizophrenia tangentially associated with cultural variables shared by members of the Haitian community. Last, it is important to emphasize that without the therapist's insight regarding a recognition of the potential impact of the therapist-client racial and or ethnic differences, the outcome of the evaluation would have been the underdiagnosis of this case (i.e., failure to diagnose this client with a mental disorder) because her symptoms were culturally related.

The Case of Isabel
Israel Cuéllar, PhD

The following case history concerns a 46-year-old Mexican-origin female married to her second husband for 10 years. She has a history of experiencing auditory hallucinations and extreme religious preoccupation. She has been treated in numerous mental health programs, including Tropical Texas Center for MHMR and the Rio Grande State Center Outreach Offices, as well as the Laredo State Center inpatient unit for the diagnosis of Psychotic Disorder NOS. She is also believed to have Schizoaffective Disorder (bipolar type) and a Generalized Anxiety Disorder. She was currently on psychotropic medications, including Resperidal and Depakote. She was referred for psychotherapy as an adjunct to treatment with psychotropic medications.

Isabel was born in Mexico and raised on a small ranch up to the age of 10 years, where she was introduced to the notion of *brujos* (witches) and *curanderos* (folk healers). She recalls as a young child in her small, rural school that the teacher taught her to say glorious praises for a local *curandero,* and the teacher would tell stories about many *brujos* that resided on the ranch itself. She believed that her cousin was a witch. Isabel was able to relate numerous instances in which her cousin was involved in creating or alleviating headaches in her mother.

Isabel's first husband was a very abusive and violent man. Isabel visited a *brujo* on numerous occasions and delivered a photograph of her husband that the *brujo* used to place a spell on her husband so that he would not be such a womanizer. She reports that he actually became more of a womanizer; however, her mother-in-law thought that he began suffering from some type of seizures following this episode with the *brujo*.

Isabel has experienced visual hallucinations on numerous occasions. Her first psychiatric treatment resulted in electroshock convulsive treatments. She reports a childhood history of being sexually molested and a history of physical abuse by her first husband. The voices she heard ordered her and informed her that her daughter-in-law was cheating on her husband as well. The voices often told her that she is the "spirit of God." Her delusions were grandiose and paranoid in nature. She believed that her first husband was currently practicing witchcraft and placed a hex (*mal puesto*) on someone via a photo and via dolls with needles in them. Her son had seen these items in his father's home on occasions during visits. Isabel has stopped attending church altogether, and she is very confused. Her second husband drinks excessively and swears he will never stop drinking and nobody will get him to quit. She has tried placing a hex on him unsuccessfully to quit drinking. She has a negative explanatory model of her illness. She is extremely sensitive, very suggestible, and suspicious. There is a strong underlying paranoid belief system and a longstanding belief in witches, evil influences, supernatural forces, and so on. She is very confused about religion and has joined, at different periods of time, the Pentecostal Church, the Jehovah's Witness Church, the Catholic Church, and the Baptist Church without long-lasting changes in her emotional well being. At times, she feels the TV is addressing her specifically.

Discussion of the Case of Isabel
Freddy A. Paniagua

General Discussion

In this case, the preliminary diagnosis of Psychotic Disorder NOS would permit the clinician to further screen Isabel's symptoms to determine which specific psychotic disorders she is experiencing. Two candidates would be Schizophrenia, Paranoid Type, (APA, 1994, p. 287) and Delusional Disorder, Grandiose Type (APA, 1994, pp. 296-297). In its current format, this vignette does not provide sufficient details to reach a diagnosis of Schizoaffective Disorder (APA, 1994, pp. 292-296) or Generalized Anxiety Disorder (APA, 1994, pp. 426-432).

Regardless of which psychiatric diagnosis is the most appropriate in this case, the critical task for the clinician would be to sort out two cultural issues prior to diagnosing Isabel. First, it is important to determine under what conditions Isabel's reports of supernatural forces, evil influences against her, and her ability to change other people's behaviors (e.g., her husband's drinking pattern) through a hex are examples of behaviors other members of her culture would consider as normal in a given context. Second, it is crucial to determine what exactly Isabel did outside this culturally normative context to require psychiatric treatment in mental health facilities staffed by Mexican American clinicians with solid understanding of cultural and ethnic issues among clients served by these facilities (e.g., Dr. Cuéllar, Mexican American, and the author of this case, is expert in the assessment and treatment of Mexican American clients; see Cuéllar, 2000). To deal with both issues, clinicians need to review cultural guidelines provided by the *DSM-IV* in the case of Schizophrenia and Other Psychotic Disorders and then determine whether or not these guidelines can be applied to this case.

The *DSM-IV* points out that "ideas that may appear to be delusional in one culture (e.g., sorcery and witchcraft) may be commonly held in another" (APA, 1994, p. 281). Many Hispanics (including Mexican Americans) believe that "evil" individuals known as "witches" (*brujos,* men; *brujas,* women) can do bad things to other people without the need to contact them directly. Therefore, when Isabel brought a photograph of her husband to the witch to assist him with his job, her belief in the power of this witch was not out of the ordinary in her own culture. Isabel also knew about the power of the hex (i.e., *mal puesto* among Hispanics, root work, voodoo death in other cultures, see APA, 1994, pp. 847-848, and Table 2.3) and used it on her second husband to force him to quit drinking. In this case, the use of the hex was probably intended to cause Isabel's second husband emotional and psychological problems forcing him to stop drinking. Again, Isabel's belief in the power of the hex was not an unusual behavior among members of her own culture, because many Mexican Americans also believe that it is possible to influence people's behavior through hexing (Martinez, 1988; Paniagua, 1998).

The *DSM-IV* also points out that "visual or auditory hallucinations with a religious content may be a normal part of religious experience (e.g., seeing the Virgin Mary or hearing God's voice" (APA, 1994, p. 281). Isabel experienced both auditory and visual hallucinations, and one would guess that her family perceived these hallucinations as normal when they involved topics culturally accepted in her community. Last, the *DSM-IV* suggests that conducting the clinical interview in the client's own language could minimize biases in the diagnosis of the case (see APA, 1994, p. 281). In the present case, Isabel was probably interviewed in Spanish because the therapist (Dr. Cuéllar) and the general staff in those mental health facilities provide mental health services in both English and Spanish. Therefore, language was not a factor in the diagnosis of this case.

If cultural variations are indeed excluded in the identification of symptoms pointing to a psychiatric illness, the question is, "What exactly Isabel did outside this culturally normative context that led Mexican American clinicians to diagnose her with a mental disorder?" In brief, Isabel reported about unseen events and supernatural experiences in ways different from other individuals' reports of similar events and experiences in her own culture. For example, Isabel *heard voices* giving her orders to behave like the "spirit of God" and the same voices told her that her daughter-in-law was cheating on her husband. Many Mexican Americans with strong religious attachment, particularly to the Catholic Church, would talk about their spiritual connection with God, not because "voices" are telling them to make that connection but because they feel that connection to God in a spiritual sense. In addition, the role of these voices in giving specific information about other individuals in the family (e.g., someone cheating in the family) is not a cultural phenomenon among Mexican Americans. In this case, Isabel would be expected to report that "Jose told me that my daughter-in-law is cheating on my husband" but not that voices inside her head told her about this relationship. Last, the fact that Isabel also felt the television addressing her specifically is an example of *referential delusions,* which clinicians must consider in the diagnosis of schizophrenia and other psychotic disorders (see APA, 1994, p. 275). In conclusion, Isabel displayed many behaviors and beliefs culturally accepted in her community. Isabel, however, is a candidate for the diagnosis of Schizophrenia, Paranoid Type, or Delusional Disorder, Grandiose Type, because her behaviors and beliefs went beyond what is culturally expected among the Mexican American community, and she also meets *DSM* criteria pointing to these two disorders.

Cultural Formulation

This case demonstrates that just because cultural elements are ubiquitous throughout the symptoms' manifestations of the psychiatric disorder, it does not mean that the patient does not have a legitimate *DSM-IV* disorder. Again, it is important to reemphasize that "too much emphasis on cultural-related syndromes [e.g., hex or mal puesto] may prevent practitioners from considering that many of these syndromes may actually include symptoms of severe psychiatric disorders" (Paniagua, 1998, p. 116). Fortunately, Isabel was assessed and treated by a Mexican American clinician who was able to distinguish between cultural variables explaining Isabel's symptoms and symptoms suggesting a mental disorder. Many idioms of distress through which Isabel communicated her symptoms (e.g., sensing that she was the "spirit of God," her supernatural ability to hex other people, her belief that others have evil influences on her) are culturally accepted by many Mexican Americans as normal behaviors and beliefs in this community. Her departure from this cultural normality was correctly noted by the clinician evaluating Isabel, who concluded that she was experiencing a psychotic disorder in terms of *DSM-IV* criteria.

In terms of the cultural identity of Isabel, it is expected that she will not stop believing in supernatural and unseen events during and after the completion of treatment because these beliefs are also common among other members of her community. Under this circumstance, the goal of treatment (e.g., cognitive-behavioral approaches in combination with medication) would not be to prevent Isabel from having these beliefs (e.g., that she is the "spirit of God") but to place them in a context culturally accepted in her community. For example, a Mexican American with extreme devotion to help people could also say that he or she is the "spirit of God" but not because a voice is saying that but in a spiritual sense of that expression.

Last, with respect to an emphasis on the cultural factors related to psychosocial environment and level of functioning (APA, 1994, p. 844), it is crucial to reestablish Isabel's church membership because the church is considered by many Mexican American clients an important component of the extended family (Paniagua, 1998). Isabel is confused about religion and apparently about which specific religious denomination she wants to join to explore changes in her emotional well-being. This type of confusion points to the V-Code, "Religious or Spiritual Problem," in the *DSM-IV* (see APA, 1994, p. 685), which should be addressed in the treatment plan.

Somatoform Disorders

Somatization and Undifferentiated Somatoform Disorder

In general, in the *DSM-IV,* the term *Somatization Disorder* is used to name a "pattern of recurring, *multiple,* clinically significant somatic complaints" (APA, 1994, p. 446; italics added) that "cannot be fully explained by a known general medical condition or the direct effect of a substance (e.g., drug abuse, a medication)" (APA, 1994, p. 450). Furthermore, during the course of these somatic complaints, the client must report at least four pain symptoms, two gastrointestinal symptoms, one sexual symptom, and one pseudoneurological symptom (e.g., paralysis, seizures; see APA, 1994, p. 449). If symptoms "are *below the threshold* for a diagnosis of Somatization Disorder" (APA, 1994, p. 445; italics added), including, for example, at least *one* unexplained medical complaint persisting for at least 6 months, only one pain symptom, absence of sexual symptoms, and so on, the appropriate diagnosis would be Undifferentiated Somatoform Disorder (see APA, 1994, pp. 450-452). In both diagnostic categories, the frequency and type of somatic symptoms may vary across cultures (Escobar, 1995). For example, people from Africa and South Asia tend to show more symptoms of burning hands and feet as well as nondelusional experiences of worms in the head or ants crawling under the skin, in comparison to individuals from North America. In cultures in which semen loss is a great concern for people, symptoms associated with male reproductive function tend to be more prevalent (see *DSM-IV,* 1994, p. 447). In India, Sri Lanka, and China, severe anxiety associated with that concern is known as *dhat* (see Table 2.3, Chapter 2). Symptoms resembling Somatization Disorder have also been reported in the case of the culture-bound syndromes *susto* and *ataques de nervios* (Table 2.3, Chapter 2; APA, 1994, p. 845; Escobar, 1995). In the specific case of Undifferentiated Somatoform Disorder, a client's reports of unexplained physical symptoms could suggest "culturally shaped 'idioms of distress' that are employed [by the client] to express concerns about a broad range of personal and social problems" (APA, 1994, pp. 450-451).

Conversion Disorder

This disorder is reported to be more frequent among low-socioeconomic-status clients from rural areas, with minimal knowledge of psychological and medical concepts (APA, 1994). Symptoms may reflect local cultural ideas about accepted and credible ways to express distress. Symptoms are common aspects of certain culturally sanctioned religious and healing rituals (APA, 1994, p. 455). Symptoms such as fainting episodes and temporary blindness might resemble the culture-bound syndromes of "ataques de nervios" among Hispanics and "falling-out" among African Americans, respectively (APA, 1994, p. 846; Chaplin, 1997).

Pain Disorder

Differences across cultural and ethnic groups exist in terms of how these groups react to pain and respond to painful stimuli (APA, 1994, p. 460; Chaplin, 1997). For example, Jewish patients tend to show pain more openly than Asian clients do. The reason for this difference is that Asians "in general are taught self-restraint and may be more reluctant to express pain" (Castillo, 1997, p. 196). The *DSM-IV* (APA, 1994) suggests that cultural variants in the evaluation and treatment of patients with Pain Disorder might be of limited utility because of the great deal of individual differences in the expression of pain across cultures. Another reason for this limitation is that it is extremely difficult to assess the severity of pain with objectivity (Castillo, 1997), which might prevent clinicians from distinguishing pain with sufficient medical justification from pain suggesting either Pain Disorder or culturally related pain in a given culture.

Hypochondriasis

Continued preoccupation with a given medical problem despite a medical evaluation and reassurance indicating that nothing is wrong should be evaluated relative to the client's cultural background and explanatory models (Chaplin, 1997). For example, traditional healers assisting Hispanics with the management of medical problems might disagree with the medical evaluation and findings provided by a physician. This disagreement could reinforce the client's folk beliefs about disease (APA, 1994, p. 464). An emphasis on the medical evaluation and the absence of significant findings to confirm the presence of a given disease would probably compete with beliefs among Hispanic clients regarding the role of bad spirits and malevolent witchcraft that could result in medical problems, as well as with the belief regarding the role of healers (*curanderos, curanderas*) in the solution of medical problems (Paniagua, 1998). As noted by Castillo (1997), clients holding these beliefs would continue looking for the "right" physician if the medical condition is not evaluated and managed with the assistance of healers in a given culture.

Body Dysmorphic Disorder

A client's concern about *imagined* physical deformities may be determined by cultural concerns about physical appearance and the importance of physical self-presentation (APA, 1994, p. 467; Castillo, 1997). For example, among some Hispanics, "thinner" is associated with being "sick," whereas "hefty" is perceived as "healthy." Among many Anglo Americans, the opposite is the accepted belief. In this context, a Hispanic client confronting these two conflicting beliefs in the North American culture would be very concerned with a "defect" involving his or her physical appearance in public. This concern, however, might be culturally appropriate in the sense that this client would be responding to racial discrimination and humiliation directed toward individuals' appearance that differ from those expected in the North American culture.

The Case of Mrs. Chang
Steven L. Chaplin, MD

Mrs. Chang, a 56-year-old married woman from Mainland China, was brought to see a psychiatrist by her daughter. Mrs. Chang was visiting the daughter, who had studied in an American university, completed a graduate degree, and now lived in the United States. In the past, Mrs. Chang had traveled to the United States and other Western countries for business reasons. This trip was strictly a social visit. The daughter had noted some strange behavior in her mother during the visit. She had given some precious items to her daughter with a solemnity that seemed uncharacteristic. She had also made numerous statements to the effect that she would not be seeing her daughter again. As the time for her mother's return to China approached, the daughter became increasingly concerned and persuaded her to see a doctor.

During the interview, Mrs. Chang told the doctor that she suffered from "weakness within the heart" and had "difficulty sleeping at night." Initially, she was reluctant to talk, but she became more animated when discussing her problems with sleep. She described intermittent, restless sleep that often prevented her from sleeping well for several days. She stated that it was because she had "too much fire in the liver," and pointed to a sore on her lip as proof of that assessment.

Upon further questioning, she related that her sleep problems had begun a year before, soon after she retired from work. She had attained a rather important position as chief architect and supervised a staff of over 100 people. She had even been able to travel outside China on business during the latter part of her career. However, she had been forced to retire in accordance with government regulations.

After retiring, she had complained that she had nothing to do, and that her life was without purpose. Her husband, also a professional, was still employed. She described him as a quiet person by nature who offered her little comfort. Later, she volunteered the information that he had an extramarital affair several years prior, and that their relationship had been strained since then.

At the conclusion of the session, the psychiatrist explained that he believed her problems were mostly related to her postretirement adjustment. He recommended that she attempt to reopen dialogue with her husband, and encouraged her to seek activities and friends outside of her home. He finally offered to prescribe medication for her "depression." She agreed to talk more with her husband and to try to cultivate outside activities. However, she claimed that she did not understand the term "depression," and reminded the doctor that she suffered "weakness within the heart," "too much fire in the liver," and "difficulty sleeping."

SOURCE: "Case 1" from "Somatization" by Steven L. Chaplin, MD (pp. 67-68), in Wen-Shing Tseng & Jon Streltzer (Eds.), Culture and Psychopathology: A Guide to Clinical Assessment (pp. 67-86). Copyright 1997 © by Brunner/Mazel, reprinted by permission of the publisher.

Discussion of the Case of Mrs. Chang
Freddy A. Paniagua

General Discussion

Mrs. Chang reported at least two somatic complaints ("difficulty sleeping at night" and "restless sleep"). In addition, it appears that no medical explanations were found in the explanation of Mrs. Chang's somatic complaints; the psychiatrist who evaluated her suggested "postretirement adjustment" as the most likely explanation of these complaints. Furthermore, Mrs. Chang did not report pain, gastrointestinal, sexual, and pseudoneurological symptoms required for a diagnosis of Somatization Disorder (APA, 1994, p. 449). These findings suggested a case of Undifferentiated Somatoform Disorder (APA, 1994, pp. 450-452). Another point to consider when making this diagnosis is that Mrs. Chang's symptoms started after she retired, suggesting that her use of various somatic idioms of distress involving medically unexplained symptoms served as a way for her to express her concern about a major personal problem or stressor she recently experienced (i.e., forced retirement because of government regulations). As noted by Chaplin (1997), many patients from Mainland China would use culturally expected idioms of distress to "communicate to a doctor the suffering they experience" (p. 79). In the case of Mrs. Chang, these somatic idioms included "weakness within the heart," and "too much fire in the liver."

Cultural Formulation

An assessment of the cultural identity of Mrs. Chang should be considered prior to the recommendation of specific treatment modalities to assist her with her "postretirement adjustment" in the absence of culturally somatic idioms of distress. For example, she traveled from China to the United States and other Western countries frequently, which apparently exposed her to different cultural and belief systems regarding the interpretation and medical treatment of her symptoms. When the psychiatrist, however, suggested that Mrs. Chang's symptoms resulted from her difficulty to adjust to a "forced" retirement and that this situation probably led to "depression" requiring "medication," she reported to be unaware of the term "depression" and reaffirmed her explanation of symptoms in terms expected culturally, somatic idioms of distress among many Asian clients experiencing similar stressors in their life. This suggests that although Mrs. Chang traveled outside China many times (for business reasons), her cultural identity with the Chinese culture was still strong. Under this circumstance, the treatment plan would have to emphasize such cultural values and belief systems Mrs. Chang still maintained in the present context (i.e., interpretation and treatment of her symptoms).

In the discussion of this case, Chaplin (1997) provided an overview of the importance of assessing the cultural identity of Mrs. Chang prior to suggesting in the treatment plan a solution to her problems: "Chinese will generally understand the idiomatic meaning of 'weakness within the heart' as implying that one's mood is down, and 'too much fire in the liver' as being anxious or irritated" (Chaplin, 1997, p. 79). In this specific case, Chaplin (1997) pointed out that the "prescribed remedy is [to encourage the client to take] the foods and drinks that are considered cold elements to reduce the excessive heat in the body" (p. 79). Therefore, in the treatment plan for Mrs. Chang, the therapist (particularly non-Chinese therapists) would have to share with Mrs. Chang these cultural idioms of distress and nontraditional treatment strategies.

Substance-Related Disorders

Alcohol-Related Disorder

In general, among all substance-related disorders, alcohol-related disorders (e.g., Alcohol Intoxication and Alcohol Withdrawal) have received most attention in the cross-cultural literature (Westermeyer, 1995). Alcohol use patterns could be the result of cultural traditions in which the consumption of alcohol is expected in family, religious, and social settings. For example, many Hispanics consider heavy drinking an acceptable behavior among Hispanic males (Canino, Burnam, & Caetano, 1992). This is particularly true for Hispanics who believe in machismo, which, among other characteristics, refers to Hispanic males' ability to consume an excessive amount of alcohol without getting drunk (Paniagua, 1998). Castillo (1997) reviewed the literature on this topic and found similar situations in Ireland, Korea, and Japan and concluded that "in these societies, heavy alcohol use is expected and . . . required by cultural customs for normal social interaction among males" (p. 162). As noted by Castillo (1997), in such societies, males who *do not engage in heavy drinking* could be exposed to "negative social and occupational consequences" (p. 162). This observation, of course, is the opposite of what one would expect in the United States where the negative consequences (both social and occupational) resulting from heavy drinking of alcohol are dramatic (e.g., social rejection, inability to find a job because of a history of alcoholism, etc.). Other substance-related disorders with brief descriptions of cultural variants in the *DSM-IV* (APA,1994) include Amphetamine-Related Disorders, Cannabis-Related Disorders, Cocaine-Related Disorders, Hallucinogen-Related Disorders, Inhalant-Related Disorders, Nicotine-Related Disorders, and Opioid-Related Disorders. In general, the *DSM-IV* does not consider these disorders as unique to specific cultures. Cultural acceptability of such disorders, however, might vary across cultures. For example, the use of the hallucinogen peyote appears more common among American Indians relative to other racial groups (Cruz, 1999; Westermeyer, 1995).

The Case of Carlos Hernandos
Virginia S. Burlingame, MSW, PhD

Every June for 5 years, Carlos Hernandos, now 59, and his three sons came to Kenosha, Wisconsin, to pick cabbages. They returned to Laredo, Texas, each October. During these summers, Mr. Hernandos missed his wife. When he was hired for a year-round factory job in Kenosha, the family moved.

Mr. Hernandos began drinking in his teens. Like many of his *compadres* and even many of his relatives, he believed that after a hard day's work in the sun, alcohol was a just reward. Eventually he was up to a six-pack daily; then he added tequila, and then pot. When he was drunk, he slept in the backyard on a cot so as not to disturb the family.

In 1996, Mr. Hernandos was arrested for driving while intoxicated. He was then hospitalized for detox. In the hospital, he was told that he had cirrhosis of the liver. Alcohol counseling had been ordered by the court, but he refused inpatient treatment because he had to support his family. The counseling fared no better. Mark T., his counselor, was a white man who struck him as phony and uninterested.

Mr. Hernandos did not consider himself an alcoholic; nor did he see drinking as a disease connected to his ill health. The only thing wrong with his drinking, he felt, was that it had caused an arrest and a fine. He was ashamed of getting caught. He hated the AA meetings where [he] had to say he would always be an "alcoholic" and must quit drinking altogether. He wouldn't go along with that. But priding himself on being a smart person, he agreed with his counselor, to fulfill the court's requirement and get it over with. He promised himself secretly that next time he would find a nondrinking, designated driver or walk home and not get into such a mess again. After the required sessions, Mark T. closed the case.

SOURCE: From *"Ethnogerocounseling: Counseling Ethnic Elders and Their Families,"* by Virginia S. Burlingame. Copyright 1999 © by Springer Publishing Company, reprinted by permission of the publishers.

Discussion of the Case of Carlos Hernandos
Freddy A. Paniagua

General Discussion

Mr. Hernandos's symptoms suggest an Alcohol-Related Disorder (APA, pp. 194-195), more likely, Alcohol Abuse (APA, 1994, p. 196). For example, although he used alcohol in a physically hazardous situation (e.g., driving while intoxicated), Mr. Hernandos did not show evidence of withdrawal, compulsive behavior associated with alcohol, or tolerance.

Cultural Formulation

Probably the most critical variable in the cultural formulation is an assessment of the cultural value of machismo in Mr. Hernandos's overall cultural identity and the culturally accepted drinking pattern among many members of the Hispanic community. Mr. Hernandos's early drinking pattern during his teens was probably socially reinforced by his family and the extended family, because among many Hispanic families, a man's ability to drink alcohol without getting drunk is a case for the cultural value of machismo (see Paniagua, 1998, p. 40). His belief in consumption of alcohol at the end of each working day was shared by many of his Hispanic friends and relatives, and this is another expected cultural belief among many Hispanic families and particularly, Hispanic men. The rejection of inpatient treatment is an example of Mr. Hernandos's belief that the family is first (*familismo*) and then his medical problems.

Future Cases

This chapter described the clinical applications of cultural variables across examples of subtypes of mental disorders in children, adolescents, and adults. For future editions of this book, I want to invite clinicians to submit cases illustrating these variables with subtypes of psychiatric disorders not covered in the present chapter (e.g., see the sections on Mood Disorders, Anxiety Disorders, and Personality Disorders, in which examples of subtypes across these disorders were selected to illustrate these variables). Please, submit new cases to Dr. Freddy A. Paniagua, Sage Publications, 2455 Teller Road, Thousand Oaks, CA 91320. In the sections to follow, additional disorders and subtypes are briefly discussed in terms of cultural considerations, and the editor will appreciate receiving cases to illustrate cultural variables with these disorders.

Delirium, Dementia, and Amnestic and Other Cognitive Disorders

During the evaluation of clients experiencing these disorders, educational and cultural backgrounds should be considered during the administration of tests to assess general knowledge, memory, and orientation (APA, 1994, pp. 125-126). These clients might not be familiar with the type of information used in these tests because it does not include culturally familiar topics (e.g., a client's lack of geographical knowledge in the United States vs. his or her knowledge of the country of origin).

Sexual Dysfunctions and Paraphilias

In Sexual Dysfunctions, the ethnic and religious background of the individual, as well as whether the client's culture emphasizes male dominance and control over female sexuality versus those that reward the opposite view should be considered during the assessment. These cultural variations may affect sexual desire, expectations, and attitudes about performance. In some societies, female sexual desire is not considered very relevant, particularly when fertility is the primary concern (APA, 1994, p. 495; Castillo, 1997). In the case of the Paraphilias, the *DSM-IV* (APA, 1994, p. 524) only suggests that these disorders might be appropriate in one culture and seen as inappropriate in other cultures; this makes the diagnosis of paraphilias across cultures and religions a complicated task for the clinician.

Eating Disorders

Eating disorders are generally more prevalent in industrialized countries, including the United States, Canada, and Japan. In Anorexia Nervosa, abundance of food and the linkage of attractiveness with being thin may explain high prevalence rates of this disorder in such countries (APA, 1994, pp. 542-543; Castillo, 1997).

Sleep Disorders

Nightmare Disorder

The importance assigned to nightmares may vary with cultural background. In some cultures, nightmares are associated with spiritual or supernatural phenomena; in other cultures, nightmares may be viewed as indicators of mental or physical disturbances (APA, 1994, p. 581).

Sleep Terror and Sleepwalking Disorders

These disorders may differ across cultures, but clear evidence regarding culturally related differences in the presentation of these disorders is lacking (APA, 1994, pp. 584-585, 589).

Sleep Disorders Related to Another Mental Disorder

Sleep complaints may be viewed as less stigmatizing in some cultures than mental disorders. For this reason, individuals from some cultures (e.g., Southeast Asian) may be more likely to show complaints of insomnia or hypersomnia rather than complaints involving symptoms of mental disorders, such as depression and anxiety (APA, 1994, p. 594).

Impulse-Control Disorders

The culture-bound syndrome *amok* is used in the *DSM-IV* (APA, pp. 610-611) to illustrate symptoms for Intermittent Explosive Disorder in cultural terms (APA, 1994, pp. 609-612). Table 2.3 provides a general description of this syndrome (see also Paniagua, 1998, p. 131). For examples of cultural variation of Pathological Gambling Disorder and Trichotillomania, see Paniagua (1998, Tables 10.1 and 10.2, respectively).

Specific cultural variables were not suggested for many other subtypes of mental disorders in the *DSM-IV*, including Catatonic and Personality Disorders Due to a General Medical Condition (APA, 1994, pp. 169-174), Factitious Disorders (APA, 1994, pp. 471-475), Gender Identity Disorder (APA, 1994, pp. 532-538), Kleptomania (APA, 1994, pp. 612-613) and Pyromania (APA, 1994, pp. 614-615); see also Table 2.2 for additional examples. Again, readers are invited to submit new cases for this chapter with emphasis on these subtypes of mental disorders (see Table 2.2).

7

Cultural Variables With Other Conditions That May Be the Focus of Clinical Attention

In Chapters 5 and 6, several case vignettes illustrated the application of two of the three guidelines suggested by the *DSM-IV* (APA, 1994) when considering "other conditions that may be the focus of clinical attention," with emphasis on the set of V-Codes described in Chapter 2. These two guidelines apply when (a) the client has a mental disorder and a given V-Code is related with this disorder and (b) the particular V-Code is unrelated to the mental disorder the client is experiencing. The following case vignettes illustrate the applicability of the third guideline, namely, those cases in which the client is not having a mental disorder, but a particular V-Code appears to be the focus of clinical attention. Similar to Chapters 5 and 6, all cases are discussed by the editor, Dr. Freddy A. Paniagua, to ensure the commonality of interpretation of cultural variables across cases.

The Case of the Preacher
Freddy A. Paniagua, PhD

The preacher is a 47-year-old Mexican American male who came to the clinic because he was "feeling very anxious and not interested in usual activities." He requested that the interview be conducted in Spanish because he wanted to explain his situation using his "own language." This request was honored. He said that he has been serving as an evangelistic preacher for over 30 years. He said that across all these years, he has enjoyed serving a large Hispanic community. Approximately 6 months ago, he was preaching to an audience of about 500 Hispanics, and during a moment of his speech, he started feeling "very sick," including difficulty in breathing, trembling and shaking, sweating, and other symptoms, which "forced him" to seek medical help. The preacher reported that he discussed this incident with his wife and children and that they advised him to seek medical attention because he was probably having "problems with [his] heart." The preacher reported that he went to see a medical doctor and that he was told that "[he] is a healthy man, with no significant medical problems." The medical doctor, Hispanic and familiar with the preacher's strong religious activities for several years, also recommended that the Preacher should see a mental health professional because those symptoms were probably psychological and not medical in nature. The preacher reported that he did not follow this recommendation immediately because he wanted to wait to see if "God could give [him] the assurance that things will be okay" the next time he preached. He tried to preach several times after that visit to the medical doctor, but he continued experiencing similar symptoms, to the point that he started feeling very afraid to go out of his house to go to church because he could not stop thinking that he will die.

During his reports of about symptoms, the preacher held a Bible all the time. He was asked to think about what events could have led to the way he is feeling. He looked at the Bible for several seconds and then said that he is having spiritual conflicts with God. When asked to elaborate on this point, he added that he knows that he should continue preaching the words of God but that after so many years preaching, he feels he should take a break. He said that each time he is at the podium preaching, he starts thinking about *that* conflict, and that is when he begins to feel symptoms resembling a panic attack. He said that he has also felt depressed at home thinking about his spiritual conflicts with God. He said several times during this intake that his conflicts with God are "telling [him]" that he is "questioning his own church membership and [his] faith in God"; thinking about this apparent lack of loyalty to his church and God was a major issue in the preacher's emotional state.

When asked about his family, he said that he is happy with his marriage. His wife and her son and three daughters and other members of his extended family had provided emotional support and encouraged him to seek mental health treatment for his emotional difficulties. He said these family members support him "both spiritually and as a good father."

The mental status indicated that he was alert and oriented. He denied suicidal ideation or attempts. His thoughts appeared coherent and within the context expected by someone heavily involved in religious matters. Psychotic and delusional symptoms were not revealed during the intake.

The preacher was told that he might be experiencing those symptoms because he recognizes that it is very difficult for him to stop serving God the way he has been doing for many years. He was asked if he would like to have individual psychotherapy to discuss in detail his spiritual conflict with God, and he said that this is "precisely [what I] want to do." He said that he needed this service immediately but that he could not return to the clinic soon because he lives too far away. He asked about assistance in looking for a mental health professional in his area who could provide the service he needed to deal with such spiritual conflicts. He was told that the present therapist is familiar with several Spanish mental health professionals in his area and that one of them could be contacted. The preacher agreed with this plan.

Discussion of the Case of the Preacher
Freddy A. Paniagua

General Discussion

Is the preacher having a mental disorder? His report of symptoms suggests a panic attack, probably Panic Disorder with Agoraphobia (APA, 1994, p. 402). The possibility of the development of Social Phobia should also be ruled out (APA, 1994, pp. 411-417). The preacher's intensive fear of having a spiritual conflict with God, however, might suggest that rather than a mental disorder, the focus of clinical attention should be related with the V-Code (62.89) "Religious or Spiritual Problem," in which a client would show symptoms for a mental disorder resulting from his or her "distressing experiences that involve loss or questioning of faith, problems associated with conversion to a new faith, or questioning spiritual values" (APA, 1994, p. 685). Therefore, with permission from the preacher, a mental health professional in his area (fluent in Spanish and familiar with the Mexican American culture in that particular area) was contacted and briefed about this case. This professional agreed that the treatment plan should emphasize assisting the preacher with the exploration of alternative, positive responses to deal with his spiritual conflicts with God.

In addition to individual psychotherapy, cognitive-behavioral interventions would also be suggested in that plan. In these interventions, emphasis would be placed on the preacher's negative thoughts involving the belief that if he takes a break from his usual preaching activities, this decision is (in that belief system) an indication that he is questioning his faith in God. The fact was that the preacher felt tired from preaching for so many years, and he thought his desire to stop preaching should be discussed with him in terms of the expected responses of someone who has been extensively involved in this activity for many years. Taking a break from his preaching activity would not necessarily indicate that he questioned his faith in God or intended to abandon his church. The extended family involvement in this treatment plan would also be critical, including not only his biological family but also church members. The goal for the inclusion of these individuals (an opportunity for the preacher to receive social and spiritual support), however, should be discussed with the preacher before the others are invited to participate in the treatment plan, designed to assist the preacher to deal positively with his spiritual conflicts with God.

Cultural Formulation

In the treatment plan, the following five elements of this formulation (see Chapter 2) should be considered: (a) language preference (the preacher asked to be interviewed in Spanish), (b) spiritual conflicts as a cultural explanation of present symptoms, (c) availability of social and spiritual support from members of the extended family, (d) availability of Spanish-speaking mental health professionals, and (e) a detailed description of the particular cultural variable selected in that plan as the focus of clinical attention.

The Case of Peter
Man Keung Ho, PhD

Peter, a 14-year-old Korean-born Asian American boy, was referred by the school counselor who was concerned about Peter's withdrawn attitude toward school and his peers. Peter did fine academic work, but he was isolated from his peers and gradually became a recluse. Peter was born in Seoul, Korea. Three months after he was born, he was adopted by a Caucasian couple who lived in a small midwestern town in the United States. Peter's adjustment in the adoptive home has been smooth. However, despite his fluency in the English language, Peter was constantly treated by his classmates and teachers as a foreigner. In addition to feeling ambivalent about others' mistaken identification of him, Peter was embarrassed by the fact that despite his Asian physical appearance, he knew nothing about the Korean culture and language. Peter's ambivalence turned into stress, particularly when he reached his 14th birthday, and there were more informal gatherings between girls and boys.

During the first two therapy sessions, Peter was guarded in his interaction with the therapist. He claimed that there was nothing wrong with wanting to be by himself. The therapist supported Peter's right and discretion in choosing to be alone. However, the therapist inquired about the nature of his thoughts while he was alone. Peter answered that he thought about a lot while alone, but could offer no specific thought patterns of subject matter that he wanted to disclose to the therapist. Peter then volunteered that he listened to music a lot while he was alone. The therapist inquired if Peter would bring his favorite music tape to the next therapy session. Peter replied, "I guess."

During the next session, Peter reluctantly played his favorite song by Garth Brooks, titled "I Got Friends in Low Places." The therapist listened with great interest. He asked Peter what particular aspect of the song he liked best. Peter answered that the son represented his feelings that he just "didn't fit into" the circle of friends he liked, and that regardless of where he was, he just felt "out of place." Upon empathizing with Peter's ambivalence and distress, the therapist engaged him in discussions about the importance of self-acceptance and his unique biculturalism. Instead of being forced to choose between races, Peter was helped to accept and take advantage of his Asian appearance and American culture and lifestyle.

SOURCE: "Peter—Korean-Born Asian American Boy." From Man Keung Ho, *Minority Children and Adolescents in Therapy* (p. 130). Copyright © 1992 by Sage Publications, Inc.

Discussion of the Case of Peter
Freddy A. Paniagua

General Discussion

Peter could be experiencing a mood disorder (e.g., Major Depression), an anxiety disorder (e.g., Social Phobia), an Adjustment Disorder with Depressed Mood, or early development of a more severe mental disorder (e.g., Schizoid Personality Disorder). However, Peter's ambivalence around his own race and how others perceived him (e.g., his physical characteristics did not match his knowledge of the Korean culture, and he was not fluent in that language) suggest a racial identity problem (i.e., V-Code 313.82 in the *DSM-IV*). If true, rather than treating Peter's "mental disorder," a better treatment strategy would be to engage Peter in discussing his ambivalence involving this racial identity problem experienced by other adolescents adopted by people who do not share either the person's race or ethnic background. This is precisely that the therapist in this case did: Music therapy was used to stimulate Peter's involvement in issues involving biculturalism and how this phenomenon could lead to a racial identity problem that then led to symptoms resembling a mental disorder.

Cultural Formulation

Peter's case is another example of the importance of considering the cultural identity of the client (see Table 2.4). In this specific case, the treatment goal would emphasize Peter's understanding of his role in the cultural reference group into which he was adopted. Peter's statement that "there was nothing wrong with wanting to be alone" may suggest a polite manner to avoid talking about the critical event, which could explain why he elected to be alone in the first place, namely, a racial identity problem and his inability to deal with this problem in terms of the display of adaptive behaviors expected by the school counselor who referred Peter to the clinic because of his withdrawn attitude toward school and his peers. The case vignette did not specify the race or ethnic background of the therapist assessing Peter's "maladaptive" behaviors, but the fact that the therapist used music therapy to promote Peter's verbalization of his feeling involving the racial identity problem is an example of a culturally sensitive approach when dealing with issues a client avoids discussing openly during the early stage of therapy (e.g., in this case, the therapist was able to deal with the core of Peter's problems during the third therapy session, using music therapy as a mediator in the facilitation of the client's willingness to talk about the central problem leading to his so-called maladaptive behaviors). In the overall cultural assessment for diagnosis and care of Peter (see Table 2.4), a clinician would point out (in the treatment plan) that symptoms reported by Peter appear to be culturally related, with emphasis on his difficulty in adjusting his Asian appearance with the American culture and styles (the central therapy goal mentioned at the end of the case).

The Case of Ron Tiger
Man Keung Ho, PhD

Ron Tiger, a 10-year-old American Indian boy, was experiencing increased difficulty both in school and at home. The most alarming incident, which brought the family to the clinic for help, was when Ron passed out from heavy glue sniffing.

Upon interviewing Ron's mother, who was a Cherokee, the therapist learned that Ron had been a "normal" child until recently, when he became withdrawn. Mrs. Tiger apologetically attributed Ron's withdrawal to her marital discord with her husband, who is a Hopi Indian. Mrs. Tiger also volunteered that a majority of her conflict with her husband centered around his passivity, especially in disciplining their son. In the therapist's interview with Mr. Tiger, who was a kind, soft-spoken, mild-mannered man, Mr. Tiger explained that in the Hopi tribe, the husband moved into his wife's household. The wife, in this particular tribe, had primary responsibility for child rearing. The husband's responsibility was to raise his sister's children, especially the male children.

Mr. Tiger moved with his parents to a large city when he was 15. When he was 20, he married his present wife. During the couple's courtship and until the couple had their first child, his wife was impressed with his interest and concern for young children, especially his sister's children. After the couple had their own child, Mrs. Tiger was disappointed with the apathy her husband showed toward the new baby. She rationalized her husband's apathetic behavior by saying he did not relate to infants as well. She later discovered that Mr. Tiger's apathetic behavior, especially with discipline, did not change as their child grew older. This began to create problems in their marriage.

The therapist inquired what efforts the couple had attempted previously to rectify the discipline problem. Mrs. Tiger disappointedly related that the couple had gone to see a marriage counselor once but never returned. Mr. Tiger did not like that counselor and felt he sided with his wife and insisted that a father should discipline his child.

With the permission of Mr. Tiger, the therapist consulted with an elder from Mr. Tiger's tribe. This elder then privately advised Mr. Tiger that his previously learned taboo of shared parental responsibility for his child applied only to marriage within the same tribe. Because his wife was from a different tribe, the prohibition did not apply.

SOURCE: "Ron Tiger—American Indian Boy." From Man Keung Ho, *Minority Children and Adolescents in Therapy* (pp. 154-155). Copyright © 1992 by Sage Publications, Inc.

Discussion of the Case of Ron Tiger
Freddy A. Paniagua

General Discussion

The case does not give enough details leading to a particular psychiatric diagnosis, but it is clear that Ron is not the individual who needs help, but his parents do. This case deals with one specific cultural variable leading to the V-Code, "Partner Relational Problem" (V61.1, APA, 1994, p. 681). Both parents were correct in their views concerning who should discipline Ron and this was precisely the factor that led to their marital difficulty requiring the attention of a mental health professional. The counselor who initially provided service to Mr. Tiger and his wife probably tried to resolve this difficulty by emphasizing cultural disciplinary norms outside the American Indian community; this is why Ron's parents did not return for additional counseling. With the second counselor, however, a culturally sensitive approach was used: consultation with an elder from Mr. Tiger's tribe. This consultation was in accord with general guidelines in the literature that recommend that individuals with great respect in the American Indian community (e.g., the elderly, tribal leaders, medicine men or women) should be consulted to minimize biases when assessing and treating clients from this racial group (see Walker & LaDue, 1986, pp. 176-177). For an extensive discussion of additional guidelines clinicians should consider to minimize bias during the assessment and treatment of this racial group and other culturally diverse groups, see Paniagua (1998, pp. 106-125).

Cultural Formulation

In the design of a treatment plan to deal with the present case, the following five areas should be addressed: (a) the cultural identity of the parents (e.g., cultural differences between Mr. and Mrs. Tiger regarding the management of their child was a key element in this case); (b) the client's cultural explanation of present problem (e.g., Mr. Tiger believed his wife was responsible for the management of Ron's behavior, not Mr. Tiger); (c) cultural factors related to psychosocial environment and level of functioning (e.g., seeking consultation from an elder, a key element in the extended family network among many American Indians); (d) the cultural elements of the relationship between the client and the clinician (e.g., a client-counselor racial or ethnic difference may prevent the counselor from providing culturally sensitive assessment and treatment); and (e) in the overall cultural formulation of this case, it is important to emphasize that the goal of treatment would be to help Mr. and Mrs. Tiger to understand that their marital difficulty is probably the result of two different cultural points of view regarding the sharing of disciplinary actions in the management of their child.

The Case of Jones
Derald Wing Sue, PhD, and David Sue, PhD

A recently divorced, 25-year-old Black medical student sought therapy for migraine headaches that were stress related. He felt that the racist environment of the training school and a particular professor were responsible for his problem. He proposed to deal with the problem directly by confronting his professor and accusing him of racism. It did appear that the professor had engaged in prejudiced behavior. However, it is very possible that directly confronting the professor in this manner would have led to the student's dismissal from the school. Jones also found that the choice of this strategy was at least particularly related to his unresolved feeling of anger over his recent divorce. This event had made him feel more vulnerable and the resulting bitter feelings helped in his choice of directly confronting the professor. As the client understood the impact of his divorce, he was able to consider a wider range of options that were open to him. He decided that it would be best to file a complaint with the minority affairs office. Although the tension between himself and the professor remained high, the student felt that he had chosen the best option and remained in school.

Discussion of the Case of Jones
Freddy A. Paniagua

General Discussion

Jones's case suggests Adjustment Disorder with Depressed Mood (APA, 1994, p. 624). Another possibility is Major Depression, Single Episode (APA, 1994, p. 340). Without additional details to rule out these two mental disorders, it appears that the main problem is Jones's social interaction in an environment he perceived as racist. The *DSM-IV* does not address this particular case in the V-Codes listed on pages 679 through 686. The closest V-Code would be "Occupational Problem" (V62.2, APA, 1994, p. 685) in which one would argue that Jones's perceived racism "is sufficiently severe to warrant independent clinical attention" (APA, 1994, p. 685). Empirical findings show that racial discrimination is a stressful event among many members of culturally diverse groups discussed in the present text (Yamamoto, Silva, Ferrari, & Nukariya, 1997) and particularly among African Americans (Klonoff, Landrine, & Ullman, 1999; Miller, 1992; Okun, 1996). A person's inability to handle this particular stressor (i.e., racial discrimination) could lead to symptoms resembling a given mental disorder (Adjustment Disorders, Mood Disorders, etc.). In the present case, however, Jones's perception of racism should be the focus of treatment rather than his "feeling of anger over his recent divorce." In this specific case, Jones's perception of "the racist environment of the training school" is a case of institutional racism (see Chapter 1, and Okun, 1996, pp. 220-222).

Cultural Formulation

Jones's strong cultural identity with the African American community should be emphasized in the treatment plan. In terms of Jones's cultural explanation of symptoms, he felt that racial discrimination was what led to such symptoms. His perception of being racially discriminated against should be validated by encouraging him to talk about racism in the United States and appropriate ways to deal with this phenomenon (e.g., Jones's approach to contact the minority affairs office). Jones's level of functioning improved (e.g., he decided to continue in school) once he decided to report this racial discrimination against him to the appropriate entity in school. Despite Jones's action, one would expect him to believe that racism is still a major social stressor he must confront in school, and this is when techniques such as problem solving and social skills training could be beneficial in exploring other alternative responses Jones could display to prevent that stressor (i.e., a perception of racism) from resulting in recurrent symptoms suggesting a mental disorder. Regardless of the racial or ethnic status of the clinician, the practitioner assigned to this case should have knowledge of historical factors leading to racial discrimination against members of the African American community (Gregory, 1996).

The Case of the Filipino Female
Danilo E. Ponce, PhD

A 15-year-old Filipino female was admitted to an adolescent psychiatric inpatient unit because of lack of sleep, not eating, withdrawal, isolation, inability or refusal to communicate, "bizarre behaviors" such as turning up the television in the "wee" hours of the morning, "hearing voices," and threats of killing herself if she were removed from home and placed elsewhere, such as in a hospital.

The patient and her family had migrated from the Philippines to the United States four years prior to admission. She was reportedly doing quite well until two years prior to admission when she abruptly refused to go to school. She had menarche during the summer of that school year, but other than that there were no significant events that might have precipitated her refusal to go to school. With mounting pressure from the school for her to return, her parents sent her back to the Philippines. While in the Philippines she also refused to go to school and continued her pattern of withdrawal, isolation, and uncommunicativeness; she just watched television. She came back to the United States after a year, in time for the start of school, but she still refused to attend school. Instead, she stayed in her small room (which she shared with siblings), and did not venture outside the house. The school requested mental health services, and the workers who saw her on home visits (as she absolutely resisted any efforts to take her out of the house) variously diagnosed her as having major depression, elective mutism, agoraphobia, psychotic disorder, or schizophrenia. There were initial speculations that she might have been severely physically or sexually abused, but this was quickly ruled out. Despite pressure from the school, the courts, mental health workers, and well-meaning relatives, the patient remained steadfastly in her room. She was placed on sertraline (an antidepressant) with no noticeable effect, and this was eventually discontinued. Her parents finally agreed to hospitalize her when her behavior became intolerably irritating, worrisome, and unintelligible to them.

While in the hospital, she initially assumed a catatonic posture—sitting in a corner, totally uncommunicative, not acknowledging the presence of anybody else, and refusing medications. On the second day of hospitalization, she surprisingly opened up to the treating male Filipino psychiatrist, who spoke to her in her dialect. She admitted to being very scared about being hospitalized, and recounted a tale of being publicly *shamed*, and *humiliated* by a teacher two years prior to admission (coinciding with the beginning of the symptoms) because "I could not hear what she was saying . . . something is wrong with my ears . . . I hear sloshing sounds . . . I vowed after that I will never go to school again, ever." A subsequent ear examination revealed a chronic middle ear infection, and a review of records also showed that she had had the ear infection more than two years earlier but that it was never adequately treated because the parents had no insurance and feared the expense. With this information, a treatment plan was developed that was successful in returning the girl to school.

SOURCE: From "Adolescent Psychopathology" (pp. 206-207) by Danilo E. Ponce. In W. Tseng and J. Streltzer (Eds.), *Culture and Psychopathology: A Guide to Clinical Assessment* (pp. 206-222). Copyright 1997 © by Brunner/Mazel. Reprinted by permission of the publisher.

Discussion of the Case of the Filipino Female
Freddy A. Paniagua

General Discussion

This adolescent showed clear symptoms suggesting Major Depressive Disorder with Psychotic Features (APA, 1994, p. 327, 340). Additional potential diagnoses include Panic Disorder with Agoraphobia (APA, 1994, pp. 402-403), Selective Mutism (APA, 1994, pp. 114-115) and Schizophrenia, Catatonic Type (APA, 1994, pp. 288-289). These disorders are included in Axis I in the *DSM-IV*. In this case, however, the chronic middle ear infection would be included in Axis III, which deals with "general medical conditions that are potentially relevant to the *understanding* [italics added] or management of the individual's mental disorder" (APA, 1994, p. 27). In this specific case, this adolescent was fortunate to be evaluated by a Filipino psychiatrist who correctly identified that medical condition as the key element in the understanding of symptoms suggesting one or more of the mental disorders listed earlier. This adolescent displayed symptoms suggesting a mental disorder as a way for her to escape from the stressor of being humiliated by her teachers in those situations in which she could not perform as expected by teachers because of her medical complication (teachers apparently were not aware of this complication). Under this circumstance, the focus of clinical attention is not a given mental disorder but to assist teachers with the understanding of the medical condition leading to such symptoms, as well as to help this adolescent with her adjustment in the school environment without the need to escape from it by displaying symptoms suggesting a mental disorder. In the general discussion of this case, Dr. Ponce correctly concluded that this adolescent was "inappropriately . . . diagnosed as having a psychiatric disorder(s), hospitalized, and treated with psychotropic medications" (Ponce, 1997, p. 208).

Cultural Formulation

Three critical elements of this formulation applicable to this case include (a) cultural factors related to psychosocial environment and level of functioning (e.g., social stressor resulting from the client's immigration status, role of the extended family, etc.), (b) a cultural explanation of symptoms, and (c) the availability of clinicians sharing the race or ethnic background (e.g., language) of the client. In the first case, for example, the patient's immigration into the United States would be considered as a potential stressor enhancing the manifestation of symptoms, and although this adolescent appeared to have the support of her extended family, this support was given in the wrong direction (agreeing to send the patient back to the Philippines, which did not resolve the symptoms, and to hospitalize the patient to treat those "mental disorders") because parents did not have a clue that their daughter was suffering from a medical complication resulting in such "psychiatric symptoms."

In the cultural explanation of symptoms, those symptoms were not the result of the medical complication (a chronic middle ear infection) but the sequence of cultural variables that significantly affect many members of the Asian community: a sense of shame, humiliation, and embarrassment (losing face) in public situations (Paniagua, 1998). In the present case, Ponce (1997) discussed these cultural variables in the following terms:

> *Shame (hiya),* and *face (amor propio)* are very important and powerful dynamics in explaining psychosocial phenomena in Filipino culture. They are even more so in the adolescent girl struggling with developmental issues of identity formation. In this case, shame and loss of face were powerful enough to cause the youngster not to attend school for two years, to withstand pressure from her school, mental health workers, the courts, and her parents. (pp. 207-208)

The third element of the cultural formulation applied to this case (i.e., clinician-client race or ethnicity background), it is evident that without the intervention of a Filipino psychiatrist, who spoke to the client in her own language, it would be very difficult to reach a conclusion other than the fact that this client, indeed, experienced symptoms suggesting a mental disorder.

The Case of Ramon
Ian A. Canino, MD, and Luis H. Zayas, PhD

Ramon, a 4-year-old Puerto Rican child born in San Juan, had been in the United States for the past two years in a bilingual preschool program. He indicated difficulties understanding words and sentences, had a limited vocabulary, and his sentence production was limited both in length and complexity for a boy of his age. There had not been early signs of language developmental delays prior to his arrival in the United States. A teacher had alarmed the parents by stating that the child had a receptive and expressive language disorder and that they should apply to a special education school for the next year. The parents sought further advice and a battery of standardized measures were administered by a bilingual and bicultural psychologist. No disorder was identified, and parents were informed that the delay seemed to be related to the acquisition of two languages in a child who was within the normal range of ability but was not particularly adept in language and verbal tasks. After an additional six months, the child was developing well.

SOURCE: From "Puerto Rican Children" by Ian Canino & Luis H. Zayas (Case Example, pp. 73-74). In G. Johnson-Powell & J. Yamamoto (Eds.), *Transcultural Child Development: Psychological Assessment and Treatment* (pp. 61-79). Copyright © 1997 by John Wiley & Sons, reprinted by permission of the publisher.

Discussion of the Case of Ramon
Freddy A. Paniagua

General Discussion

The teacher in this case "alarmed the parents" with the "finding" that Ramon was experiencing two communication disorders namely, Expressive Language Disorder (APA, 1994, pp. 55-58) and Mixed Receptive-Expressive Language Disorder (APA, 1994, pp. 58-61). (In the *DSM-IV,* a receptive language problem is assumed to be accompanied by an expressive language problem. For this reason, a child experiencing a receptive language disorder would be diagnosed with a Mixed Receptive-Expressive Language problem.) Two alternative learning disorders the teacher "missed" (and Ramon's parents were probably glad the teacher missed them) were Reading Disorder (APA, 1994, pp. 48-50) and Disorder of Written Expression (APA, 1994, pp. 51-53). In the case of a reading disorder, Ramon probably had difficulty reading at the level expected by the teacher; in the second disorder, Ramon probably displayed poor paragraph organization, multiple spelling errors, and excessively poor handwriting, all of which are important features in diagnosing a child with a Disorder of Written Expression (see APA, 1994, p. 52). In the assessment of these disorders, however, the *DSM-IV* is very explicit about taking into account the individual's cultural language. This is particularly important to emphasize for persons growing up in bilingual settings, which is true of Puerto Rico in which both English and Spanish are spoken. This is the point that the teacher missed, and it also explains why the therapists in this case were correct in not diagnosing Ramon with a communication disorder. Ramon also received a series of standardized measures of language development and of nonverbal intellectual capacity relevant to his culture and linguistic group.

Clinicians assessing the possibility of language and intellectual problems in Hispanic children are advised to seek appropriate cultural consultation from mental health professionals trained in the use of psychometric tests (e.g.,

Golden, 1990) prior to concluding that the particular client is experiencing a given communication disorder (or for that matter, any other disorder in which language and intellectual difficulties are the central features, such as in the diagnosis of mental retardation, learning disorders, and communication disorders; see APA, 1994, pp. 39-65).

Cultural Formulation

The treatment plan in this case would explore cultural variations between academic settings in Puerto Rico and similar settings in the United States and then present these variations to teachers as an alternative in the explanation of the assumed mental disorder. The diagnostic team correctly concluded that Ramon was not experiencing a mental disorder but rather academic problems resulting from his exposure to an academic setting different from the one he experienced at the age of 2 in Puerto Rico. Under this circumstance, the V-Code "Academic Problem" (APA, 1994, p. 685) would be considered as the focus of clinical attention but with emphasis on potential cultural variables preventing Ramon from performing (academically) at the level expected by his teachers. The fact that Ramon's parents were alarmed with the teacher's conclusion regarding Ramon's academic difficulties suggests that they did not perceive the same difficulties in their son and decided (rightly) to seek a second opinion. The diagnostic team selected a bilingual and bicultural psychologist in response to the parents' request. This scenario points to a recognition of the cultural identity of the client and his family (both from Puerto Rico), as well as an effort to prevent misdiagnosing Ramon with a mental disorder by controlling cultural and ethnic differences between the client and the diagnostician (see APA, 1994, p. 844).

The Case of Natalia
Ian A. Canino, MD, and Luis H. Zayas, PhD

Natalia, a Puerto Rican second grader, is the oldest of two daughters of an intact Puerto Rican family who had recently moved to a middle-income suburban community. Her mother was expecting a third child and her father was employed as a handyman in a small apartment complex where they resided. Her teacher became concerned with how shy, reticent, apparently anxious, and unassertive Natalia was in the classroom. Natalia seldom spoke up in class, never raised her hand, and answered only questions posed to her by the teacher. Natalia did not present any behavioral problems, but in fact was exceedingly cooperative when asked by the teacher to assist her (e.g., running an errand to the principal's office). At recess, Natalia chatted animatedly with other girls, according to the teacher, but would become quiet when an adult approached. In a routine teacher-parent conference, the teacher raised her concerns with Natalia's mother, whose English was quite limited. Hearing that the teacher was "worried" about Natalia alarmed the mother. Natalia's mother discussed her concerns with her husband, who had been unable to attend the meeting. More fluent in English than his spouse, Natalia's father spoke with the teacher and could not understand why the teacher was so concerned when Natalia was doing quite well. Tension developed between the parents and the teacher, with the parents feeling that Natalia was being targeted and the teacher feeling that the parents were overlooking Natalia's inhibitions in the classroom. In consultation with a Puerto Rican psychologist, it was apparent that both parents held to relatively traditional Puerto Rican child-rearing beliefs about the importance that children demonstrate respect and deference to adult authority, and that children comply with teachers' requests, conform to rules of the classroom, and not question the teacher or speak out of turn. When the teacher was helped to understand the cultural influences on Natalia's classroom demeanor, she became less concerned with what she had first thought to be excessive inhibition. The parents were also assisted in understanding the value held by American teachers that pupils be assertive, creative, and independent in their learning.

SOURCE: From "Puerto Rican Children" by Ian Canino & Luis H. Zayas (Case Example, pp. 67-68). In G. Johnson-Powell & J. Yamamoto (Eds.), *Transcultural Child Development: Psychological Assessment and Treatment* (pp. 61-79). Copyright © 1997 by John Wiley & Sons, reprinted by permission of the publisher.

Discussion of the Case of Natalia
Freddy A. Paniagua

General Discussion

The teacher in this case was concerned that Natalia's behavioral pattern in school appeared to differ from what is expected among "normal" non-Hispanic students. A clinician unfamiliar with cultural variants affecting Natalia's symptoms in school would conclude that she is experiencing an early development of mental disorder. For example, Natalia's symptoms might be early indication of the development of a Pervasive Developmental Disorder, most likely Childhood Disintegrative Disorder (APA, 1994, pp. 73-75), Selective Mutism (APA, 1994, pp. 114-115) and Social Phobia (1994, pp. 411-417). For *Pervasive Developmental Disorders,* the *DSM-IV* did not include a discussion of potential cultural variables that clinicians should consider when diagnosing children with these disorders. Cervantes and Arroyo (1995), however, suggested that behavioral difficulties suggesting Pervasive Developmental Disorders could be significantly influenced by culture. For example, Cervantes and Arroyo pointed out that "some Hispanic children may be judged as being impaired if comparing above behaviors to non-Hispanic behavioral norms" (p. 143), which appears to apply to the teacher reporting her concern to Natalia's parents.

For Selective Mutism, the *DSM-IV* suggests that unfamiliarity with the English language or being uncomfortable with this language could lead to mutism in immigrant children (see APA, 1994, p. 114). Natalia, however, "chatted animatedly with other girls," suggesting that English was not a problem in her communication with other people in school. Natalia, however, could still be diagnosed with Selective Mutism by an uninformed clinician about potential cultural variables affecting this case because she still *selected* a specific group (other children) and setting (e.g., recess) to interact verbally and seldom spoke in the classroom and to teachers.

For Social Phobia, the *DSM-IV* points out that "in certain cultures . . . individuals with [this disorder] may develop persistent and excessive fears of giving offense to others in social situations, instead of being embarrassed" (APA, 1994, p. 413). Extreme anxiety might result from the thought that "blushing, eye-to-eye contact, or one's body odor will be offensive to others" (APA, 1994, p. 413). As noted earlier, among Asians, this type of anxiety is known as *taijin kyofusho,* which is an example of culture-bound syndromes in the *DSM-IV* (see APA, 1994, p. 849, Guarnaccia, 1997, p. 12, and Table 2.3). From the overall narrative of this vignette, one would assume that in addition to being shy and anxious, and unwilling to talk in class, Natalia also refused to maintain eye-to-eye contact in the presence of her teacher and other adults in school, suggesting that she wanted to avoid being "offensive" to her teacher and other adults. If true, the diagnosis of Social Phobia would not be applied in this case because symptoms appear to be associated with a specific cultural context (e.g., fear that eye contact may be offensive to others).

Cultural Formulation

This case is an example of the V-Code "Relational Problem Not Otherwise Specified" (APA, 1994, pp. 681-682). It appears that Natalia's pattern of interaction between herself and the teacher led to the teacher's interpretation of that pattern as dysfunctional. This relational problem involved Natalia and her teacher as well as the teacher and parents. The treatment team correctly identified this relational problem as the focus of clinician attention, rather than a given mental disorder (which was not considered a possibility by the diagnostic team in this case). The source of that relational problem centered on Natalia's strong sense of *respeto* (respect) and deference to adult authority (see Paniagua, 1998, pp. 40-41).

Many Hispanic parents expect their children to comply with teachers' demands, follow adults' rules without questioning them, and not to speak without asking to do so (e.g., Natalia's case). Hispanic children behaving this way are considered "well-educated children" (Paniagua, 1998). Therefore, Natalia's behaviors indicated to her parents that she was "una persona bien educada" (a well-educated person), and they appeared confused to know that the teacher perceived their "educated" child having problems because Natalia engaged in behaviors culturally expected by members of the Hispanic community. Once the teacher learned about this cultural explanation of Natalia's symptoms, reports of excessive inhibition in the classroom decreased over time, which led to improved interpersonal relationships between Natalia and her teacher, as well as between this American teacher and the Hispanic parents. These improved relations also served to maintain the cultural identity of Natalia, particularly in terms of her intention to display behaviors culturally expected by Hispanic children. Because Natalia would have to adapt and use certain cultural patterns expected by American teachers (e.g., assertiveness and independence in American classrooms), assisting parents to understand the need to deal with these cultural patterns without neglecting the cultural identity of Natalia was a culturally sensitive approach in this case.

The Case of Susan
Man Keung Ho, PhD

Susan, a 15-year-old Black adolescent of [Jamaican] descent, was very angry at her mother's restriction of her excessive interaction with her peers. During the conjoint family session with Susan and her mother, who was also a single parent, Susan repeatedly wanted her mother to "chill out" and leave her alone. The mother, in turn, accused Susan of being "immature," "too Americanized," and caring only for herself and nobody else in the family.

In joining the family for therapy, the therapist utilized the technique of cultural reframing (Falicov & Karrer, 1984). By using this technique, the demands or expectations made by both Susan and her mother were analyzed in relation to the cultural values that constituted the background for the demands. Hence, the mother's demand that Susan interact less frequently with her peers and stay at home more was viewed as expressing a cultural value of familism that family takes priority over the individual. Susan's demand for greater freedom was viewed as expressing a value of individualism over family. Each value was understood to be functional, or adaptive, within its social context. The mother's definition of the situation was based upon the traditional value of the family over the individual, whereas the middle-class American value of the individual above the family is implicit in Susan's request.

Focusing on cultural differences allowed the mother-daughter conflict to shift from the individual blame of Susan or the mother to the acculturation process, which placed different demands on the adolescent and parent generations. After Susan and her mother were led to see the problem or conflict differently, from person to culture, an impartial model of the family life-cycle progression through the stages of adolescence was presented. As blaming and hostility disappeared, mother and daughter began to develop mutual trust, which in turn allowed the mother to openly share with the daughter her reluctance to see her grow up and leave her. A compromise was arranged whereby Susan would have a weekly preplanned outing with her friends and be at home at a time acceptable to her mother.

SOURCE: "Susan—Black Adolescent." From Man Keung Ho, *Minority and Adolescents in Therapy* (pp. 153-154). Copyright © 1992 by Sage Publications, Inc.

Discussion of the Case of Susan
Freddy A. Paniagua

General Discussion

Susan's symptoms do not point to a mental disorder. The following V-Codes appear to be the focus of clinical attention: Parent-Child Relational Problem (APA, 1994, p. 681) and Acculturation Problem (APA, 1994, p. 685).

Cultural Formulation

This case is a classic example of the impact of cultural variables on children and adolescents struggling to assimilate values, norms, and lifestyles of the dominant culture and the negative impact of this assimilation process on parent-child relationships. Excessive interaction with peers, a desire to be Americanized, and being an independent individual *are not maladaptive behaviors* per se, except when they are *evaluated against a culture that does not value such characteristics*. This is precisely the problem that Susan confronted with her mother. The strategy taken by the clinician to deal with this cultural conflict between Susan and her mother was not to determine who was right or wrong but to clarify cultural differences resulting from different levels of acculturation. This culturally sensitive strategy preserved the cultural identity of both Susan and her mother, brought to the attention of the family a cultural explanation of Susan's apparent maladaptive behaviors, and reestablished a sense of familism in Susan's interactions with her mother. In addition, this case also illustrates the central argument in the universalistic hypothesis described earlier (see Chapter 6, The Case of Sylvia, and Paniagua, 1998, pp. 6-8): that the racial or ethnic match between the client and the clinician is not a critical variable in the assessment and treatment of culturally diverse clients in those cases when the clinician is able to show cultural sensitivity and cultural competence with a given racial or ethnic group (which is the case with Susan, black adolescent, assessed and treated by an Asian clinician).

8

Practicing Clinical Cases

General Guidelines for Practicing Cases

The following cases should be used to practice clinical applications of cultural variables. This exercise includes two elements across cases, namely, (a) the clinical assessment of the case with emphasis on cultural variables and (b) the cultural formulation of the case. In the clinical assessment, three steps are suggested: (a) discussion of the *DSM-IV* Multiaxial Classification (Axes I-V, APA, 1994) should be undertaken, with emphasis on possible cultural variables explaining the disorder under consideration; (b) identification of other conditions that might be related with this disorder (i.e., V-Codes in the *DSM-IV*) and considered the focus of clinical attention should be listed and discussed; and (c) if the case does not meet criteria for any of the *DSM-IV* disorders in Axes I and II (APA, 1994), but one or more V-Codes are identified as the focus of clinical attention, a brief explanation for the reason in making this decision should be provided. Once the three steps have been fulfilled, each element of the cultural formulation should be considered (APA, 1994, Appendix I). Write a brief sentence or paragraph about each element of the cultural formulation in relation to the case being considered. For group practices, discuss among members of the group the alternative cultural explanations provided by individual members of the group (the name of the reviewer should be noted in those cases when this practice must be evaluated by an instructor prior to its discussion in class or for grading purposes). Appendix I in the *DSM-IV* should be reviewed before working on this portion of this exercise (see APA, 1994, pp. 843-849). This chapter begins with child and adolescent cases and are followed by adult cases.

CHILD AND ADOLESCENT CASES

The Case of Todd
Amor S. Del Mundo, MD

Todd is a 15-year-old African American male who was referred by his pediatrician after minor legal problems. He lives with both of his natural parents and two younger siblings. His father is an automobile mechanic and is described as even-tempered; the mother does complain that the father could be more involved with the children. His referral resulted after mental health recommended an admission for alcohol and drug rehabilitation. The mother wished to maintain him locally. His family relocated 2 years past from an inner-city neighborhood to a rural setting. Apparently, Todd did not adjust well to the transition, finding the city to be much more stimulating. He perceived his prior neighborhood as being his primary support group, whereas in his current, more rural location, he reported minimal social support from new neighbors and friends.

The history showed that Todd affiliated with friends older than he who engaged in delinquent acts (e.g., shoplifting) performed as a group (e.g., three or more boys his age or older). He denied being confrontational with theft and only shoplifted. He never confronted a victim. He endorsed only mild violent behavior and no fights. There was no use of weapons, no cruelty to animals or children, or vandalism in his history. During the clinical evaluation, Todd was already homebound because of signaling behavior problems at school and "acting as a class clown." Multiple school suspensions were also reported in the past because of similar maladaptive behaviors. His academic performance, however, was reported as above average in the past. Rating scales (e.g., Conners' scales; see Barkley, 1990) were used to supplement the clinical presentation of symptoms, and Todd scored above the cutoff scores suggesting significant problem behaviors. Todd's mother reported a great deal of irritability and anger expressed by Todd at home, as well as a tendency for Todd to awaken in an extremely irritable mood in the mornings and be quite unapproachable. The history also revealed that Todd had never been treated with long-term psychotherapy for the management of his emotional difficulties at home and in school.

Todd's family psychiatric history is extremely significant, for both parents had a history of crack cocaine abuse; however, both parents were in remission and maintaining full-time employment in the rural area, which was reported as the primary reason for their move from the city. Alcoholism in one of Todd's grandparents was also reported. Todd endorsed the use of some marijuana. He denied alcohol or other street drug use. A urine screening by his pediatrician at time of presentation was negative for drugs other than marijuana, which was reported as a consistent finding throughout the course of Todd's behavioral problems.

During the mental status exam, Todd was very well dressed and well groomed. He appeared much older than his stated age. He was initially only marginally cooperative with the exam but became more cooperative as the interview progressed. He maintained eye contact and appeared comfortable interacting with the examiner. His posture was relaxed. He was oriented to person, place, time, and situation. Evidence of psychomotor agitation or psychomotor retardation was not noted. His speech was at a normal rate, volume, and tone. Todd described his mood as "OK" and denied instances of irritability previously reported by his mother. His affect was congruent with depression, with a somewhat blunted intensity. He thought content was negative for suicidal or homicidal ideation. No evidence of paranoid delusions or grandiosity was noted. His thought content did suggest a running theme of despair with his current social situation and a certain feeling of hopelessness. His thought processes were linear and coherent, and he demonstrated good insight and judgment regarding the impact of emotional difficulties in his life and the life of others around him. Todd was diagnosed with Dysthymia and Cannabis abuse, mild and socialized. [Readers are encouraged to explore additional diagnoses and potential V-Codes in this case.] Several social stressors were identified in Axis IV (APA, 1994), including moving to a different location, which Todd did not appear to enjoy; a history of relationships with a deviant peer group, and being under probation for his maladaptive behaviors with delinquent tendencies. His current overall global assessment was GAF = 45, and 65 in the past year.

The patient was stabilized initially using SSRIs. Paxil was initially administered, supplemented with Depakote to help Todd to manage his anger. Prior to the administration of this medication, Todd had been extremely disruptive at school, including being aggressive and combative with teachers, which resulted in in-school suspension for a prolonged period. Todd did not meet criteria for admission to a local psychiatric hospital. However, the treatment team argued that Todd would benefit from inpatient treatment, in which medication management would be carefully stabilized and monitored in combination with other forms of therapy (e.g., individual psychotherapy). During this acute hospitalization, Todd continued on Paxil and Depakote and was transferred to a residential home following substantial progress in the management of his emotional difficulties. He continued in the residential home for a period of 9 months with continued improvement, including his academic performance (e.g., Todd achieved a 4.0 GPA during this residential treatment period). He continued on Depakote on returning home and maintained positive behavior at expected level in school and at home. Suspensions or detention from schools were not reported. His mother, however, continued reporting minimal instances of irritability and anger at home. Todd began to show noncompliance with the Depakote because he felt that he would become too dependent on this medication; he was also afraid of the stigma attached to seeing a psychiatrist if it became known to people outside his immediate family. To manage Todd's noncompliance with this aspect of his treatment (e.g., V-Code 15.81, "Noncompliance with Treatment" in the *DSM-IV,* APA, 1994, p. 683), he was informed that if he allowed the teachers to complete rating scales and the scores showed that he continued improving (i.e., scores below cutoff points for symptoms suggesting behavioral problems), he would be allowed to remain off the medication. Todd agreed with this stipulation, and teachers continued assessing significant improvement in Todd's general behaviors with the assistance of these scales, resulting in the removal of the medication. Todd also found a job at a local telemarketing firm and received very good evaluations from his employer. This job was within walking distance of his home, but Todd felt that he was getting behind in school and chose to discontinue his employment to concentrate his time on school tasks. Another significant improvement was that Todd's most recent urine drug screening was negative.

In conclusion, during the initial evaluation of this case, the diagnostic team considered that Todd was at risk for substance abuse from a genetic point of view. Both parents had been crack cocaine abusers and dependent on substances. It was apparent that Todd's engagement in similar maladaptive behaviors was the result of his exposure to these situations. In terms of his aggressive behavior, Todd lived in an inner-city neighborhood where he was exposed to violent behavior and also apparently modeled them over time. In addition, the parents' decision to locate the family outside the city limits and Todd's inability to change this situation probably contributed to his symptoms.

CASE: TODD   **REVIEWED BY:**_____

Clinical Assessment

List the main *DSM-IV* diagnosis or diagnoses: _____
_____

List the differential diagnosis or diagnoses: _____
_____

List V-Code(s) related with the disorder(s) _____
_____

If this case does not meet criteria for a mental disorder, which specific V-Code(s) would you consider as the focus of clinical attention and why?_____
_____

Which cultural variables might be considered in the diagnosis and differential diagnosis of this case? _____
_____

Cultural Formulation

Cultural identity of the client:_____
_____

Cultural explanation of the individual's illness: _____
_____

Cultural factors related to psychosocial environment and level of functioning:_____
_____

Cultural elements of the relationship between the client and the clinician: _____
_____

Overall cultural assessment for diagnosis and care of the present mental disorder:_____
_____

The Case of Chow

Larke Nahme Huang, PhD, and Yu-Wen Ying, PhD

Mrs. Chow requested therapy for the family because of her fourteen-year-old son's outbursts in the home, his poor school grades, and her concerns that he would become a "delinquent." Their first session was with a Chinese American female therapist. Mrs. Chow and her son did most of the talking. She focused on her son's unmanageable behavior, speaking angrily toward him, and then began blaming the father for his inability to control his son. The son, experiencing severe identity conflicts, also seemed angry and accused his father of being too "Chinesey." His father remained quiet, contributing little to the interaction. However, the family failed to return for subsequent sessions, never directly canceling the sessions with the therapist but leaving messages with excuses in response to the therapist's inquiries.

SOURCE: From "Chinese American Children and Adolescents," by Larke Nahme Huang & Yu-Wen Ying. In J. T. Gibbs & L. N. Huang (Eds.), *Children of Color: Psychological Interventions With Culturally Diverse Youth* (pp. 33-67). Copyright © 1998 by Jossey-Bass Publishers, reprinted by permission of the publisher.

CASE: CHOW   **REVIEWED BY:**_____

Clinical Assessment

List the main *DSM-IV* diagnosis or diagnoses: _____

_____

List the differential diagnosis or diagnoses: _____

_____

List V-Code(s) related with the disorder(s) _____

_____

If this case does not meet criteria for a mental disorder, which specific V-Code(s) would you consider as the focus of clinical attention and why?_____

_____

Which cultural variables might be considered in the diagnosis and differential diagnosis of this case? _____

_____

Cultural Formulation

Cultural identity of the client:_____

_____

Cultural explanation of the individual's illness: _____

_____

Cultural factors related to psychosocial environment and level of functioning:_____

_____

Cultural elements of the relationship between the client and the clinician: _____

_____

Overall cultural assessment for diagnosis and care of the present mental disorder:_____

_____

The Case of Diana
Kokab Saeed, MD

Diana, a 12-year-old Chinese American female, came because her grades were declining due to her mind being preoccupied with saying prayers excessively. Exploration revealed a 3-year history of compulsive hand washing and motor and vocal tics. There was no history of prior treatment. Her biological parents were born and raised in China and came to America in their 20s. They were divorced when the patient was 3 years old. The father was reported as a genius, with a PhD in physics, who did not believe in psychological disorders. He lived in town but never became involved in evaluation and treatment. The mother reluctantly started dispensing medication (Luvox) to Diana and kept the dosage at half the recommended dose. Diana began feeling happier, her concentration and grades improved, but the tics and compulsive behavior remained. Mother decided to discontinue medication after 5 months of treatment, claiming a friend's advice to do so.

CASE: DIANA   REVIEWED BY:_____

Clinical Assessment

List the main *DSM-IV* diagnosis or diagnoses: _____

_____

List the differential diagnosis or diagnoses: _____

_____

List V-Code(s) related with the disorder(s) _____

_____

If this case does not meet criteria for a mental disorder, which specific V-Code(s) would you consider as the focus of clinical attention and why?_____

_____

Which cultural variables might be considered in the diagnosis and differential diagnosis of this case? _____

_____

Cultural Formulation

Cultural identity of the client:_____

_____

Cultural explanation of the individual's illness: _____

_____

Cultural factors related to psychosocial environment and level of functioning:_____

_____

Cultural elements of the relationship between the client and the clinician: _____

_____

Overall cultural assessment for diagnosis and care of the present mental disorder:_____

_____

The Case of Nag
Kokab Saeed, MD

A Vietnamese mother brought her 6-year-old daughter, Nag, with a 3-day history of fever. Further history revealed a decrease in appetite and loss of energy and activity secondary to continuous fever. The mother denied use of antipyretics. Physical examination revealed a sick, febrile, dehydrated child who had no focus of infection. Her skin was dry, hot, and flushed, with significant bruises in a regular pattern. On inquiry about the bruises, the mother told about rubbing a coin on the skin to relieve the temperature. Child abuse was suspected, and Child Protective Services (CPS) was called. Mother was very upset with medical staff for accusing her of abuse. She added, "my mother used to practice coin rubbing when I had fever."

CASE: NAG   **REVIEWED BY:**_____

˙ Clinical Assessment

List the main *DSM-IV* diagnosis or diagnoses: _____

_____

List the differential diagnosis or diagnoses: _____

_____

List V-Code(s) related with the disorder(s) _____

_____

If this case does not meet criteria for a mental disorder, which specific V-Code(s) would you
consider as the focus of clinical attention and why?_____

_____

Which cultural variables might be considered in the diagnosis and differential diagnosis of this
case? _____

_____

Cultural Formulation

Cultural identity of the client:_____

_____

Cultural explanation of the individual's illness: _____

_____

Cultural factors related to psychosocial environment and level of functioning:_____

_____

Cultural elements of the relationship between the client and the clinician: _____

_____

Overall cultural assessment for diagnosis and care of the present mental disorder:_____

_____

The Case of Ken
Donna K. Nagata, PhD

Ken, a sixteen-year-old Japanese American male, reported feeling depressed and fatigued. Upon further inquiry, Ken noted that his depression had increased at the same time that recent conflicts with his parents had arisen. Ken's parents, both Nisei who had been interned as adolescents, owned and operated a family grocery store that had been in the family for two generations. They hoped that Ken, the oldest son, would take over the store after they retired. Conflicts between Ken and his parents centered on his resistance to working in the store after school and on Saturdays. Ken's parents expected him to contribute his part to the family business, but Ken resented having to spend his free time working for his parents. He pointed out that none of his Caucasian American friends had such restrictions on their schedules. In fact, Ken stated, several of his peers made fun of the fact that he was "still tied to his parent's apron strings."

Ken noted that his mother and father just "didn't understand" him. Rather than listen to him, they admonished his verbal outbursts of anger by telling him it was disrespectful to challenge their authority. Ken grew increasingly frustrated with this situation and began experiencing depressive feelings and fatigue as he internalized his frustration more and more, withdrawing from his parents and eventually his peers as well.

SOURCE: From "The Assessment and Treatment of Japanese American Children and Adolescents" by Donna K. Nagata. In J. T. Gibbs & L. N. Huang (Eds.), *Children of Color: Psychological Interventions With Culturally Diverse Youth* (pp. 68-111). Copyright 1998 © by Jossey-Bass Publishers, reprinted by permission of the publisher.

CASE: KEN   REVIEWED BY:_____

Clinical Assessment

List the main *DSM-IV* diagnosis or diagnoses: _____

_____

List the differential diagnosis or diagnoses: _____

_____

List V-Code(s) related with the disorder(s) _____

_____

If this case does not meet criteria for a mental disorder, which specific V-Code(s) would you
consider as the focus of clinical attention and why?_____

_____

Which cultural variables might be considered in the diagnosis and differential diagnosis of this
case? _____

_____

Cultural Formulation

Cultural identity of the client:_____

_____

Cultural explanation of the individual's illness: _____

_____

Cultural factors related to psychosocial environment and level of functioning:_____

_____

Cultural elements of the relationship between the client and the clinician: _____

_____

Overall cultural assessment for diagnosis and care of the present mental disorder:_____

_____

The Case of Sergio and Laura
Oscar Ramirez, PhD

Sergio, (fifteen), Laura (thirteen), and their family were seen because of the parents' concern about Sergio's "bad temper" and Laura's sexual behavior. The parents complained about Sergio's anger, poor impulse control, and self-destructive behavior, and Laura's overt interest in boys. Sergio, Mr. C. (forty-three, migrated from Mexico to the United States thirteen years before), Mrs. C. (thirty-four, born and raised in the United States), and Laura attended the first session. The Anglo intake therapist had reported that the mother was the family spokesperson, but later it was determined that the father spoke only Spanish, and the therapist was not Spanish-speaking. Accordingly, the family was transferred to the author for subsequent treatment.

The mother reported that the father was having difficulty as the children reached adolescence and began to assert themselves more, which he viewed as blatant disrespect. Both teenagers reported that they were doing well in school and related very well to the therapist. Mr. C. was emotional and articulate as he complained about his children's exposure to values and standards of morality that were considerably "lower" than what he wanted for them and what he had learned from his strict father. Sergio agreed that his father accurately described their defiant attitudes toward his values, and he explained that he and Laura constantly felt torn in two opposite directions. On the one hand was his father's strict, "old world" view of family life, in which children unquestionably accept the high moral and ethical standards set for them; on the other hand was the constant peer pressure to go along with the crowd. The adolescents pleaded with the therapist to help their father understand that they felt very conflicted emotionally and had resorted to hurting themselves as a way of releasing their tension and frustration. The therapist ended the session by translating for the father what his children had said in English and assuring him of their loyalty, love, and respect for him but also explaining the pressure they felt to be accepted by their peers at school. The therapist made three recommendations to the family: first, that all corporal punishment cease immediately; second, that the family members discuss in Spanish how they had been feeling so that the father could understand his children's emotional dilemma; and finally, that Sergio be allowed to stay temporarily with someone in the extended family in order to reduce the immediate tension in the home.

Over the next several sessions, the family improved dramatically, the level of tension decreased significantly, and there were no outbursts of aggression by anybody. Family therapy involved finding some middle ground for each teenager between the father's rules and the peer pressure to do "illicit" things for group acceptance. The mother, who was more modern in her views, acted as a mediator between her husband and the children. Finally, the father was encouraged to express nurturance and support toward his teenagers, whose earlier views of him as playful and affectionate had been replaced by experiences with him as angry and disapproving.

SOURCE: From "Mexican American Children and Adolescents," by Oscar Ramirez. In J. T. Gibbs & L. N. Huang (Eds.), *Children of Color: Psychological Interventions With Culturally Diverse Youth* (pp. 215-239). Copyright 1998 © by Jossey-Bass Publishers, reprinted by permission of the publisher.

CASE: SERGIO AND LAURA   **REVIEWED BY:**_____

Clinical Assessment

List the main *DSM-IV* diagnosis or diagnoses: _____

_____

List the differential diagnosis or diagnoses: _____

_____

List V-Code(s) related with the disorder(s) _____

_____

If this case does not meet criteria for a mental disorder, which specific V-Code(s) would you consider as the focus of clinical attention and why?_____

_____

Which cultural variables might be considered in the diagnosis and differential diagnosis of this case? _____

_____

Cultural Formulation

Cultural identity of the client:_____

_____

Cultural explanation of the individual's illness: _____

_____

Cultural factors related to psychosocial environment and level of functioning:_____

_____

Cultural elements of the relationship between the client and the clinician: _____

_____

Overall cultural assessment for diagnosis and care of the present mental disorder:_____

_____

The Case of Jill
Jewelle Taylor Gibbs, PhD

Jill, the nineteen-year-old daughter of a black mother and white father, was from a well-to-do Eastern family. After growing up in a white neighborhood and attending an exclusive prep school, she enrolled in a West Coast university for a "change of scenery." Her first year was difficult because she preferred to socialize with the white students from similar backgrounds and felt that the African American students were very hostile to her. After an unsuccessful affair with an older white male who physically abused her, she became very depressed and stopped going to classes. She was brought into the student mental health clinic by her roommate after she took an overdose of sleeping pills, and she was hospitalized for several days. Jill confided in the therapist that she felt as if she had a foot in two worlds but couldn't stand on both feet in the white world or the black world. She was very angry at her parents "for treating me like I was white and not preparing me for the real world as a black person.

SOURCE: From "Biracial Adolescents" by Jewelle Taylor Gibbs. In J. T. Gibbs & L. N. Huang (Eds.), *Children of Color: Psychological Interventions With Culturally Diverse Youth* (pp. 305-332). Copyright 1998 © by Jossey-Bass Publishers, reprinted by permission of the publisher.

CASE: JILL   **REVIEWED BY:**_____

Clinical Assessment

List the main *DSM-IV* diagnosis or diagnoses: _____

_____

List the differential diagnosis or diagnoses: _____

_____

List V-Code(s) related with the disorder(s) _____

_____

If this case does not meet criteria for a mental disorder, which specific V-Code(s) would you consider as the focus of clinical attention and why?_____

_____

Which cultural variables might be considered in the diagnosis and differential diagnosis of this case? _____

_____

Cultural Formulation

Cultural identity of the client:_____

_____

Cultural explanation of the individual's illness: _____

_____

Cultural factors related to psychosocial environment and level of functioning:_____

_____

Cultural elements of the relationship between the client and the clinician: _____

_____

Overall cultural assessment for diagnosis and care of the present mental disorder:_____

_____

The Case of Wei Lee
Larke Nahme Huang, PhD, and Yu-Wen Ying, PhD

Wei Lee, a nineteen-year-old male, was referred to the therapist by an in-patient mental health crisis unit for follow-up treatment on an inpatient basis. Wei's diagnosis was paranoid schizophrenia. Many of his delusions were race related; his feelings of persecution were based on being Chinese American and being rejected by his surrounding community. After one session with Wei, and with Wei's consent, the therapist invited his parents to meet with her. Mr. and Mrs. Lee, immigrants from China, had resided in the United States for more than twenty years, and both worked as civil servants for the city government. They were a rather traditional couple, Mr. Lee being the clear, dominant authority and Mrs. Lee being silent, in the background, and considerably more emotional. Wei was their fourth child and had been born in the United States.

Although Mr. and Mrs. Lee recognized the bizarre behavior of their son, they expressed anger and frustration toward the mental health system. They said that very little information had been shared with them, that there was no discussion of his diagnosis or treatment plan, and that after he was discharged, Wei had returned home, again became withdrawn, and stopped his medications. They reported that this was Wei's second hospitalization in two years and the pattern was exactly the same. Their questions remained unasked and unanswered, and Wei had refused to continue treatment.

The therapist discussed the diagnosis and range of possible implications, answered questions about the hospitalization and the mental health system, discussed insurance and disability payments, and employed the parents as collaborators in the treatment plan. She acknowledged the boundaries and limits of confidentiality in the individual therapy with Wei, but she also invited any calls or questions from the parents. She listened and empathized with their frustrations with their son and the mental health system, and she acknowledged Mrs. Lee's concerns about possible relations between events during her pregnancy and Wei's disorder. The meeting went beyond the designated fifty minutes.

The therapy with Wei continued for three and a half years with the support of his parents. The payment of a reduced fee was shared by Wei and his parents. Wei learned to identify environmental and personal factors that triggered his delusions and developed methods to cope with them. He began to be able to distinguish reality-based racism from his own projections. No further meetings were held with his parents, although they initiated telephone contact with the therapist about once a month. Wei made considerable gains, lived independently, worked as a grocery clerk, and visited his family regularly.

SOURCE: From "Chinese American Children and Adolescents," by Larke Nahme Huang & Yu-Wen Ying. In J. T. Gibbs & L. N. Huang (Eds.), *Children of Color: Psychological Interventions With Culturally Diverse Youth* (pp. 33-67). Copyright 1998 © by Jossey-Bass Publishers, reprinted by permission of the publisher.

CASE: WEI LEE   **REVIEWED BY:**_____

Clinical Assessment

List the main *DSM-IV* diagnosis or diagnoses: _____

_____

List the differential diagnosis or diagnoses: _____

_____

List V-Code(s) related with the disorder(s) _____

_____

If this case does not meet criteria for a mental disorder, which specific V-Code(s) would you consider as the focus of clinical attention and why?_____

_____

Which cultural variables might be considered in the diagnosis and differential diagnosis of this case? _____

_____

Cultural Formulation

Cultural identity of the client:_____

_____

Cultural explanation of the individual's illness: _____

_____

Cultural factors related to psychosocial environment and level of functioning:_____

_____

Cultural elements of the relationship between the client and the clinician: _____

_____

Overall cultural assessment for diagnosis and care of the present mental disorder:_____

_____

The Case of Andrew
Jewelle Taylor Gibbs, PhD

Andrew was a nineteen-year-old [African American] sophomore in a private "elite" college. He was referred to the counseling center for assaulting a white male student in his dormitory. After initially acting very suspicious and hostile toward the female therapist, he eventually formed a good working alliance with her, facilitated by a positive transference that was not interpreted. Andrew reported that he had attacked the student after a series of incidents in which several white students had made fun of his southern accent, his Afro haircut, and his clothes, all of which he interpreted as racist comments. The short-term treatment focused on helping Andrew to express his feelings about being a "token" African American who was always under a microscope, his doubts about his ability to achieve in the highly competitive environment, and his anger about being rejected by a white girlfriend. His self-esteem and feelings of competence were enhanced by encouraging him to identify the talents and skills that had gained him admission to college, and to review his actual college performance, which was above average. In addition, his ambivalence toward socializing with other African American students was explored and he was able to reevaluate and reframe his social options. Finally, the therapist helped Andrew to recognize those situations that particularly triggered his rather explosive temper, and to develop more socially acceptable ways of channeling his anger.

SOURCE: From "African American Adolescents," by Jewelle Taylor Gibbs. In J. T. Gibbs & L. N. Huang (Eds.), *Children of Color: Psychological Interventions With Culturally Diverse Youth* (pp. 171-214). Copyright 1998 © by Jossey-Bass Publishers, reprinted by permission of the publisher.

CASE: ANDREW   **REVIEWED BY:**_____

Clinical Assessment

List the main *DSM-IV* diagnosis or diagnoses: _____

_____

List the differential diagnosis or diagnoses: _____

_____

List V-Code(s) related with the disorder(s) _____

_____

If this case does not meet criteria for a mental disorder, which specific V-Code(s) would you consider as the focus of clinical attention and why?_____

_____

Which cultural variables might be considered in the diagnosis and differential diagnosis of this case? _____

_____

Cultural Formulation

Cultural identity of the client:_____

_____

Cultural explanation of the individual's illness: _____

_____

Cultural factors related to psychosocial environment and level of functioning:_____

_____

Cultural elements of the relationship between the client and the clinician: _____

_____

Overall cultural assessment for diagnosis and care of the present mental disorder:_____

_____

CLINICAL ADULT CASES

The Case of Mr. Diaz
Antonio E. Puente, PhD, and Gabriel D. Salazar, BA

Mr. Diaz is a 25-year-old Mexican male quadriplegic confined to a wheelchair as a result of a work-related accident in which he fell out of a tree. He is unable to meander without the assistance of this machine. However, he is very adept at it. Mr. Diaz's history, clinical evaluation, and cultural issues will be discussed in further detail.

Mr. Diaz was born in rural Mexico to a semiliterate farmer and an illiterate seamstress. As a child, he did not learn to walk until he was almost 2 years old. Mr. Diaz did not like school and was not a particularly good learner. Although he can read and write (in Spanish only), he terminated school in the fifth grade. Mr. Diaz then began to work and began working full time around the age of 15 at a car assembly plant as well as in construction.

Mr. Diaz has been in the United States for 4 years, working primarily as a construction worker. His mother came a year ago to help him after the accident. Up until about 3 months before the accident, Mr. Diaz was a copious consumer of alcohol, drinking on a regular daily basis. He is one of 12 siblings, with 5 brothers and 6 sisters. They are all unskilled laborers. Two of his brothers are deceased, one of diabetes and the other in a motor vehicle accident. Five of his other siblings live in the United States. They all apparently have a good relationship.

An interview was conducted with Mr. Diaz's primary caregiver (his youngest sister), and she said that his behavior is very erratic. Sometimes, he wants to leave the house, and other times, he just wants to sleep. She says he is also paranoid about other people's intentions and is disoriented as to time and location. She also noted that he spent 4 months in a nursing home where he did not receive adequate care. Mr. Diaz's mother added that he forgets things very easily and repeats himself regularly. It is also difficult for him to make decisions and needs others to assist him.

Mr. Diaz recalled how bad life has been since the accident. It is interesting that he talks more about his traumatic response to the events that have occurred since the accident rather than the accident itself. He describes in vivid detail how terrible it was to be in the nursing home where people ignored his requests for different kinds of assistance or how they inadvertently dropped him on the floor for an extended period of time and how they did not make an effort to try and deal or understand his requests or demands. He seemed traumatized by the event and continues experiencing difficulties in adjusting to limitations associated with his current situation at home. He says he is extremely depressed from staying at home and does not know what to do. The insurance company is handling his care, and Mr. Diaz is having trouble understanding how Workmen's Compensation and rehabilitation work.

Mr. Diaz's diagnosis is depression superimposed on closed head injury. He attends for only small amounts of time, and his vocabulary is very limited. He has difficulty handling the demands of his situation. As a consequence, most people, including his family, do not realize how complicated life is for him.

Mr. Diaz presents a rare case in that he is quadriplegic. Not only is he unclear about the Worker's Compensation system, he is also having trouble understanding his legal case, rehabilitation, and intervention. These factors, coupled with the fact that neither he nor his family speak English, make his case even more complicated.

CASE: MR. DIAZ   **REVIEWED BY:**_____

Clinical Assessment

List the main *DSM-IV* diagnosis or diagnoses: _____

_____

List the differential diagnosis or diagnoses: _____

_____

List V-Code(s) related with the disorder(s) _____

_____

If this case does not meet criteria for a mental disorder, which specific V-Code(s) would you consider as the focus of clinical attention and why?_____

_____

Which cultural variables might be considered in the diagnosis and differential diagnosis of this case? _____

_____

Cultural Formulation

Cultural identity of the client:_____

_____

Cultural explanation of the individual's illness: _____

_____

Cultural factors related to psychosocial environment and level of functioning:_____

_____

Cultural elements of the relationship between the client and the clinician: _____

_____

Overall cultural assessment for diagnosis and care of the present mental disorder:_____

_____

The Case of Elena Rodriguez
Virginia S. Burlingame, PhD

Elena Rodriguez, age 64, the eldest of five, was born in San Juan in 1933 to poor parents who migrated to New York City when Elena was 3. They hoped for employment and a better life but did not find either. The father became disabled from polio. The mother, overwhelmed with family responsibilities, had serious episodes of depression that required hospitalization. Neighbors helped but mostly Elena, who dropped out of school in ninth grade, kept house and cared for her siblings. The family, on general relief, survived marginally in Brooklyn and never revisited Puerto Rico.

Later Elena was proud to assure her mother she was a good girl and virgin when she married a coworker, Carlos Rodriguez. Soon afterward, Marita and Pepe were born. The family was fairly happy despite financial struggles. Mrs. Rodriguez counseled her two sisters—one on drugs, the other, a runaway—she nursed her sickly mother, and raised her own children. She never saw her brothers.

Carlos Rodriguez, a strict father and possessive husband, was protective of his family, but on weekends he partied with friends, leaving Mrs. Rodriguez at home. In 1970, he was fatally shot in a drive-by shooting. His wife said that her devotion to Catholicism, which incorporated what she called spiritualism and *espiritistas,* helped her through. She believed *fatalismo,* that "there was always a reason."

When her mother developed cancer, Mrs. Rodriguez gave her herbs from Brazil and the West Indies as well the doctor's medicine. She sang a song at "Mommi's" funeral, honoring her as a "saint," knowing she was now entering the gates of heaven and all was now perfect.

Mrs. Rodriguez was referred to a Puerto Rican agency—the Instituto—by a home care worker because she was not eating or sleeping well, cried often, and wanted to die. Now obese, and with hypertension, gallstones, and heart disease, she was homebound, alone in public housing. Her children seldom came to see her. This was due to conflict over Marita's sexual behaviors—an illegitimate baby and a series of live-in boyfriends—and Pepe's gang membership, with its culture of drugs and jail.

Mrs. Rodriguez made no secret of the fact that her children were causing her illness and unhappiness. She herself had done what her mother wanted and had always been there for her mother. Now, at her own hour of need, her children were not there for her. This was her worst disappointment.

Although she was a law-abiding person, Mrs. Rodriguez had many confrontations with the legal system over Pepe's problems. She also felt ashamed about trying to get Marita and the baby onto AFDC. Therefore, she viewed the referral to the Instituto with suspicion.

Carmen M., a Spanish-speaking worker with both *personalismo* and *dignidad,* was assigned to her case. Ms. M. engaged Mrs. Rodriguez in talk about their homeland and offered concrete help with home services. Mrs. Rodriguez asked her some personal questions. Lonely and abandoned, she liked talking about commonalities and she got Ms. M. to do practical things—help move this; get that out of the refrigerator. Because of the client's many needs, the worker's visits lengthened. "Mrs. Rodriguez has no one to talk to," Ms. M. told her supervisor, but she knew that these long visits were causing her to work overtime and to neglect her other clients.

Ms. M. and her supervisor revised the care plan. Because of the good rapport she had developed with Mrs. Rodriguez, Ms. M. was able to explain the new limits so that the client would not feel rejected. A Spanish-speaking telephone reassurance service was tried and a goal was to enlist Marita. Ms. M. advised Marita: "Even if you don't think your mother deserves your special attention now, you might feel better about yourself for helping her—so do it for yourself. It is *familismo.*

Ms. M. knew that Mrs. Rodriguez would soon need a nursing home. The client was relying heavily on home remedies from *botanicas* and herbalists, and she liked spicy, salty foods; thus she was noncompliant with her medical regimen. Ms. M. was surprised when Pepe and Marita vetoed the nursing home, saying, "We don't believe in that." Ms. M. felt stuck.

SOURCE: From *"Ethnogerocounseling: Counseling Elders and Their Families,"* by Virginia S. Burlingame, copyright 1999 © by Springer Publishing Company, reprinted by permission of the publisher.

CASE: ELENA RODRIGUEZ   **REVIEWED BY:_____**

Clinical Assessment

List the main *DSM-IV* diagnosis or diagnoses: _____

_____

List the differential diagnosis or diagnoses: _____

_____

List V-Code(s) related with the disorder(s) _____

_____

If this case does not meet criteria for a mental disorder, which specific V-Code(s) would you consider as the focus of clinical attention and why?_____

_____

Which cultural variables might be considered in the diagnosis and differential diagnosis of this case? _____

_____

Cultural Formulation

Cultural identity of the client:_____

_____

Cultural explanation of the individual's illness: _____

_____

Cultural factors related to psychosocial environment and level of functioning:_____

_____

Cultural elements of the relationship between the client and the clinician: _____

_____

Overall cultural assessment for diagnosis and care of the present mental disorder:_____

_____

The Case of Lucy Longfeather
Virginia S. Burlingame, PhD

Lucy Longfeather, age 79, lived her entire life on the Jemez Pueblo near Santa Fe, New Mexico. This small compact village, a family-clan in itself, is chiefly agricultural. Mrs. Longfeather's life centered on child care, crafts, and housekeeping. Except for infrequent trips to the IHS in Santa Fe, she seldom left the pueblo, as she lacked transportation and had little facility in English. She spoke some Spanish, but she preferred her native Towa language, and that often created problems of communication with the outside world and even with her grandchildren.

Mrs. Longfeather married Jim Longfeather in 1936 and they later had four children. They lived in terraced adobe with no modern conveniences; thus they had to carry water in, use an outhouse, and chop wood for heat.

Jim Longfeather died of cancer in 1987. Throughout his illness, the family had refused to talk about his condition or to touch him. He was buried in an unmarked grave without ado; but yearly, on November 1, All Soul's Day, the family members bring his favorite foods and celebrate with his spirit at the grave.

Mrs. Longfeather tried living alone in her home, relying on her granddaughter for transportation. She took meals at the tribal meal site for sociability, or meals were delivered to her home when she took care of her great grandchildren, who were not eligible for the senior meal program. Most health care—monitoring her arthritis and cataracts—was provided on the pueblo and financed by Medicare, Medicaid, and the IHS. In 1990, her children noticed that she was confused at night and that her thinking was disorganized. She couldn't remember and was often lost.

The family moved Mrs. Longfeather into a daughter's new adobe ranch home, which had modern conveniences but was isolated and even further from the pueblo. Mrs. Longfeather was not comfortable there, even with a telephone and a television set. A large extended family resided there, and she tried hard to take care of the very young children while others were gone for many hours during the day. Her condition worsened. She was finally taken to the IHS hospital in Santa Fe with added presenting symptoms: impaired gait, incontinence, and confusion. A geriatric multidisciplinary team made the diagnosis of Alzheimer's-type dementia.

The patient's support system was also assessed. Dorothy G., the social worker, with the cooperation of Mrs. Longfeather's eldest son, invited the entire family for sessions. The tribal elder code was consulted, and although the sons were not expected to become caregivers, they were specified as spokespersons. Ms. G. told the family about a nursing home in the area staffed by a few American Indian nurses who spoke Towa. Native

foods were offered, and Mrs. Longfeather could have day passes to celebrate powwows and feast days with the family. Ms. G. emphasized that
Mrs. Longfeather would not have a male nurse, that no one at the nursing
home would throw away any of her hair, etc.

Dorothy G. complimented the family members for their concern but
pointed out that they could no longer help Mrs. Longfeather in the old way.
She gave basic concrete information about the needs of Alzheimer's patients, levels of nursing care, and the dementia unit; and she stressed that
Mrs. Longfeather was not crazy. She noted that no caregivers' support
groups were available.

The family resisted, saying that the pueblo would criticize them and talk
about them. It was wrong to make such a decision. Dorothy G. reframed
their concerns and said that it might look like they were neglecting their
mother by *not* getting her the help she needed. She reminded them that
they mustn't neglect their own children or their jobs but also that they
could not leave their mother alone anymore. She suggested that they try a
30-day nursing home respite. She also offered to help them get permission
for placement from their tribal council, and to get the medicine man's ap-
proval as well.

SOURCE: From "*Ethnogerocounseling: Counseling Elders and Their Families,*" by Virginia S.
Burlingame, copyright 1999 © by Springer Publishing Company, reprinted by permission of the
publisher.

CASE: LUCY LONGFEATHER   **REVIEWED BY:**_____

Clinical Assessment

List the main *DSM-IV* diagnosis or diagnoses: _____
_____

List the differential diagnosis or diagnoses: _____
_____

List V-Code(s) related with the disorder(s) _____
_____

If this case does not meet criteria for a mental disorder, which specific V-Code(s) would you consider as the focus of clinical attention and why?_____
_____

Which cultural variables might be considered in the diagnosis and differential diagnosis of this case? _____
_____

Cultural Formulation

Cultural identity of the client:_____
_____

Cultural explanation of the individual's illness: _____
_____

Cultural factors related to psychosocial environment and level of functioning:_____
_____

Cultural elements of the relationship between the client and the clinician: _____
_____

Overall cultural assessment for diagnosis and care of the present mental disorder:_____
_____

The Case of Mr. Jimenez
Antonio E. Puente, PhD, and Gabriel D. Salazar, BA

Mr. Jimenez is a 40-year-old Hispanic male who is currently on trial for first degree murder. He has been in jail for about 11 years. He is illiterate both in his native Spanish as well as English. Mr. Jimenez has also used drugs such as cocaine and Valium extensively. He was tested in prison for 8 hours and given a battery of tests in Spanish. He does not seem to understand others very well, thus his inability to participate in his defense at the trial.

Mr. Jimenez was born in Puerto Rico, the youngest of 10 children. At the age of 1, he lost his father. His mother then had to work to support the family. Five of his siblings died as infants. Two others died, one of an overdose of heroin and the other of high blood pressure. Two of his brothers are currently in jail for dealing drugs, and his sister is the only immediate family member not dead or incarcerated.

As a child, Mr. Jimenez was not provided with much. His house had no gas, water, plumbing, or electricity. He went to school on a regular basis and did very poorly. He got into a lot of fights and claims he was hit several times in the head with a loss of consciousness. At the age of 14 and in the 3rd grade, Mr. Jimenez decided to quit school. He says he was "too big" and could not learn.

Mr. Jimenez worked in the sugarcane fields for about a year. Soon thereafter, he came to the United States and found work as a candle maker. He claims it was the best job he ever had. He also made tables for about a year. He then lost his job and began to experiment with drugs.

Mr. Jimenez began to sell drugs as a means of using them. His drugs of choice were Valium, cocaine, and heroin. He preferred Valium to the other two because he felt "good" when he used it, usually 10 to 30 pills per day. He also used cocaine frequently and had been doing heavy drugs for approximately 3 years. As a consequence of his heavy drug use, Mr. Jimenez's wife left him after 3 years of marriage. He has a 20-year-old son, a 16- year-old daughter, and a 16-year-old son from an affair he had in Puerto Rico.

Presently, Mr. Jimenez sits in his cell 23 hours a day. There are no English classes offered, and his inability to read and understand English is a major obstacle, preventing him to grasp the cognitive challenges associated with the legal system as well as standard psychotherapy. He does, however, see a psychiatrist once a month regarding his sleep medication.

Neuropsychological testing was given, and Mr. Jimenez could barely recite the alphabet and could only count up to 50. Therefore, validity of other psychological tests administered was probably not achieved. In general, however, the minimal amount of neurological and related information collected suggests significant problems, including, but not limited to, retardation and neuropsychological deficits. The possibility of a preexist-ing personality disorder was also considered. Significant limitations, how-ever, were noted in terms of the data that was gathered and the method of information gathering, resulting in potentially questionable validity of the results and an equating of cultural differences with personality disorder.

CASE: MR. JIMENEZ   **REVIEWED BY:**_____

Clinical Assessment

List the main *DSM-IV* diagnosis or diagnoses: _____

_____

List the differential diagnosis or diagnoses: _____

_____

List V-Code(s) related with the disorder(s) _____

_____

If this case does not meet criteria for a mental disorder, which specific V-Code(s) would you
consider as the focus of clinical attention and why?_____

_____

Which cultural variables might be considered in the diagnosis and differential diagnosis of this
case? _____

_____

Cultural Formulation

Cultural identity of the client:_____

_____

Cultural explanation of the individual's illness: _____

_____

Cultural factors related to psychosocial environment and level of functioning:_____

_____

Cultural elements of the relationship between the client and the clinician: _____

_____

Overall cultural assessment for diagnosis and care of the present mental disorder:_____

_____

The Case of Mrs. W.

Helen A. Mendes, DSW

Mrs. W., a 38-year-old Afro-American woman, sought treatment because of depression and anxiety. For 15 years, Mrs. W. had been married to a man who was financially irresponsible and had had numerous affairs. In spite of her unhappiness, Mrs. W. was able to neither improve her marriage nor leave it. "I'm going 'round in circles," she said, " and it's driving me crazy."

During the first therapeutic session, Mrs. W. mentioned in passing that she was a practicing Catholic, that her sons attended parochial school, and that she and her sons went to mass every Sunday. During that first session, the worker tried to find out if Mrs. W. saw any connection between her religious beliefs and her problems. Mrs. W. denied that she saw any connection.

The worker, however, noted that Mrs. W., who had a strict Catholic upbringing, gave birth to her first son out of wedlock and was pregnant with a second child when she married Mr. W. (Both children were his.) The worker's knowledge of Catholicism led her to suspect that, in spite of Mrs. W.'s denial, religious beliefs were potent influences in Mrs. W.'s marriage and self-identity. The worker suspected that Mrs. W. was, perhaps unconsciously, experiencing a great deal of guilt and that this was behind her depression and anxiety.

After working with Mrs. W. for six months, the worker grew in her conviction about the significance of Mrs. W.'s religious beliefs. Trusting the strength of the good client-worker relationship, the worker, instead of asking, asserted that she believed that Mrs. W.'s religious beliefs greatly influenced how she functioned as a wife and mother. Mrs. W., who was normally a talkative woman, grew silent for some time as she reflected upon the worker's statement. Mrs. W. then began to recall her experiences with the nuns and priests during her youth. The theme of her recollections was that it was a mark of holiness to suffer, to endure pain. The worker was impressed with the fact that Mrs. W. had only extracted the "negatives," i.e., prohibitions and renunciations from her religion. Mrs. W. expressed none of the "positives," i.e., affirmations.

The worker, who was not Catholic, but was knowledgeable about Catholicism, challenged Mrs. W.'s understanding of the faith. In order to do this, the worker indicated an acceptance of Mrs. W.'s religious paradigm. Mrs. W. listened intently as the worker reminded Mrs. W. of the affirmations or "positives" of Christianity.

That session was a turning point in the treatment process, as it opened the discussion of sin, guilt, and suffering. The worker encouraged Mrs. W.

to get in touch with her long-standing guilt about her sexual behavior and to avail herself of her religion's rituals of atonement and receiving of forgiveness. Mrs. W. did so, and began to make and sustain real gains in freeing herself from depression and anxiety. She also began to make demands upon her husband, and their relationship improved.

SOURCE: "Mrs. W." From "The role of religion in psychotherapy with Afro-Americans" by Helen A. Mendes. In B. A. Bass, G. E. Wyatt, & G. J. Powell (Eds.), *The Afro-American Family: Assessment, Treatment and Research Issues* (pp. 203-210), copyright 1982 © by the Psychological Corporation, reprinted by permission of the publisher.

CASE: MRS. W.   **REVIEWED BY:**_____

Clinical Assessment

List the main *DSM-IV* diagnosis or diagnoses: _____
_____

List the differential diagnosis or diagnoses: _____
_____

List V-Code(s) related with the disorder(s) _____
_____

If this case does not meet criteria for a mental disorder, which specific V-Code(s) would you consider as the focus of clinical attention and why?_____
_____

Which cultural variables might be considered in the diagnosis and differential diagnosis of this case? _____
_____

Cultural Formulation

Cultural identity of the client:_____
_____

Cultural explanation of the individual's illness: _____
_____

Cultural factors related to psychosocial environment and level of functioning:_____
_____

Cultural elements of the relationship between the client and the clinician: _____
_____

Overall cultural assessment for diagnosis and care of the present mental disorder:_____
_____

The Case of Mrs. Chuppa
Jeff Baker, PhD

Mrs. Chuppa, 31 years old, was referred to the Orthopaedics Spine Surgery Clinic for an evaluation regarding the psychological overlay to her chronic low back pain. Mrs. Chuppa had newly immigrated to the United States from India less than 2 years before. She reported that several members of her husband's family lived close by. She came to the United States to join her husband who had been in the United States for approximately 5 years and had opened a small convenience store. She has been married for 11 years and has no children. She reports a history of low back pain that started approximately 3 years prior to being seen in the pain clinic. She currently reports depressive symptoms that include sleep difficulties, sadness, spontaneous crying, and loss of appetite that has become severe within the past 6 months. She also reports significant stressors as a result of the intensity of the pain. She currently rated her pain as a 9/10 with 10 being the very worst pain she has experienced. She also reports significant stress due to her inability to conceive a child. She has attempted this over the past 10 years, and even though her husband was in the States, he made frequent trips back to India where they continued trying to conceive on his short visits home. This stressful situation appears to result from the fact that Mrs. Chuppa feels that she cannot fulfill a critical role expected from spouses in the Asian Indian culture, namely, having children. Mrs. Chuppa realized that her inability to conceive children is against the cultural and gender expectations in the Asian Indian community, and this situation also appears critical in the origin of her symptoms.

The patient reports that family gatherings are stressful due to "hurtful remarks" regarding her lack of children and his family's nonunderstanding of her chronic pain. Her husband appears supportive and nonjudgmental or critical of her situation. It is reported that her husband has had to take up more traditional tasks that she had once been responsible for (washing dishes, laundry, cleaning the house, etc.).

Mrs. Chuppa reported that her relationship with her husband is somewhat strained as he presents himself as supportive but also appears tired of being responsible for so much of the home responsibilities in addition to working long hours at a 24-hour convenience store that sells gasoline and groceries. She denied sexual or physical abuse and reported that her husband was part of an arranged marriage contracted by her parents, which is a culturally accepted norm in her country but not generally practiced in the United States. She appeared unhappy with this type of marriage arrangement. She reported that she loves her husband but that she is really not in love with him. She expects this love to mature as children are added to the household. She is interested in conceiving but has a difficult time with sexual intercourse, which is also complicated regarding her feelings of intimacy toward her husband. She also reported that it is not that important to her to be "in love" with her husband, but expectations from family regarding her inability to conceive children has complicated the cultural and gender expectations that she has for herself.

She reports a childhood that included servants and her being treated very special because she was the youngest child. She could not recall being denied any request that she had made while growing up. Mrs. Chuppa also reported attending private schools where her education was directed by nuns from a Catholic order in her home country of India. These reports suggested Mrs. Chuppa's clear understanding of the Asian Indian system of privilege toward Indian women. Mrs. Chuppa spoke and described this system as a naturally occurring activity in her country of origin but reported significant difficulty adjusting herself to the U.S. cultural norms and, particularly, local customs of Texas. She finds the United States a strange country and has had difficulty adjusting to the lack of privileges she experiences here. She admits this has caused her significant stress, and she has had difficulty accepting this characteristic of herself. Fortunately, Mrs. Chuppa is part of a very close-knit community that provides social, educational, and religion support to a significant number of Asian Indians living in southeast Texas.

The treatment plan included an in-depth medical and psychological evaluation to determine "the factors involved in the etiology and maintenance of the pain [reported by Mrs. Chuppa] (APA, 1994, p. 458), as well as an evaluation of potential mental disorders suggested from Mrs. Chuppa's reports of symptoms. The psychological evaluation included the MMPI-2, Beck Depression Inventory, a coping-skills inventory, and a clinical interview (Dana, 1993a; Golden, 1990; Zalewski & Green, 1996). Behavioral group pain management was recommended regarding the patient's management of chronic low back pain. The treatment team determined that Mrs. Chuppa's symptoms of pain were associated with both psychological factors and a general medical condition [for practicing purposes, see APA, 1994, p. 458 for more details regarding this point]. The treatment team recommended surgery to Mrs. Chuppa to correct a spinal problem. Mrs. Chuppa, however, was also told that counseling would be necessary prior to and after surgery to deal with underlying psychological issues associated with her symptoms of pain. This portion of the treatment plan included discussion of Mrs. Chuppa's expectations of gender role, her social cultural expectations, and her immigrant status. Another important issue involved Mrs. Chuppa's apparent rejection of cultural norms in her own community, which suggests a potential cultural identity conflict to be carefully addressed first during individual psychotherapy and then during family therapy with her husband. Mrs. Chuppa also appears to have

some dynamics of learned helplessness, which may or may not be culturally influenced, and this situation should be also explored in the treatment
plan. Additional treatment modalities planned with this case include the
programming of cognitive-behavioral interventions, which work pretty
well with clients experiencing pain problems. During these interventions,
some of the acculturation issues lend themselves to assisting the client to a
better understanding of mind-body issues and allow the patient to move
away from dichotomous and negative thinking. The cognitive-behavioral
interventions should also be used to prevent Mrs. Chuppa from erroneously believing that surgery will lower her pain to zero (which is not expected in most cases of this nature). Assertiveness training, communication skills, issues of gender role, and learned helplessness are also helpful
for the patient to identify and articulate her feelings of sadness, grief, and
loneliness.

Mrs. Chuppa attended group pain management sessions along with her
spouse, who also gained insight into the patient's physical and psychological pain due to the hurtful comments of his family. Over the course of
treatment with these interventions, Mrs. Chuppa was able to practice and
demonstrate assertive communication as well as a better understanding of
mind-body issues, and she also received support through group participation regarding her loneliness at the loss of her culture and her own family
support. The patient attended six individual medical psychotherapy sessions and six group pain management sessions and was able to undergo
the surgical procedure with more realistic expectations. Her recovery had
a couple of setbacks as she immediately became focused on becoming
pregnant and needed two follow-up sessions to remind her of the expectations she places on herself and others.

CASE: MRS. CHUPPA   **REVIEWED BY:**_____

Clinical Assessment

List the main *DSM-IV* diagnosis or diagnoses: _____

_____

List the differential diagnosis or diagnoses: _____

_____

List V-Code(s) related with the disorder(s) _____

_____

If this case does not meet criteria for a mental disorder, which specific V-Code(s) would you consider as the focus of clinical attention and why?_____

_____

Which cultural variables might be considered in the diagnosis and differential diagnosis of this case? _____

_____

Cultural Formulation

Cultural identity of the client:_____

_____

Cultural explanation of the individual's illness: _____

_____

Cultural factors related to psychosocial environment and level of functioning:_____

_____

Cultural elements of the relationship between the client and the clinician: _____

_____

Overall cultural assessment for diagnosis and care of the present mental disorder:_____

_____

The Case of Don
Freddy A. Paniagua, PhD

Don is a 14-year-old African American male brought to the clinic by his aunt, Ms. J. Don was reluctant to talk about the reason for being here today and asked his aunt to explain why he was in the clinic. According to Ms. J., 3 years before, the aunt's brother killed the patient's mother. The father and mother were married for several years and had three children (the patient and his two sisters, approximately his age). Ms. J. reported that Don learned about the killing when he was on a short vacation in Corpus Christi with other family members. Don was 11 years old when his mother was killed by his biological father. His father is now in jail and will continue in jail for the next 20 years. Ms. J. reported that after learning about the unexpected death of his mother, Don started having recurrent recollections of this traumatic event and distressing dreams. Ms. J. reported that the patient does not want to talk about the event and that in many instances, she had seen him crying and depressed, including having suicidal ideation but without attempts. Don also has showed over the years a severe decrease in participation in social activities, irritability and anger toward other members of the family from the father's side, and a feeling that he is detached from others. Ms. J. also reported that the patient sometimes feels "like he is afraid that I [Ms. J.] will leave him if I am not on time to pick him up from some place" (e.g., malls, school).

  When asked about that traumatic event, Don said that it is true that he does not want to talk about it. Don also agreed with his aunt's reports about symptoms. Don added that he feels that he does not "fit" in the family because "everybody has a mother and a father," but he does not have his parents (mother dead, father in jail for killing patient's mother). Patient currently lives with Ms. J. and one cousin (aunt's son, 13 years old). When asked about his anger toward family members, Don said that he does not feel happy living with his aunt (Ms. J.) because she reminds him of his father. He said that he has not talked about this feeling with Ms. J., but that he does not "hate" Ms. J. the way he feels about his father whom patient does not consider as his "real father" because he killed his mother. When asked about his two sisters, he replied "they are not my sisters." Don was asked to explain why he felt this way toward his two sisters, and he replied "I hate them because they decided to move with my father's family." Don used to live with his sisters and the family from his father's side, but because of his emotional difficulties dealing with the stress of living with this family and his recurrent thoughts of that traumatic event, Ms. J. took legal custody of Don and brought him to her house to live with her and her 13-year-old son. Ms. J. reported that this move has apparently helped Don to deal with these stressful events but that he is still having difficulties in handling these events in a "mature" way.

During the mental status exam, Don was alert and oriented. His thoughts were coherent and without psychotic features. He scored 60 (past year = 55) on the Global Assessment of Functioning Scale (APA, 1994, p. 32). Don reported past suicidal ideation but said that he is not currently suicidal and that he does not plan to do this "stupid thing" because it is against "God" and added he feels his church is helping him in dealing with his emotional problems. Don reported going to church each Sunday morning with his aunt and cousin but said that he has not discussed his feelings with the minister yet but this is something he would like to do. Don appeared to have a problem with his self-image and self-esteem in that he reported that if he does not look "good and well dressed," he cannot interact with peers in school. He dressed casually during this meeting, but he did not perceive himself as being dressed "nice."

Don and his aunt were told that individual psychotherapy could benefit Don in dealing with feelings associated with the traumatic events and his difficulties in interacting with his sisters and other family members. Ms. J. was told that because of Don's lack of key members in his nuclear family, family therapy would be programmed later, after Don feels comfortable talking about his feelings toward his sisters and his difficulty with his current living situation (i.e., living with his father's sister). Ms. J. asked about medication, and she was told that medication management of Don's symptoms also could be explored in subsequent sessions. Don was specifically told to continue going to church each Sunday and that after several individual psychotherapy sessions, he would be able to talk about his symptoms with his minister.

CASE: DON   **REVIEWED BY:**_____

Clinical Assessment

List the main *DSM-IV* diagnosis or diagnoses: _____

_____

List the differential diagnosis or diagnoses: _____

_____

List V-Code(s) related with the disorder(s) _____

_____

If this case does not meet criteria for a mental disorder, which specific V-Code(s) would you
consider as the focus of clinical attention and why?_____

_____

Which cultural variables might be considered in the diagnosis and differential diagnosis of this
case? _____

_____

Cultural Formulation

Cultural identity of the client:_____

_____

Cultural explanation of the individual's illness: _____

_____

Cultural factors related to psychosocial environment and level of functioning:_____

_____

Cultural elements of the relationship between the client and the clinician: _____

_____

Overall cultural assessment for diagnosis and care of the present mental disorder:_____

_____

The Case of Maria Elena Z.
Cervando Martinez, Jr., MD

The patient, Maria Elena Z., is a 29-year-old, single, unemployed Mexican American woman who was seen in the outpatient psychiatry clinic accompanied by her father. She has been mentally ill since her freshman year at the state university in a nearby city, when she became preoccupied with romantic overtures that she believed a male classmate was making toward her. In subsequent years, she developed paranoid delusions, auditory and visual hallucinations, and bizarre behavior requiring several admissions to psychiatric inpatient facilities. During her outpatient visits after release, she was usually accompanied by her mother who was from Mexico, spoke only Spanish, and was employed full time and gradually developed a fairly sound understanding of her daughter's illness and needed care.

Several months before the present clinic visit, Maria Elena again discontinued her medication and had abruptly become more and more disorganized and psychotic. She was admitted to the psychiatric unit and after a short stay was released to outpatient care, still very delusional and almost incoherent. Her mother accompanied her to her first clinic follow-up visit, and they were told that because of the continuing severity of her symptoms, it would be necessary to see her weekly for follow-up. At the next visit, her father accompanied her to save the mother having to take time off work.

After a brief conversation with the patient, the interviewer approached Mr. Z. to elicit his perspective on his daughter's illness. Mr. Z. related how his daughter had gone off to the university in good health, on scholarship, and then how several months later, something had gone wrong. He also described a possible romance she had had and how, after this ended, she began to change. He wondered whether the ex-boyfriend's new girlfriend might have been jealous (*celosa*) of his daughter and alluded to the possibility of a poison that could have been given to her that might have caused brain damage. He added that he did not think that X-rays of her brain had ever been done (he was correct—no CT scan or MRI had ever been done at the present facility, only routine lab tests). He said that, after all, *males* (bad things) do occur, and perhaps something like this had happened to her. It was not clear, even after an attempt to clarify was made, whether he meant *mal* in the sense of "bad things" or a hex. Throughout, although cooperative and nonresistant, he seemed to have difficulty communicating clearly, even in Spanish, appearing disjointed, vague, and suspicious.

CASE: MARIA ELENA Z.   **REVIEWED BY:**_____

Clinical Assessment

List the main *DSM-IV* diagnosis or diagnoses: _____
_____

List the differential diagnosis or diagnoses: _____
_____

List V-Code(s) related with the disorder(s) _____
_____

If this case does not meet criteria for a mental disorder, which specific V-Code(s) would you consider as the focus of clinical attention and why?_____
_____

Which cultural variables might be considered in the diagnosis and differential diagnosis of this case? _____
_____

Cultural Formulation

Cultural identity of the client:_____
_____

Cultural explanation of the individual's illness: _____
_____

Cultural factors related to psychosocial environment and level of functioning:_____
_____

Cultural elements of the relationship between the client and the clinician: _____
_____

Overall cultural assessment for diagnosis and care of the present mental disorder:_____
_____

References

Alarcon, R. D. (1983). A Latin-American perspective on *DSM-III*. In R. L. Spitzer, J. B. Williams, & A. E. Skodol, *International perspectives on DSM-III* (pp. 243-249). Washington, DC: American Psychiatric Press.

American Psychiatric Association. (1980). *Diagnostic and statistical manual of mental disorders* (3rd ed.). Washington, DC: Author.

American Psychiatric Association. (1987). *Diagnostic and statistical manual of mental disorders* (3rd ed.-rev.). Washington, DC: Author.

American Psychiatric Association. (1994). *Diagnostic and statistical manual of mental disorders* (4th ed.). Washington, DC: Author.

Anastasi, A. (1988). *Psychological testing* (6th ed.). New York: Macmillan.

Arnold, B. R., & Matus, Y. E. (2000). Test translation and cultural equivalence methodologies for use with diverse populations. In I. Cuéllar & F. A. Paniagua (Eds.), *Handbook of multicultural mental health: Assessment and treatment of diverse populations* (pp. 121-136). New York: Academic Press.

Arroyo, J. A. (1996). Psychotherapist bias with Hispanics: An analog study. *Hispanic Journal of Behavioral Sciences, 18,* 21-28.

Baker, F. M. (1988). Afro-Americans. In L. Comas-Díaz & E. E. H. Griffith (Eds.), *Clinical guidelines in cross-cultural mental health* (pp. 151-181). New York: John Wiley.

Baker, F. M., & Lightfoot, O. B. (1993). Psychiatric care of ethnic elders. In A. C. Gaw (Ed.), *Culture, ethnicity, and mental illness* (pp. 517-552). Washington, DC: American Psychiatric Press.

Barkley, R. A. (1990). *Attention-deficit hyperactivity disorder: A handbook for diagnosis and treatment* (2nd ed.). New York: Guilford.

Berg, I. K., & Jaya, A. (1993). Different and same: Family therapy with Asian-American families. *Journal of Marital and Family Therapy, 19,* 31-38.

Berg-Cross, L. (1997). *Couples therapy.* Thousand Oaks, CA: Sage.

Bernal, E. M. (1990). Increasing the interpretive validity and diagnostic utility of Hispanic children's scores on tests of achievement and intelligence. In F. C. Serafica, A. I. Schwebel, R. K. Russell, P. D. Isaac, & L. B. Myers (Eds.), *Mental health of ethnic minorities* (pp. 108-138). New York: Praeger.

Bernal, G., & Gutierrez, M. (1988). Cubans. In L. Comas-Díaz & E. E. H. Griffith (Eds.), *Clinical guidelines in cross-cultural mental health* (pp. 233-261). New York: John Wiley.

225

Bernstein, D. M. (1997). Anxiety disorders. In Wen-Shin Tseng & J. Streltzer (Eds.), *Culture and psychopathology* (pp. 46-66). New York: Brunner/Mazel.

Bernstein, R. L., & Gaw, A. C. (1990). Koro: Proposed classification for the *DSM-IV. American Journal of Psychiatry, 147*, 1670-1674.

Berry, J. W., Poortinga, Y. H., Segall, M. H., & Dasen, P. R. (1992). *Cross-cultural psychology: Research and applications.* Cambridge, UK: Cambridge University Press.

Boehnlein, J. K., & Kinzie, J. D. (1995). Refugee trauma. *Transcultural Psychiatric Research Review, 32*, 223-252.

Boyd-Franklin, N. (1989). *Black family therapy: A multisystems approach.* New York: Guilford.

Boyd-Franklin, N., Aleman, J., Jean-Gilles, M. M., & Lewis, S. Y. (1995). Cultural sensitivity and competence. In N. Boyd-Franklin, G. L. Steiner, & M. G. Boland (Eds.), *Children, families, and HIV/AIDS* (pp. 53-77). New York: Guilford.

Burlingame, V. S. (1999). *Ethnogerocounseling: Counseling ethnic elders and their families.* New York: Springer.

Campinha-Bacote, J. (1992). Voodoo illness. *Perspectives in Psychiatry Care, 28*, 11-117.

Canino, G., Burnam, A., & Caetano, R. (1992). The prevalence of alcohol abuse/dependence in two Hispanic communities. In J. Helzer & G. Canino (Eds.), *Alcoholism in North America, Europe and Asia* (pp. 131-155). New York: Oxford University Press.

Canino, I. A., & Canino, G. J. (1993). Psychiatric care of Puerto Ricans. In A. C. Gaw (Ed.), *Culture, ethnicity, and mental illness* (pp. 467-499). Washington, DC: American Psychiatric Press.

Canino, I. A., & Spurlock, J. (1994). *Culturally diverse children and adolescents: Assessment, diagnosis, and treatment.* New York: Guilford.

Canino, I. A., & Zayas, L. H. (1997). Puerto Rican children. In G. Johnson-Powell & J. Yamamoto (Eds.), *Transcultural child development: Psychological assessment and treatment* (pp. 61-79). New York: John Wiley.

Castillo, R. J. (1997). *Culture and mental illness.* Pacific Grove, CA: Brooks/Cole.

Cervantes, R. C., & Arroyo, W. (1995). Cultural considerations in the use of *DSM-IV* with Hispanic children and adolescents. In A. M. Padilla (Ed.), *Hispanic psychology* (pp. 131-147). Thousand Oaks, CA: Sage.

Chaplin, S. L. (1997). Somatization. In Wen-Shin Tseng & J. Streltzer (Eds.), *Culture and psychopathology: A guide to clinical assessment* (pp. 67-86). New York: Brunner/Mazel.

Cheng, S. T. (1996). A critical review of Chinese Koro. *Culture, Medicine and Psychiatry, 20*, 67-82.

Chowdhury, A. N. (1996). The definition and classification of Koro. *Culture, Medicine and Psychiatry, 20*, 41-65.

Chung, D. K. (1992). Asian cultural commonalities: A comparison with mainstream American culture. In A. M. Furuto, R. Biswas, D. K. Chung, Murase, K., & Roff-Sheriff, F. (Eds.), *Social work practice with Asian Americans* (pp. 27-44). Newbury Park, CA: Sage.

Comas-Díaz, L. (1988). Cross-cultural mental health treatment. In L. Comas-Díaz & E. E. H. Griffith (Eds.), *Clinical guidelines in cross-cultural mental health* (pp. 337-361). New York: John Wiley.

Comas-Díaz, L., & Duncan, J. W. (1985). The cultural context: A factor in assertiveness training with mainland Puerto Rican women. *Psychology of Women Quarterly, 9*, 463-476.

Comas-Díaz, L., & Griffith, E. E. H. (Eds.). (1988). *Clinical guidelines in cross-cultural mental health.* New York: John Wiley.

Constantino, G., Malgady, R. G., & Rogler, L. H. (1988). *Technical manual: The TEMAS Thematic Apperception Test.* Los Angeles: Western Psychological Services.

Cruz, M. (1999). Alcohol and solvent abuse. In J. M. Galloway, B. W. Goldberd, & J. S. Alper (Eds.), *Primary care of Native American patients: Diagnosis, therapy and epidemiology* (pp. 263-268). Boston: Butteworth Heinemann.

Cuéllar, I. (1998). Cross-cultural clinical psychological assessment of Hispanic adolescents. *Journal of Personality Assessment, 70*, 71-86.

Cuéllar, I. (2000). Acculturation and mental health: Ecological, transactional relations and adjustment. In I. Cuéllar & F. A. Paniagua (Eds.), *Handbook of multicultural mental health: Assessment and treatment of diverse populations* (pp. 45-62). New York: Academic Press.

Cuéllar, I., Arnold, B., & Maldonado, R. (1995). Acculturation rating scale for Mexicans-II: A revision of the original ARSMA scale. *Hispanic Journal of Behavioral Sciences, 17,* 275-304.

Cuéllar, I., Harris, L. C., & Jasso, R. (1980). An acculturation scale for Mexican American normal and clinical populations. *Hispanic Journal of the Behavioral Sciences, 2,* 199-217.

Cuéllar, I., & Paniagua, F. A. (Eds.). (2000). *Handbook of multicultural mental health: Assessment and treatment of diverse populations.* New York: Academic Press.

Cuffe, S., McCullough, E., & Pumariega, A. (1994). Co-morbidity of attention deficit hyperactivity disorder and post-traumatic stress disorder: A case report. *Journal of Child and Family Studies, 3,* 327-336.

Dana, R. H. (1993a, November). *Can "corrections" for culture using moderator variables contribute to cultural competence in assessment?* Paper presented at the Annual Convention of the Texas Psychological Association, Austin, Texas.

Dana, R. H. (1993b). *Multicultural assessment perspectives for professional psychology.* Boston: Allyn & Bacon.

Dana, R. H. (1997). *Understanding cultural identity in intervention and assessment.* Thousand Oaks, CA: Sage.

De La Cancela, V. (1993). Rainbow warriors: Reducing institutional racism in mental health. *Journal of Mental Health Counseling, 15,* 55-71.

Dillard, J. L. (1973). *Black English: Its history and use in the United States.* New York: Vintage.

Escobar, J. I. (1995). Transcultural aspects of dissociative and somatoform disorders. *The Psychiatric Clinics of North America, 18,* 555-569.

Eysenck, H. J., & Eysenck, S. B. S. (1975). *Manual for the Eysenck Personality Questionnaire.* San Diego, CA: Educational and Industrial Testing Service.

Fairchild, H. H. (1985). Black, Negro, or African American? The differences are crucial. *Journal of Black Studies, 16,* 47-55.

Falicov, C., & Karrer, B. (1984). Therapeutic strategies for Mexican-American families. *International Journal of Family Therapy, 6,* 18-30.

Fleming, C. M. (1992). American Indians and Alaska Natives: Changing societies past and present. In M. Orlandi & R. Weston (Eds.), *Cultural competence for evaluators* (pp. 147-171). Rockville, MD: U.S. Department of Health and Human Services.

Franco, J. N. (1983). An acculturation scale for Mexican American children. *Journal of General Psychology, 108,* 175-181.

French, L. A. (1993). Adapting projective tests for minority children. *Psychological Reports, 72,* 15-18.

Friedman, S. (Ed.). (1997). *Cultural issues in the treatment of anxiety.* New York: Guilford.

Fujii, J. S., Fukushima, S. N., & Yamamoto, J. (1993). Psychiatric care of Japanese Americans. In A. C. Gaw (Ed.), *Culture, ethnicity, and mental illness* (pp. 305-345). Washington, DC: American Psychiatric Press.

Garcia, M., & Lega, L. I. (1979). Development of a Cuban ethnic identity questionnaire. *Hispanic Journal of the Behavioral Sciences, 1,* 247-261.

Garza-Trevino, E., Ruiz, P., & Venegas-Samuels, K. (1997). A psychiatric curriculum directed to the care of the Hispanic patient. *Academic Psychiatric, 21,* 1-10.

Gaw, A. C. (Ed.). (1993a). *Culture, ethnicity, and mental illness.* Washington, DC: American Psychiatric Press.

Gaw, A. C. (1993b). Psychiatric care of Chinese Americans. In A. C. Gaw (Ed.), *Culture, ethnicity, and mental illness* (pp. 245-280). Washington, DC: American Psychiatric Press.

Geisinger, K. F. (Ed.). (1992). *Psychological testing of Hispanics.* Washington, DC: American Psychological Association.

Gibbs, J. T. (1998a). African American adolescents. In J. T. Gibbs & L. H. Huang (Eds.), *Children of color: Psychological interventions with culturally diverse youth* (pp. 171-214). San Francisco: Jossey-Bass.

Gibbs, J. T. (1998b). Biracial adolescents. In J. T. Gibbs & L. H. Huang (Eds.), *Children of color: Psychological interventions with culturally diverse youth* (pp. 305-332). San Francisco: Jossey-Bass.

Gibbs, J. T., & Huang, L. N. (1998). *Children of color: Psychological interventions with culturally diverse youth.* San Francisco: Jossey-Bass.

Golden, C. J. (1990). *Clinical interpretation of objective psychological tests* (2nd ed.). Needham, MA: Allyn & Bacon.

Good, B. J. (1996). Culture and *DSM-IV*: Diagnosis, knowledge and power. *Culture, Medicine, and Psychiatry, 20,* 127-132.

Gregory, S. (1996). "We've been down this road already." In S. Gregory & R. Sanjek (Eds.), *Race* (pp. 18-38). New Brunswick, NJ: Rutgers University Press.

Griffith, E. E. H., & Baker, F. M. (1993). Psychiatric care of African Americans. In A. C. Gaw (Ed.), *Culture, ethnicity, and mental illness* (pp. 147-173). Washington, DC: American Psychiatric Press.

Griffith, E. E. H., English, T., & Mayfield, V. (1980). Possession, prayer, and testimony: Therapeutic aspects of the Wednesday night meeting in a Black church. *Psychiatry, 43,* 120-128.

Guarnaccia, P. J. (1997). A cross-cultural perspective on anxiety disorders. In S. Friedman (Ed.), *Cultural issues in the treatment of anxiety* (pp. 3-20). New York: Guilford.

Helms, J. E. (1986). Expanding racial identity theory to cover the counseling process. *Journal of Counseling Psychology, 33,* 62-64.

Helms, J. E. (1987). Cultural identity in the treatment process. In P. Pedersen (Ed.), *Handbook of cross-cultural counseling and therapy* (pp. 339-354). New York: Praeger.

Ho, M. K. (1987). *Family therapy with ethnic minorities.* Newbury Park, CA: Sage.

Ho, M. K. (1992). *Minority children and adolescents in therapy.* Newbury Park, CA: Sage.

Hoffmann, T., Dana, R., & Bolton, B. (1985). Measured acculturation and MMPI-168 performance of Native American adults. *Journal of Cross-Cultural Psychology, 16,* 243-256.

Holzer, C. E. (2000). Personal communication with editor.

Holtzman, W. H. (1988). Beyond the Rorschach. *Journal of Personality Assessment, 52,* 578-609.

Honda, Y. (1983). *DSM-IV* in Japan. In R. L. Spitzer, J. B. Williams, & A. E. Skodol, *International perspectives on DSM-III* (pp. 185-201). Washington, DC: American Psychiatric Press.

Huang, L. N. (1998). Southeast Asian refugee children and adolescents. In J. T. Gibbs & L. N. Huang (Eds.), *Children of color: Psychological interventions with culturally diverse youth* (pp. 264-304). San Francisco: Jossey-Bass.

Huang, L. N., & Ying, Y. W. (1998). Chinese American children and adolescents. In J. T. Gibbs & L. N. Huang (Eds.), *Children of color: Psychological interventions with culturally diverse youth* (pp. 33-67). San Francisco: Jossey-Bass.

Hughes, C. C. (1993) Culture in clinical psychiatry. In A. C. Gaw (Ed.), *Culture, ethnicity, and mental illness* (pp. 3-41). Washington, DC. American Psychiatric Press.

Ivey, A. E., Ivey, M. B., & Simek-Morgan, L. (Eds.). (1996). *Counseling and psychotherapy: A multicultural perspective.* Boston: Allyn & Bacon.

Jackson, M. L. (1995). Counseling youth of Arab ancestry. In C. C. Lee (Ed.), *Counseling for diversity: A guide for school counselors and related professionals* (pp. 41-60). Boston: Allyn & Bacon.

Jenkins, J. O., & Hunter, K. C. (1991). Minorities. In M. Hersen, A. E. Kazdin, & A. S. Bellack (Eds.), *The clinical psychology handbook* (pp. 724-740). New York: Pergamon.

Jones, A. C. (1992). Self-esteem and identity in psychotherapy with adolescents from upwardly mobile middle-class African American families. In L. A. Vargas & J. D. Koss-Chioino (Eds.), *Working with culture: Psychotherapeutic interventions with ethnic minority children and adolescents* (pp. 25-42). San Francisco: Jossey-Bass.

Joyce, P. R., & Paykel, E. S. (1989). Predictors of drug response in depression. *Archives of General Psychiatry, 46,* 89-99.

Kaufman, S., Kamphaus, R. W., & Kaufman, N. L. (1985). New directions in intelligence testing: The Kaufman Assessment Battery for Children (K-ABC). In B. B. Wolman (Ed.), *Handbook of intelligence: Theories, measurements, and applications* (pp. 663-698). New York: John Wiley.

Kilgus, M. D., Pumariega, A. J., & Cuffe, S. P. (1995). Influence of race on diagnosis in adolescent psychiatric inpatients. *Journal of the American Academy of Child and Adolescent Psychiatry, 34,* 67-72.

Kim, S., McLeod, J. H., & Shantzis, C. (1992). Cultural competence for evaluators working with Asian-American communities: Some practical considerations. In M. Orlandi & R. Weston (Eds.), *Cultural competence for evaluators* (pp. 203-260). Rockville, MD: U.S. Department of Health and Human Services.

Kinzie, J. D., & Edeki, T. (1998). Ethnicity and psychopharmacology: The experience of Southeast Asians. In S. O. Okpaku (Ed.), *Clinical methods in transcultural psychiatry* (pp. 171-190). Washington, DC: American Psychiatric Press.

Kinzie, J. D., & Leung, P. K. (1993). Psychiatric care of Indochinese Americans. In A. C. Gaw (Ed.), *Culture, ethnicity, and mental illness* (pp. 281-304). Washington, DC: American Psychiatric Press.

Kinzie, J. D., Manson, S. D., Do, T. V., Nguyen, T. T., Anh, B., & Than, N. P. (1982). Development and validation of a Vietnamese-language depression rating scale. *American Journal of Psychiatry, 139,* 1276-1281.

Kirmayer, L. J., Dao, T. H. T., & Smith, A. (1998). Somatization and psychologization: Understanding cultural idioms of distress. In S. O. Okpaku (Ed.), *Clinical methods in transcultural psychiatry* (pp. 233-265). Washington, DC: American Psychiatric Press.

Kirmayer, L. J., Young, A., & Hayton, B. (1995). The cultural context of anxiety disorders. *Psychiatric Clinics of North America, 18,* 503-521.

Klonoff, E. A., Landrine, H., & Ullman, J. B. (1999). Racial discrimination and psychiatric symptoms among blacks. *Cultural Diversity and Ethnic Minority Psychology, 5,* 329-339.

Koss-Chioino, J., & Vargas, L. A. (1999). *Working with Latino youth.* San Francisco: Jossey-Bass.

Kratochwill, T. R., & Bergan, J. R. (1990). *Behavioral consultation in applied settings: An individual guide.* New York: Plenum.

Kuhn, T. S. (1962). *The structure of scientific revolutions.* Chicago: University of Chicago Press.

LaFromboise, T. D., Dauphinais, P., & Rowe, W. (1980). Indian students' perception of positive helper attitudes. *Journal of American Indian Education, 111,* 11-15.

Lange, A. J., & Jakubowski, P. (1976). *Responsible assertive behavior.* Champaign, IL: Research Press.

Levin, J. S., & Taylor, R. J. (1993). Gender and age differences in religiosity among Black Americans. *The Gerontologist, 33,* 16-23.

Lewis-Fernandez, R. (1996). Cultural formulation of psychiatric diagnosis. *Culture, Medicine, and Psychiatry, 20,* 133-144

Lewis-Fernandez, R., & Kleinman, A. (1995). Cultural psychiatry: Theoretical, clinical, and research issues. *Psychiatric Clinics of North America, 18,* 433-448.

Lineberger, M. H., & Calhoun, K. S. (1983). Assertive behavior in Black and White American undergraduates. *Journal of Psychology, 13,* 139-148.

Lonner, W. J., & Ibrahim, F. A. (1996). Appraisal and assessment in cross-cultural counseling. In P. B. Pedersen, J. G. Draguns, W. J. Lonner, & J. E. Trimble (Eds.), *Counseling across cultures* (pp. 293-322). Thousand Oaks, CA: Sage.

López, S. R. (1989). Patient variable biases in clinical judgement: Conceptual overview and methodological considerations. *Psychological Bulletin, 106,* 184-203.

Marcos, L. R. (1976). Bilinguals in psychotherapy: Language as an emotional barrier. *American Journal of Psychotherapy, 30,* 552-560.

Marin, G., & Marin, B. V. (1991). *Research with Hispanic populations.* Newbury Park, CA: Sage.

Marsella, A. J., & Yamada, A. M. (2000). Culture and mental health: An introduction and overview of foundations, concepts, and issues. In I. Cuéllar & F. A. Paniagua (Eds.), *Handbook of multicultural mental health: Assessment and treatment of culturally diverse populations* (pp. 3-24). New York: Academic Press.

Martinez, C. (1986). Hispanic psychiatric issues. In C. Wilkinson (Ed.), *Ethnic psychiatry* (pp. 61-87). New York: Plenum.

Martinez, C. (1988). Mexican-Americans. In L. Comas-Díaz & E. E. H. Griffith (Eds.),*Clinical guidelines in cross-cultural mental health* (pp. 182-203). New York: John Wiley.

Martinez, C. (1993). Psychiatric care of Mexican Americans. In A. C. Gaw (Ed.), *Culture, ethnicity, and mental illness* (pp. 431-466). Washington, DC: American Psychiatric Press.

Masuda, M., Matsumoto, G. H., & Meredith, G. M. (1970). Ethnic identity in three generations of Japanese Americans. *Journal of Social Psychology, 81,* 199-207.

Matheson, L. (1986). If you are not an Indian, how do you treat an Indian? In H. P. Lefley & P. B. Pedersen (Eds.),*Cross-cultural training for mental health professionals* (pp. 115-130). Springfield, IL: Charles C Thomas.

McAdoo, H. P. (Ed.). (1993). *Family ethnicity: Strength in diversity.* Thousand Oaks, CA: Sage.

McCarthy, P. R., Katz, I. R., & Foa, E. B. (1991). Cognitive-behavioral treatment of anxiety in the elderly: A proposed model. In C. Salzman & B. D. Lebowitz (Eds.), *Anxiety in the elderly: Treatment and research.* New York: Springer.

McNeil, D. W., Kee, M., & Zvolensky, M. J. (1999). Culturally related anxiety and ethnic identity in Navajo college students. *Cultural Diversity and Ethnic Minority Psychology, 5,* 56-64.

Mendes, H. A. (1982). The role of religion in psychotherapy with Afro-Americans. In B. A. Bass, G. E. Wyatt, & G. J. Powell (Eds.), *The Afro-American family: Assessment, treatment and research issues* (pp. 203-210). New York: Psychological Corporation.

Mendoza, R. H. (1989). An empirical scale to measure type and degree of acculturation in Mexican-American adolescents and adults. *Journal of Cross-Cultural Psychology, 20,* 372-385.

Mercer, J., & Lewis, J. (1978). *System of multicultural pluralistic assessment.* New York: Psychological Corporation.

Miller, F. S. (1992). Network structure support: Its relationship to psychosocial development of Black females. In A. K. H. Burlew, W. C. Banks, H. P. McAdoo, & D. A. Azibo (Eds.), *African American psychology* (pp. 105-126). Newbury Park, CA: Sage.

Milliones, J. (1980). Construction of a black consciousness measure: Psychotherapeutic implications. *Psychotherapy: Theory, Research, and Practice, 17,* 175-182.

Moffic, H. S., & Kinzie, J. D. (1996). The history and future of cross-cultural psychiatric services. *Community Mental Health Journal, 32,* 581-592.

Mollica, R. F. (1989). Developing effective mental health policies and services for traumatized refugee patients. In D. R. Koslow & E. P. Salett (Eds.), *Crossing cultures in mental health* (pp. 101-115). Washington, DC: International Counseling Center.

Mollica, R. F., & Lavelle, J. (1988). Southeast Asian refugees. In L. Comas-Díaz & E. E. H. Griffith (Eds.), *Clinical guidelines in cross-cultural mental health* (pp. 262-293). New York: John Wiley.

Mueller, J., Kiernan, R. J., & Langston, J. W. (1992). The mental status examination. In H. H. Goldman (Ed.), *Review of general psychiatry* (pp. 109-117). San Mateo, CA: Appleton & Lange.

Murphy, J. M. (1978). The recognition of psychosis in non-Western societies. In R. L. Spitzer & D. F. Klein (Eds.), *Critical issues in psychiatric diagnosis* (pp. 1-13). New York: Raven.

Nagata, D. K. (1998). The assessment and treatment of Japanese American children and adolescents. In J. T. Gibbs & L. N. Huang (Eds.), *Children of color: Psychological interventions with culturally diverse youth* (pp. 68-111). San Francisco: Jossey-Bass.

Neff, J. A., & Hoppe, S. K. (1993). Race/ethnicity, acculturation, and psychological distress: Fatalism and religiosity as cultural resources. *Journal of Community Psychology, 21,* 3-20.

Nguyen, N. A. (1992). Living between two cultures: Treating first-generation Asian Americans. In L. A. Vargas & J. D. Chioin (Eds.), *Working with culture: Psychotherapy interventions with ethnic minority children and adolescents* (pp. 204-222). San Francisco: Jossey-Bass.

Norris, A. E., Ford, K., & Bova, C. A. (1996). Psychometrics of a brief acculturation scale for Hispanics in a probability sample of urban Hispanic adolescents and young adults. *Hispanic Journal of Behavioral Sciences, 18,* 29-38.

O'Brien, S. (1989). *American Indian tribal governments.* Norman: University of Oklahoma Press.

Okun, B. F. (1996). *Understanding diverse families: What practitioners need to know.* New York: Guilford.

Organista, K. C., & Dwyer, E. V. (1996). Clinical case management of cognitive-behavior therapy: Integrated psychosocial services for depressed Latino primary care patients. In P. Manoleas (Ed.), *The cross-cultural practice of clinical case management in mental health* (pp. 119-143). New York: Haworth.

Paniagua, F. A. (1994). *Assessing and treating culturally diverse clients: A practical guide.* Thousand Oaks, CA: Sage.

Paniagua, F. A. (1996). Cross-cultural guidelines in family therapy practice. *The Family Journal: Counseling and Therapy for Couples and Families, 4,* 127-138.

Paniagua, F. A. (1998). *Assessing and treating culturally diverse clients: A practical guide* (2nd ed.). Thousand Oaks, CA: Sage.

Paniagua, F. A. (2000). Culture-bound syndromes, cultural variations, and psychopathology. In I. Cuéllar & F. A. Paniagua (Eds.), *Handbook of multicultural mental health: Assessment and treatment of diverse populations* (pp. 139-169). New York: Academic Press.

Paniagua, F. A., & Baer, D. M. (1981). A procedural analysis of the symbolic forms of behavior therapy. *Behaviorism, 9,* 171-205.

Paniagua, F. A., & Black, S. A. (1990). Management and prevention of hyperactivity and conduct disorders in 8-10 year old boys through correspondence training procedures. *Child and Family Behavior Therapy, 12,* 23-56.

Paniagua, F. A., O'Boyle, M., Tan, V. L., & Lew, A. S. (2000). *Self-evaluation of biases and prejudice.* Manuscript submitted for publication.

Paniagua, F. A., Tan, V. T., & Lew, A. S. (1996). A summary of cultural variations in the *DSM-IV. Sociotam: International Journal of Social Sciences and Humanities, 6,* 33-57.

Paniagua, F. A., Wassef, A., O'Boyle, M., Linares, S. A., & Cuéllar, I. (1993). What is a difficult mental health case? An empirical study of relationships among domain variables. *Journal of Contemporary Psychotherapy,* 77-98.

Pedersen, P. B. (1987). *Handbook of cross-cultural counseling and therapy.* London: Greenwood.

Pedersen, P. B. (1997). *Culture-centered counseling interventions: Striving for accuracy.* Thousand Oaks, CA: Sage.

Pedersen, P. B. (1999). *Multiculturalism as a fourth force.* Philadelphia, PA: Taylor & Francis.

Pedersen, P. B., Draguns, J. G., Lonner, W. J., & Trimble, J. E. (1996). *Counseling across cultures.* Thousand Oaks, CA: Sage.

Pierce, R. C., Clark, M., & Kiefer, C. W. (1972). A "bootstrap" scaling technique. *Human Organization, 31,* 403-410.

Ponce, D. E. (1997). Adolescent psychopathology. In W. Tseng & J. Streltzer (Eds.), *Culture and psychopathology: A guide to clinical assessment* (pp. 206-222). New York: Brunner/Mazel.

Ponterotto, J. G., Casas, J. M., Suzuki, L. A., & Alexander, C. M. (Eds.). (1995). *Handbook of multicultural counseling.* Thousand Oaks, CA: Sage.

Ponterotto, J. G., Rieger, B. P., Barrett, A., & Sparks, R. (1994). Assessing multicultural counseling competence: A review of instrumentation. *Journal of Counseling and Development, 72,* 316-322.

Pope-Davis, D. B., & Coleman, H. L. K. (1997). (Eds.). *Multicultural counseling competencies: Assessment, education and training, and supervision.* Thousand Oaks, CA: Sage.

Puente, A. E., & Perez-Garcia, M. (2000). Neurological assessment of ethnic minorities: Clinical uses. In I. Cuéllar & F. A. Paniagua (Eds.), *Handbook of multicultural mental health: Assessment and treatment of diverse populations* (pp. 419-435). New York: Academic Press.

Pumariega, A. J., & Cross, T. (1997). Cultural competence in child psychiatry. In J. Noshpitz & N. Alessi (Eds.), *Handbook of child & adolescent psychiatry* (pp. 473-484). New York: John Wiley.

Raajpoot, U. A. (2000). Multicultural demographic developments: Current and future trends. In I. Cuéllar & F. A. Paniagua (Eds.), *Handbook of multicultural mental health: Assessment and treatment of diverse populations* (pp. 79-94). New York: Academic Press.

Radloff, L. S. (1977). The CES-D scale: A self-report depression scale for research in the general public. *Applied Psychological Measurement, 1,* 385-401.

Ramirez, M. (1984). Assessing and understanding biculturalism-multiculturalism in Mexican-American adults. In J. L. Martinez & R. H. Mendoza (Eds.), *Chicano psychology* (pp. 77-94). Orlando, FL: Academic Press.

Ramirez, O. (1984). Mexican American children and adolescents. In J. T. Gibbs & L. N. Huang (Eds.), *Children of color: Psychological interventions with culturally diverse youth* (pp. 215-239). San Francisco: Jossey-Bass.

Ramirez, S. Z., Wassef, A., Paniagua, F. A., Linskey, A. O., & O'Boyle, M. (1994). Perceptions of mental health providers concerning cultural factors in the evaluation of Hispanic children and adolescents. *Hispanic Journal of Behavioral Sciences, 16,* 28-42.

Richardson, E. H. (1981). Cultural and historical perspectives in counseling American Indians. In D. W. Sue (Ed.), *Counseling the culturally different: Theory and practice* (pp. 216-255). New York: John Wiley.

Rogler, L. H. (1999). Methodological sources of cultural insensitivity in mental health. *American Psychologist, 54,* 424-433.

Rosenthal, R. H., & Akiskal, H. S. (1985). Mental status examination. In M. Hersen & S. M. Turner (Eds.), *Diagnostic interviewing* (pp. 25-52). New York: Plenum.

Roubideaux, Y. (1999). Cross-cultural aspects of mental health and culture-bound illness. In J. M. Galloway, B. W. Goldberd, & J. S. Alper (Eds.), *Primary care of Native American patients: Diagnosis, therapy and epidemiology* (pp. 269-272). Boston: Butteworth Heinemann.

Ruiz, R. A. (1981). Cultural and historical perspectives in counseling Hispanics. In D. W. Sue (Ed.), *Counseling the culturally different: Theory and practice* (pp. 186-215). New York: John Wiley.

Samuda, R. J. (1998). *Psychological testing of American minorities.* Thousand Oaks, CA: Sage.

Sandoval, M. C., & De La Roza, M. C. (1986). A cultural perspective for serving Hispanic clients. In H. P. Lefley & P. B. Pedersen (Eds.), *Cross-cultural training for mental health professionals* (pp. 151-181). Springfield, IL: Charles C Thomas.

Schneider, B. H., Karcher, M. J., & Schlapkohl, W. (1999). Relationship counseling across cultures: Cultural sensitivity and beyond. In P. Pedersen (Ed.), *Multiculturalism as a fourth force* (pp. 167-190). Philadelphia: Taylor & Francis.

Silver, B., Poland, R. E., & Lin, K. (1993). Ethnicity and the pharmacology of tricyclic antidepressants. In K. Lin, R. E. Poland, & G. Nakasaki (Eds.), *Psychopharmacology and psychobiology of ethnicity* (pp. 61-89). Washington, DC: American Psychiatric Press.

Simons, R. C., & Hughes, C. C. (1993). Cultural-bound syndromes. In A. C. Gaw (Ed.), *Culture, ethnicity, and mental illness* (pp. 75-93). Washington, DC: American Psychiatric Press.

Skerry, P. (1993). *Mexican Americans: The ambivalent minority.* New York: Free Press.

Skinner, B. F. (1953). *Science and human behavior.* New York: Macmillan.

Smart, D. W., & Smart, J. F. (1997). *DSM-IV* and culturally sensitive diagnosis: Some observations for counselors. *Journal of Counseling & Development, 75,* 392-398.

Smith, E. J. (1981). Cultural and historical perspectives in counseling Blacks. In D. W. Sue (Ed.), *Counseling the culturally different: Theory and practice* (pp. 141-185). New York: John Wiley.

Smith, M., & Mendoza, R. (1996). Ethnicity and pharmacogenetics. *The Mount Sinai Journal of Medicine, 63,* 285-290.

Smith, T. W. (1992). Changing racial labels: From "colored" to "Negro" to "Black" to "African American." *Public Opinion Quarterly, 56,* 496-544.

Smither, R., & Rodriguez-Giegling, M. (1982). Personality, demographics, and acculturation of Vietnamese and Nicaraguan refugees to the United States. *International Journal of Psychology, 17,* 19-25.

Smitherman, G. (1995). *Black talk.* Boston: Houghton Mifflin.

Spitzer, R. L., & Endicott, J. (1978). *The schedule for affective disorders and schizophrenia* (3rd ed.). New York: New York State Psychiatric Institute.

Spitzer, R. L., Gibbon, M., Skodol, A. E., Williams, J. W., & First, M. B. (1994). *DSM-IV Casebook: A learning companion to the Diagnostic and Statistical Manual of Mental Disorders, Fourth Edition.* Washington, DC: American Psychiatric Press.

Spitzer, R. L., & Klein, D. F. (Eds.). (1978). *Critical issues in psychiatric diagnosis.* New York: Raven.

Spitzer, R. L., Williams, J. B., & Skodol, A. E. (1983). *International perspectives on DSM-III.* Washington, DC: American Psychiatric Press.

Sue, D. W., Bingham, R. P., Porce-Burke, L., & Vasquez, M. (1999). The diversification of psychology: A multicultural revolution. *American psychologist, 54,* 1061-1069.

Sue, D. W., & Sue D. (1987). Asian-Americans and Pacific Islanders. In P. Pedersen (Ed.), *Handbook of cross-cultural counseling and therapy* (pp. 141-146). London: Greenwood.

Sue, D. W., & Sue, D. (1990). *Counseling the culturally different: Theory and practice* (2nd ed.). New York: John Wiley.

Sue, D. W., & Sue, D. (1999). *Counseling the culturally different: Theory and practice* (3rd ed.). New York: John Wiley.

Sue, S. (1999). Science, ethnicity, and bias: Where have we gone wrong? *American Psychologist, 54,* 1070-1077.

Sue, S., Fujino, D. C., Hu, L., Takeuchi, D. T., & Zane, N. W. S. (1991). Community mental health services for ethnic minority groups: A test of the cultural responsiveness hypothesis. *Journal of Consulting and Clinical Psychology, 59,* 433-540.

Suinn, R. M., Rickard-Figueroa, K., Lew, S., & Vigil, S. (1987). The Suinn-Lew Asian Self-Identity Acculturation scale: An initial report. *Education and Psychological Measurement, 47,* 401-407.

Szapocznik, J., Scopetta, M. A., Arnalde, M., & Kurtines, W. (1978). Cuban value structure: Treatment implications. *Journal of Consulting and Clinical Psychology, 46,* 961-970.

Takahashi, Y., & Berger, D. (1996). Cultural dynamics and the unconscious in suicide in Japan. In A. Leenars & D. Lester (Eds.), *Suicide and the unconscious* (pp. 248-258). Northvale: Jason Aronson.

Takeshita, J. (1997). Psychosis. In W. Tseng & J. Streltzer, (Eds.), *Culture and psychopathology: A guide to clinical assessment* (pp. 124-138). New York: Brunner/Mazel.

Takeuchi, J. (2000). Treatment of a biracial child with schizophrenic form disorder: Cultural formulation. *Cultural Diversity and Ethnic Minority Psychology, 6,* 93-101.

Tanaka-Matsumi, J., & Higginbotham, H. N. (1996). Behavioral approaches to counseling across cultures. In P. B. Pedersen, J. G. Draguns, W. J. Lonner, & J. E. Trimble (Eds.), *Counseling across cultures* (pp. 266-292). Thousand Oaks, CA: Sage.

Tapscott, B. L. (1976). *Elementary applied symbolic logic.* Englewood Cliffs, NJ: Prentice Hall.

Tharp, R. G. (1991). Cultural diversity and treatment of children. *Journal of Consulting and Clinical Psychology, 59,* 799-812.

Thompson, J., Walker, R. D., & Silk-Walker, P. (1993). Psychiatric care of American Indians and Alaska Natives. In A. C. Gaw (Ed.), *Culture, ethnicity, and mental illness* (pp. 189-243). Washington, DC: American Psychiatric Press.

Trimble, J. E., & Fleming, C. M. (1989). Providing counseling services for Native American Indians: Client, counselor, and community characteristics. In P. B. Pedersen, J. G. Draguns, W. J. Lonner, & J. E. Trimble (Eds.), *Counseling across cultures* (3rd ed., pp. 177-204). Honolulu: University of Hawaii Press.

Tseng, W., & Streltzer, J. (1997). Integration and conclusions. In W. Tseng & J. Streltzer (Eds.), *Culture and psychopathology* (pp. 241-252). New York: Brunner/Mazel.

U.S. Bureau of the Census. (1996). *Statistical abstract of the United States.* Washington, DC: Government Printing Office.

U.S. Department of Health and Human Services. (1991). *Health status of minorities and low-income groups: Third Edition.* Washington, DC: Health Resources and Services Administration, U.S. Department of Health and Human Services.

Walker, R. D., & LaDue, R. (1986). An integrative approach to American Indian mental health. In C. B. Wilkinson (Ed.), *Ethnic psychiatry* (pp. 143-199). New York: Plenum.

Weiss, G., & Hechtman, L. T. (1993). *ADHD in children, adolescents, and adults* (2nd ed.). New York: Guilford.

Weiss, M. G. (1995). Eating disorders and disordered eating in different cultures. *Psychiatric Clinics of North America, 18,* 537-553.

Westermeyer, J. J. (1993). Cross-cultural psychiatric assessment. In A. C. Gaw (Ed.), *Culture, ethnicity, and mental illness* (pp. 125-144). Washington, DC: American Psychiatric Press.

Westermeyer, J. (1995). Cultural aspects of substance abuse and alcoholism. *Psychiatric Clinics of North America, 18,* 589-605.

Wilkinson, C. B., & Spurlock, J. (1986). The mental health of black Americans: Psychiatric diagnosis and treatment. In C. B. Wilkinson (Ed.), *Ethnic psychiatry* (pp. 15-59). New York: Plenum.

Wong-Rieger, D., & Quintana, D. (1987). Comparative acculturation of Southeast Asians and Hispanic immigrants and sojourners. *Journal of Cross-Cultural Psychology, 18,* 145-162.

Yamamoto, J. (1986). Therapy for Asian American and Pacific Islanders. In B. C. Wilkinson (Ed.), *Ethnic psychiatry* (pp. 89-141). New York: Plenum.

Yamamoto, J., Lam, J., Choi, W. I., Reece, S., Lo, S., Hahn, D., & Fairbanks, L. (1982). The psychiatric status schedule for Asian-Americans. *American Journal of Psychiatry, 139,* 1181-1184.

Yamamoto, J., Silva, J. A., Ferrari, M., & Nukariya, K. (1997). Culture and psychopathology. In G. Johnson-Powell & J. Yamamoto (Eds.), *Transcultural child development* (pp. 34-57). New York: John Wiley.

Yamamoto, J., Silva, J. A., Justice, L. R., Chang, C. Y., & Leong, G. B. (1993). Cross-cultural psychotherapy. In A. C. Gaw (Ed.), *Culture, ethnicity, and mental illness* (pp. 101-124). Washington, DC: American Psychiatric Press.

Zalewski, C., & Green, R. L. (1996). Multicultural use of the MMPI-2. In L. A. Zuzuki, P. J. Meller, & J. G. Ponterotto (Eds.), *Handbook of multicultural assessment: Clinical, psychological, and educational applications* (pp. 77-114). San Francisco: Jossey-Bass.

Zapata, J. T. (1995). Counseling Hispanic children and youth. In C. C. Lee (Ed.), *Counseling for diversity: A guide for school counselors and related professionals* (pp. 85-108). Boston: Allyn & Bacon.

Zuzuki, L. A., Meller, P. J., & Ponterotto, J. G. (1996). *Handbook of multicultural assessment: Clinical, psychological, and educational applications.* San Francisco: Jossey-Bass.

Author Index

235

Subject Index

About the Editor

Freddy A. Paniagua, PhD, is Professor in the Department of Psychiatry and Behavioral Sciences, University of Texas Medical Branch at Galveston, where he teaches general cross-cultural mental health seminars with emphasis on the assessment and treatment of African American, American Indian, Asian, and Hispanic clients. He also teaches a specialty postgraduate seminar for Residents in General and Child and Adolescent Psychiatry with emphasis on cultural variants discussed across psychiatric disorders in the *DSM-IV* (APA, 1994). In 1989, he received a 6-year training grant from the National Institute of Mental Health to provide postdoctoral and postmaster's training to mental health professionals representing different multicultural groups, with emphasis on the assessment, diagnosis, and treatment of emotionally disturbed clients. He received his doctorate from the University of Kansas and postdoctoral training at Johns Hopkins University School of Medicine.

He has published over 40 scientific articles, including basic and applied research and theoretical contributions. The first edition of his first book, *Assessing and Treating Culturally Diverse Clients: A Practical Guide* became a bestseller in the cross-cultural field, is in its second edition, and has been adopted in over 200 colleges and universities nationally and abroad. Among his many honors, in 1998, he received the Dr. Martin Luther King, Jr. Service Award from the University of Texas Medical Branch (UTMB) Affirmative Action Advisory Committee "for significant contributions in promoting equity within the UTMB community."

About the Contributors

Please note: Titles and affiliations were selected from submission of new cases or publication of original cases.

Jeff Baker, PhD—Associate Professor, Department of Orthopedics and Rehabilitation, University of Texas Medical Branch, Galveston, Texas.

David M. Bernstein, MD—Assistant Professor, Department of Psychiatry, University of Hawaii School of Medicine.

Daphne C. Brazile, MD,—Chief Resident, Child and Adolescent Psychiatry, University of Texas Medical Branch, Galveston, Texas.

Virginia S. Burlingame, MSW, PhD—Professor, Wisconsin Gerontology Institute at University of Wisconsin-Parkside, Kenosha, Wisconsin.

Ian A. Canino, MD—Clinical Professor, Department of Psychiatry, College of Physicians and Surgeons, Columbia University, New York, New York, and New York Psychiatric Institute, New York.

Richard Castillo, PhD—Associate Professor, Department of Psychology, University of Hawaii at West Oahu.

Steven L. Chaplin, MD—Clinical Assistant Professor, Department of Psychiatry, University of Hawaii School of Medicine.

Israel Cuéllar, PhD,—Professor, Department of Psychology and Anthropology, University of Texas Pan American, Edinburg, Texas.

Amor Del Mundo, MD—Assistant Professor, Department of Psychiatry and Behavioral Sciences, James H. Quillen College of Medicine, East Tennessee State University, Johnson City, Tennessee.

Lee E. Emory, MD—Private Practice, Galveston, Texas.

Albert Gaw, MD—Professor of Psychiatry, University of Massachusetts Medical School, Worcester, Massachusetts.

Jewelle Taylor Gibbs, PhD—The Zellerbach Family Professor of Social Policy, Community Change, and Practice at the School of Social Welfare, University of California at Berkeley, California.

Xiao-yan He, MD—Child and Adolescent Psychiatry Resident, University of Texas Medical Branch, Galveston, Texas.

Man Keung Ho, PhD—Professor of Social Work, University of Oklahoma.

Larke Nahme Huang, PhD—Consulting Psychologist, National Technical Assistance Center for Children's Mental Health Services, Georgetown University Child Development Center.

James P. Lavelle, MSW—Program Director, Indochinese Psychiatric Clinic, St. Elizabeth Hospital, Brighton, Massachusetts, and Adjunct Assistant Professor of Social Work, Boston University, Boston, Massachusetts.

Ruth Levine, MD—Associate Professor, Department of Psychiatry and Behavioral Sciences, University of Texas Medical Branch, Galveston, Texas.

Angela S. Lew, PhD—Madison Center for Children, South Bend, Indiana.

Cervando Martinez, Jr., MD—Professor, Department of Psychiatry and Behavioral Sciences, University of San Antonio Health Sciences Center, San Antonio, Texas.

Helen A. Mendes, DSW—Associate Professor, School of Social Work, University of Southern California, Los Angeles, California.

Richard F. Mollica, MD, MAR—Assistant Professor, Department of Psychiatry, Harvard Medical School, Massachusetts General Hospital, and Clinical Director, Indochinese Psychiatric Clinic at St. Elizabeth Hospital, Brighton, Massachusetts.

Donna K. Nagata, PhD—Associate Professor of Clinical Psychology, University of Michigan, Ann Arbor, Michigan.

Nga Anh Nguyen, MD—Associate Professor, Department of Psychiatry and Behavioral Sciences, University of Texas Medical Branch, Galveston, Texas.

Michael O'Boyle, MD, PhD—Professor, Department of Psychiatry and Behavioral Sciences, University of Texas Medical Branch, Galveston, Texas.

Freddy A. Paniagua, PhD—Professor, Department of Psychiatry and Behavioral Sciences, University of Texas Medical Branch, Galveston, Texas.

Danilo E. Ponce, PhD—Professor, Department of Psychiatry, University of Hawaii School of Medicine.

Antonio E. Puente, PhD—Professor of Psychology, University of North Carolina, Wilmington, North Carolina.

Andrés J. Pumariega, MD—Professor and Chairman, Department of Psychiatry and Behavioral Sciences, James H. Quillen College of Medicine, East Tennessee State University, Johnson City, Tennessee.

Oscar Ramirez, PhD—Clinical Associate Professor of Psychiatry, University of Texas Health Sciences Center, San Antonio, Texas.

Kokab Saeed, MD—Clinical Assistant Professor, General Academic Division of Pediatrics, University of Texas Medical Branch, Galveston, Texas.

Gabriel D. Salazar, BA—Research Assistant, Department of Psychology, University of North Carolina, Wilmington, North Carolina.

Rita Sommers-Flanagan, PhD—Professor, Counselor Education, University of Montana, Missoula, Montana, Clinical Consultant, Missoula Vet Center.

Jeanne Spurlock, MD—Professor, Psychiatry, Pediatrics and Child Health Center, Howard University College of Medicine, Washington, DC.

David Sue, PhD—Professor of Psychology, Department of Psychology, Western Washington University, Bellingham, Washington.

Derald Wing Sue, PhD—Professor, California School of Professional Psychology, Alameda California State University, Hayward, California.

Yu-Wen Ying, PhD—Professor, School of Social Welfare, University of California at Berkeley, California.

Luis H. Zayas, PhD—Associate Professor, Graduate School of Social Service, Fordham University, New York, New York.